Planning
Non-Traditional
Programs

AN ANALYSIS OF THE ISSUES
FOR POSTSECONDARY EDUCATION

K. Patricia Cross

John R. Valley

and Associates

PLANNING
NON-TRADITIONAL
PROGRAMS

 Jossey-Bass Publishers
San Francisco · Washington · London · 1974

PLANNING NON-TRADITIONAL PROGRAMS
An Analysis of the Issues for Postsecondary Education
by K. Patricia Cross, John R. Valley, and Associates

Copyright © 1974 by: Jossey-Bass, Inc., Publishers
615 Montgomery Street
San Francisco, California 94111
&
Jossey-Bass Limited
3 Henrietta Street
London WC2E 8LU

Library of Congress Catalogue Card Number LC 73-18505

International Standard Book Number ISBN 0-87589-217-5

Manufactured in the United States of America

JACKET DESIGN BY WILLI BAUM

FIRST EDITION

Code 7409

The Jossey-Bass
Series in Higher Education

A publication of the
COMMISSION ON NON-TRADITIONAL STUDY
Samuel B. Gould, Chairman

Preface

In February 1971 the Commission on Non-Traditional Study was established under the joint auspices of the College Entrance Examination Board and Educational Testing Service with a grant from the Carnegie Corporation of New York. Its mission was to achieve a national perspective on the issues surrounding non-traditional alternatives and to make recommendations for fulfilling the promise of the movement.

To guide their efforts, Commission members agreed that non-traditional study was "more an attitude than a system and thus can never be defined except tangentially." Nevertheless, "this attitude puts the student first and the institution second, concentrates more on the former's need than the latter's convenience, encourages diversity of individual opportunity rather than uniform prescription, and deemphasizes time, space, and even course requirements in favor of competence and, where applicable, performance. It has concern for the learner of any age and circumstance, for the degree aspirant as well as the person who finds sufficient reward in enriching life through constant, periodic, or occasional study" (Commission on Non-Traditional Study, 1973, p. xv).

Commission members were aware that this definition raises more questions than it answers. What are the "needs" of non-traditional learners? How can "competence" and "performance" be determined? What is the nation presently doing to demonstrate its "concern for the learner of any age and circumstance"? Because these questions can be answered only through a systematic and co-ordinated effort, the research committee of the Commission recommended a unified program of research about student interests, institutional offerings, the use and promise of new technologies to deliver instruction, and the issues to consider in awarding credit and setting standards for accreditation.

Although information about these topics must be obtained from different respondents and sources, educators planning non-traditional programs need to know how information from one source relates to that from another. They must know, for example, not only how much importance adults place on academic credit, but how institutions, through the constituted authority of the faculties, are dealing with credit for out-of-class learning. What measures to assess learning are available or possible? How do new credit arrangements and new delivery systems affect institutional accreditation? A useful research design would thus consist of a tightly interlocking set of studies.

Educational Testing Service proposed such a research program, and it was funded by the Carnegie Corporation of New York and the Educational Foundation of America. *Planning Non-Traditional Programs* reports the findings of these studies. The individual authors have assembled information from students and potential students, from colleges and universities, from people with experience and expertise in such technical fields as educational measurement, the new technologies, and accreditation, and from the research literature. Thus after an overview of the interrelationships that exist among these factors in Chapter One, Chapter Two presents the learning interests and experiences of a national sample of adults between the ages of eighteen and sixty. Chapter Three presents the results of a survey of colleges and universities to determine the number and nature of non-traditional opportunities available in the spring of 1972. Source materials for Chapters Four, Five, and Six are experts who were interviewed or whose writings were read to give perspective to technology, credit, and accreditation in relation to non-traditional study. And the sources for Chapter Seven consist of a vast literature of some 885 documents from libraries, clearinghouses of the Educational Resources Information

Center (ERIC), and personal files of scholars of the non-traditional study movement.

The authors of Chapters Two through Seven prepared initial drafts of these reports for the Commission on Non-Traditional Study to use in forming final recommendations in its report, *Diversity by Design* (1973). These initial documents were cited in Appendix B of that report, and the Commission referred to some of the data they contain in the report itself. But because these studies contain so much valuable information for educators throughout higher education, the authors have rewritten their earlier drafts for *Planning Non-Traditional Programs* and its wider audience.

The chapters are aimed both at leaders of non-traditional programs, who can use them to set their own work in national perspective, and at educators interested in planning new programs, who can benefit from the reports here of experiences, trends, and problems. Different readers will find different sections of particular use to them, and can pick and choose among the chapters as from any volume of multiple resources.

We are grateful to our colleagues in this effort for their willingness to share their findings with a national audience in this way. We hope the results help further the goal of the Commission on Non-Traditional Study in encouraging diversity of educational opportunity for learners of every age and circumstance.

Berkeley   K. PATRICIA CROSS
Princeton   JOHN R. VALLEY
January 1974

Contents

Contributors

ABRAHAM CARP, *director of research, Educational Testing Service, Berkeley*

K. PATRICIA CROSS, *senior research psychologist, Educational Testing Service, Berkeley; research educator, Center for Research and Development in Higher Education, University of California, Berkeley*

LUCY ANN GEISELMAN, *assistant dean of extension programs, University of California*

JB LON HEFFERLIN, *director of special projects, Jossey-Bass, Inc., Publishers*

WILLIAM A. MAHLER, *associate reseach psychologist, Educational Testing Service, Princeton*

RICHARD PETERSON, *research psychologist, Educational Testing Service, Berkeley*

PAMELA ROELFS, *senior research assistant,*
  Educational Testing Service, Berkeley

JANET RUYLE, *associate specialist, Center for*
  Research and Development in Higher
  Education, University of California, Berkeley

JOHN R. VALLEY, *co-director, Office of New Degree*
  Programs, Educational Testing Service,
  Princeton, and College Entrance Examination
  Board, New York

WESLEY W. WALTON, *executive associate,*
  Educational Testing Service, Princeton

JONATHAN R. WARREN, *research psychologist,*
  Educational Testing Service, Berkeley

*Planning
Non-Traditional
Programs*

AN ANALYSIS OF THE ISSUES
FOR POSTSECONDARY EDUCATION

Non-Traditional Study: An Overview

K. Patricia Cross
John R. Valley

꧁꧁꧁꧁꧁꧁꧁꧁꧁꧁꧁꧁꧁꧁꧂꧂꧂꧂꧂꧂꧂꧂꧂꧂꧂꧂꧂꧂

*F*ew innovations in higher education have met with more ready acceptance by a diversity of people and institutions than non-traditional study and its various forms—external degree, Extended University, Open University, University Without Walls, and others. Although the movement that gave birth to these models and plans is difficult to define with any precision, people share a common understanding about the nature of this new concept of education. Its greatest departure from traditional education is its explicit recognition that education should be measured by what the student knows rather than how or where he learns it. Beyond that it builds upon two basic premises—that opportunity should be equal for all who wish to learn and that learning is a lifelong process unconfined to one's youth or to campus classrooms. Few would quarrel with the logic of these concepts, but the implementation of educational programs to meet such new needs requires considerable imagination, thought, and study.

The purpose of this chapter is to present an overview of

the variables and the complicated interrelationships that must be considered if these new programs are to meet their objectives. Changes in one part of the educational system create new pressures and demand new responses from other components. For example, changing the nature of the student body changes the interests and needs of learners. Should it change the content of the curriculum as a result? New methods of teaching change the processes of learning. Should they change the manner in which learning is evaluated? Changes in content and evaluation change the role of colleges which, in turn, changes the role of accreditation. How should accrediting agencies respond?

In this research overview, we center our analysis on the changing student body and its impact on almost all other aspects of education, for it is the attitude that "puts the student first and the institution second, concentrates more on the former's need than the latter's convenience" that is the focal point of the non-traditional movement.

Curriculum Content

In general, adults do not value learning for its own sake or for its liberating influence. The majority of respondents to the research of Carp, Peterson, and Roelfs (Chapter Two) express an interest in the utility of knowledge. Knowledge that leads to better jobs, that helps in practical daily living, and that teaches the skills and pleasures associated with leisure-time activities holds greater interest for the typical American adult than the subjects that colleges and universities are most interested in teaching. For example, the biological, physical, and social sciences as well as community problems and public affairs rank low in relation to how-to-do-it subjects, such as how to improve business skills, how to invest money wisely, how to cook and garden, and how to repair things around the home. Respondents show interest in learning more about sports, games, crafts, physical fitness, travel, and leisure-time activities. While the order of preference in subjects may vary among different people, a substantial discrepancy arises between what adults want to learn and what colleges offer to teach.

The research of Ruyle and Geiselman (Chapter Three)

shows that colleges and universities offering programs considered non-traditional in one or more respects are most likely to develop programs that cater to the vocational interests of adults, frequently directing attention to particular occupational groups. After this concordance, the fit between adult interests and college offerings diverge. The second most popular college offering is the traditional curriculum, which appeals to relatively few of the adults—less than 10 percent. The second most popular adult interest is recreational and leisure-time activities, which rank low in college offerings— fewer than 10 percent of the non-traditional programs. (This percentage may be an underestimate because the research concentrated on programs, and recreational activities may not be listed as programs.)

At present, few people worry about the lack of correspondence between student interests and institutional offerings. Colleges take the position that their task is to offer their curriculum to those who want it, and students who want courses in crafts, child care, and investments find other agencies to provide the instruction.

Certainly the research indicates that there are enough people who *do* want the traditional academic disciplines to make non-traditional delivery of traditional education quite worthwhile. We find, for example, that 8 percent of the potential learners would like to know more about the biological sciences. When that relatively small percentage is converted to numbers, it means that there may be as many as 6.4 million potential students of biology in this country. Likewise, in 1972 8 percent of the adults surveyed, or a possible 8.3 million people, actually found most instruction in hobbies and handicrafts outside of traditional educational institutions.

Perhaps no dramatic agitation compels change in the traditional college curriculum. Potential learners are not generally criticizing colleges for not offering the courses they want to take. And yet 12 percent of the respondents in the national survey did complain that they are deterred from further learning because the courses they want are not available. Other complaints are implied about the traditional academic curriculum—9 percent do not enjoy studying; 6 percent are tired of school; 13 percent feel that their grades are too low; 6 percent say they do not meet requirements. Millions of potential learners are admittedly not reached by the traditional content emphasized in programs presumably designed for non-traditional learners. While it is undoubtedly beneficial to increase access to traditional content for those previously excluded, it is not a sufficient response to the needs of the new learners.

Part of the impetus for the non-traditional movement is to provide equal educational opportunity. The experience of Open University in Britain and the research presented in this book indicate that those who already have the most education are those who are most likely to engage in further study. Furthermore, the traditional curriculum consisting of the academic disciplines is likely to appeal especially to those with the best educational backgrounds. Thus, the net result of delivering the traditional curriculum to non-traditional students who want it may be to increase the educational gap between the haves and the have nots. The trend to offer adults more practical courses, on the other hand, appeals to low-income groups and attracts them to college programs.

The readiness of colleges to provide career-oriented education is a new trend, responsive to the interests of the new learners as well as to societal pressures for equality of educational opportunity. The research demonstrates that newer programs designated non-traditional are more likely to offer an occupational or career focus, whereas the older programs tend to retain a liberal arts curriculum. Newer programs, as opposed to older programs, attempt to increase practical learning through job-related learning experiences such as field work, cooperative education, and instruction at business sites.

In summary, the data related to curriculum content indicate that perhaps eighty million people would like to participate in formal learning activities. But they are primarily interested in knowledge that is useful in their daily lives as workers, parents, homeowners, and people with recreational interests. Colleges are beginning to respond to these interests by changes in content as well as changes in methods of delivery.

Methods of Delivery

Much of the talk about non-traditional programs has emphasized the need for reaching people who are unable or unwilling to come to the campus. Furthermore, the research indicates that

institutions presently offering non-traditional programs are con-
centrating on "new ways of teaching old subjects to new students
rather than new subjects as such." But a closer examination of the
data reveals that the new methods are not really very new. In
particular, the new technologies are not yet making their predicted
impact. Most non-traditional programs use the old standby of
lectures and class discussion; they just transport it to off-campus
locations, usually regional learning centers.

The new learners are apparently receptive to this delivery
system; lectures or classes are rated the most popular method of
instruction. One can argue that people are getting what they want.
But only a fourth of the people who say they would like to learn
prefer lectures, and these are the better educated people in the upper
socioeconomic levels. Lectures are more popular among actual
students than in the preference ratings of would-be students.

The trend is in the direction of offering a variety of instructional techniques but it is by no means dramatic. Recent non-traditional programs emphasize field work and business and industrial
sites rather than regional learning centers, and on-the-job training
is more widely used today than it was a decade ago. There is also
a tendency to offer more instruction via the new technologies, especially in programs designed for the economically disadvantaged.
But unlike the use of other methods, where the demand seems to
create the supply, the use of the new technologies reported by
institutions is somewhat ahead of the expressed desire of the new
learners. Less than 2 percent of American adults express interest in
the prospect of learning with television, radio, or video or audio
cassettes.

Overall, the data on methods of instruction seem to demonstrate that people are more apt to like what they know than to
know what they like. People who have learned with lectures are
likely to prefer that method of delivery; people who have learned
on the job seem to prefer that; workshops are popular with business
and professional people who have experienced them. Very few
people have learned with the new media, and more experience
with it will show if it creates the predicted revolution in education.

In Chapter Four Walton discusses the impressive potential
of the media to transform education. If by the end of the 1970s

cable television serves 40 to 60 percent of all American homes
and if videocassettes fulfill their early promise, then not only will
demand rise for instruction via the media, but the learning society
of the future will undergo sweeping changes. Those studying the
potential of the media are already urging us to think not of what
the media will add to education, but rather how new tools of communication will change the entire educational process.

Academic Credit

An immediate problem to face in expanding learning opportunities to non-traditional learners is the matter of academic credit.
Not surprisingly, granting credit has become a central issue in the
non-traditional movement. The new learners are interested not only
in useful learning, but also in the credentials that provide an entry
ticket to desired ends—further schooling, jobs, or professional advancement. The national survey of potential learners indicates that
the desire for college credit is strong among those eligible for it—
those with a high school diploma but not a baccalaureate degree.
But neither colleges nor the accrediting agencies have clearly defined
just what is signified by *credit* and a *college degree*.

Data from numerous sources suggests that if time-free,
space-free, non-classroom learning could be measured in terms comparable to the more familiar (although not necessarily more accurate) classroom assessments, it might remove three of the four
major obstacles that respondents to the institutional survey say
inhibit the development of non-traditional programs—difficulty in
assessing classroom learning, concern for academic standards, and
faculty resistance. But present measures of learning are not so
adequate that we should delay the introduction of non-traditional
alternatives; our present concept of degrees and credit is acceptable
more because of familiarity than because of logic.

Warren asserts in his analysis of the credit issue (Chapter
Five) that "no rational foundation for the degree and credit
structure exists in the higher educational system." Like the dollar,
the academic unit of credit is valuable only as long as people have
confidence in it. Credit and the degree are primarily measures of
time served. Furthermore, the amount of learning associated with

a unit of credit is highly variable from instructor to instructor, from campus to campus, from academic subject to subject, and its value varies from time to time.

Improved measures of educational achievement are important to non-traditionalists because of their conviction that what the student knows is more important than where or how he learned it. The present credit system tells us only that the student met professor Y's requirements, which usually involve an argeed-upon, well-established set of procedures. There is no real reason why professor Y's judgment could not be relied upon with equal confidence to assess out-of-class learning. According to Warren, "measurement of non-classroom learning ought to be no more difficult, in principle, than measurement of learning in the classroom."

Warren (Chapter Five) gives numerous examples of assessment measures that appear to have as much, if not more, promise for assessing learning than the traditional methods. Data from the institutional survey show, however, that by far the most acceptable measures of out-of-class learning are paper-and-pencil examinations, especially national programs such as the Advanced Placement Program and the College Level Examination Program (CLEP). These examinations seem to bridge the credibility gap because of their similarity to traditional measures. But despite some new flexibilities, institutions are moving cautiously. Although most now grant credit-by-examination, few grant a degree by examination. The latter, however, is rapidly becoming a reality in states that are in the vanguard of seeking alternatives to traditional education.

In the final analysis, says Warren, the solution to the credit problem lies in a sensible organization of education toward stated goals rather than the arbitrary time spans that now define credit and degrees. And that eventuality will be as salutary for traditional education as for non-traditional.

Accreditation

The assessment of institutional performance is undergoing the same examination as the assessment of student performance, with one major difference. Most institutions are not using accrediting procedures as an excuse to avoid introducing new flexibilities for the non-traditional learner. Respondents to the institutional questionnaire did not expect to run into difficulties with accrediting agencies, nor did they worry about non-traditional students experiencing problems in securing vocational licenses or jobs. Strangely enough, the leading outside threat to the acceptance of the non-traditional experiences of students comes from inside the educational establishment—the graduate schools. Hefferlin (Chapter Six) asserts that "all of the regulatory agencies and accrediting associations combined have not approached the restrictive power that university graduate schools have held and continue to hold over unconventional undergraduate programs." Hefferlin also recognizes that non-traditional alternatives will quite likely prosper (or fail) only to the extent that they "work" for people studying by non-traditional means. If people learn what they want to learn and if the credentials open the right doors to jobs or further study, then non-traditional methods will prosper whether they are accredited or not.

Nevertheless, accrediting agencies play an important role, inside and outside of the non-traditional movement, in the preservation of academic standards. Some programs riding on the crest of the popularity of the non-traditional movement should feel more threatened by the accreditation process than they do. And how can accrediting agencies encourage flexibility in non-traditional studies while protecting the public against fraud? Above all, they will have to evaluate educational programs by student performance—a variable that rarely enters into present evaluations which concentrate on institutional procedures.

Local Planning

The Commission on Non-Traditional Study operated from a national perspective to find reasonable generalizations regarding students, curriculum content, delivery systems, academic credit, and accreditation. Can these national data be used for planning at the local level as well? What implications does the research information have for those in individual institutions and agencies who are planning new programs?

Local planners should study the data in terms of overall

trends and averages, and they should look for specific facts that, while perhaps off the central theme, seem to relate significantly to their institution. They can then test local circumstances against the general findings and ask: Are we the same as or different from most? If different, how are we different? On this dimension do we want to be the same or do we want to be different? And is it good or bad or right or wrong that we are the same or that we are different?

For example, issues of student assessment have loomed large in planning non-traditional programs, constituting a central point of concern for many institutions. A local planner should therefore be prepared to give early and substantial attention to issues of assessment and to ask: What philosophical foundations should underpin assessment in our new program? And what assessment procedures and techniques will provide adequate data to these ends? The planner can note the practices of other colleges as presented in Chapter Three by Janet Ruyle and Lucy Ann Geiselman, consider the recommendations of Jonathan Warren from Chapter Five, and review the literature identified by William Mahler in Chapter Seven. He can also make an inventory of campus resources as well as community assistance, advice, and counsel. Involving local experts in consideration of the problems encountered and the solutions proposed elsewhere should prove both expeditious and effective.

If the planner has accurate and current information pertaining to local conditions, there is probably no need to repeat at the local level the surveys described in this volume. Yet, on critical elements, the planner should not make unwarranted assumptions about the local scene. Undertaking within the service area of an institution the type of market survey reported by Abraham Carp, Richard Peterson, and Pamela Roelfs in the next chapter, for example, may not only prevent unrealistic planning on the basis of inadequate data but also point to unique local opportunities for institutional service impossible to predict from national statistics.

It is not easy for institutions to be creative and innovative in a wide variety of areas all at the same time. To reach new learners by new methods with the content that they want and need, while maintaining quality educational programs, is a complex undertaking. And yet that is the task which non-traditional education has set for itself. The Commission on Non-Traditional Study has presented their recommendations about this task in their report, *Diversity by Design*. This book presents the research findings that provided one source of information for the Commission. We hope that it helps planners to think about the development of local programs in the perspective of national data and helps make their work and the resulting programs as effective as possible in terms of offering all who wish to learn an education that serves their needs.

Adult Learning Interests
and Experiences

ABRAHAM CARP

RICHARD PETERSON

PAMELA ROELFS

ᝡᝡᝡᝡᝡᝡᝡᝡᝡᝡᝡᝡᝡᝡᝣᝣᝣᝣᝣᝣᝣᝣᝣᝣᝣᝣ

Few people need reminding that education in America has been changing rapidly in the past decade. Of the many trends, two relate especially to adults. The first is an expanding awareness among adult Americans of the value of continued learning throughout their lifetimes. The second is a new understanding among educators that learning need not be limited to the classroom and the campus—that learning can occur through a variety of "non-traditional" modes.

But how large has the potential market for adult learning grown? Among adults, what are their subject matter interests, their preferences among settings for learning, their reasons for continued

We wish to acknowledge the contribution of Barbara Greenberg, Andrew York, and Carol Vale of ETS-Berkeley in constructing the questionnaire described in this chapter and tabulating responses, and to Reuben Cohen and Charlotte Slider of the Response Analysis Corporation for their cooperation in data-gathering.

11

learning? And what subjects are currently being studied, under what instructional methods, by men and women who *are* in fact continuing their education?

While answers to these questions had been gathered a decade ago (see Johnstone and Rivera, 1965), the Commission on Non-Traditional Study needed current data on which to base its 1972 recommendations and sponsored the present study as a result. To gather this information, the Berkeley office of Educational Testing Service designed a survey questionnaire (Appendix A) which the Commission termed its "demand study" in its final report, *Diversity by Design* (1973) and which Cyril O. Houle mentioned in his report for the Commission, *The External Degree* (1973).

Survey Method

This survey was designed to allow respondents to indicate their own learning interests from among a wide range of topics— including basic education, citizenship, and even occult sciences— besides the academic and vocational subjects traditionally offered by colleges. Likewise it allowed respondents to report their preferred mode of learning from among extension courses, correspondence courses, on-the-job training, private lessons, televised classes, and independent study, as well as standard classroom instruction. Other questions focused on the respondents' preferred place of study, reasons for learning, willingness to pay, desire for credit, perceived barriers to learning, any recent enrollment in courses, and the usual items of biographical information.

These thirty-four precoded multiple-choice questions were designed to be self-administering and simple to answer and to require only an average of thirty minutes to complete. (Most questions were answered by about 95 percent of the respondents, but only 85 percent—the lowest response—answered the question on family income.)

DATA COLLECTION

Sample selection and data collection were subcontracted to the Response Analysis Corporation (RAC), a commercial survey organization, of Princeton, New Jersey. From the survey universe of approximately 104 million persons between the ages of eighteen and sixty who were living in private households in the continental United States and who were not full-time students in mid-1972, RAC derived a national probability sample of 2515 households. To do so, it used the most recent census information and systematic random procedures to select specific geographic locations, households, and individuals. In the summer of 1972 RAC interviewers succeeded, after as many as four visits, in determining at 83 percent of these households if an eligible respondent was in residence. At 78 percent of these screened households that had one or more eligible respondents, up to two questionnaires were left, completed by the designated respondents, and picked up on a return visit by the interviewer. About 3 percent of the questionnaires were completed through personal interviews with respondents who were illiterate, non-English-reading, or handicapped in such a way that they needed RAC assistance.

Of the 2974 people who were asked to respond, 2004 (or 67 percent) in a total of 1248 households completed the form. Another 7 percent could not be reached after three return visits, and the remaining 26 percent refused to participate for one reason or another.

For the purposes of this report, the responses of the 111 full-time students who were surveyed have been omitted from analysis. Each of the remaining 1893 respondents in the final sample was assigned a weight to make the sample comparable to the general American adult population exclusive of full-time students. This weight combined three adjustments, accounting for (1) the size of the respondent's household; (2) its geographic location; and (3) the age, sex, race, and educational attainment of the respondent. These adjustments resulted in a weighted sample size of 3910, which is the basis for all further statistics in this chapter.

DATA INTERPRETATION

The purpose for this weighting was to enable sample results to be projected to the total survey population. To estimate the number of adult Americans that corresponds to any of the following percentages, one can use 104 million people as this survey population to equal 100 percent of the total weighted sample of 3910. The size of population *sub*groups can be similarly estimated from Table 1—which indicates the relative size of each demographic subsample within the total weighted sample—and subsequent tables. For example, the number of Black adult Americans interested in learning vocational subjects is approximately 4 million, based on the 9 percent of respondents in the right column of Table 1 who are Black and the 56 percent of these Blacks in the first column of Table 3 who indicated an interest in vocational fields.* Such population estimates should, however, be made with caution, since percentages of a nationwide sample of this size can have a margin of error of as much as 3 percent—representing more than three million people—and percentages of subsamples are subject to much larger margins of error. Hence the data in this report are not population projections but instead percentages of the weighted sample or its subsamples.

Among the many surprising results of the survey, some will be heartening to educators, such as the finding that some three-fourths of all American adults express interest in continued learning of some kind. Others will be sobering for academic professionals, such as the respondents' relatively small interest in academic subjects as compared to vocational and avocational topics. All these results should be regarded as *general* indicators of learning interests and activities, rather than as *definitive* descriptions. Educational market surveys such as this one have consistently shown a sizable discrepancy between stated intentions and actual behavior—between an interest in some kind of study and actually enrolling for the study. Caution is particularly appropriate in interpreting the data from the various *sub*samples delineated in the survey—Black adults, recipients of postgraduate degrees, widowed or divorced people, and so forth—because of the relatively small number of respondents in these categories. Nonetheless, the information in these pages should be of considerable use to educational planners in weighing policy

---

* Most of the demographic subgroups are self-explanatory from the labels used in these tables, but Appendix A explains categorization for the educational, occupational, and geographic subsamples.

proposals for the continuing learning of American adults. For readers who require substantially more data in tabular form, a longer project report is available from the authors.

Learners and Would-Be Learners

The two subgroups of the survey sample whose learning interests and experiences are the main elements in the analyses of this report can best be labeled Learners and Would-Be Learners. The Learners are the 1207 weighted respondents among the total weighted sample of 3910 who reported receiving instruction in some subject or skill within the past twelve months. The Would-Be Learners are the 3001 weighted individuals (including 1142 Learners) who reported an *interest* in some kind of further learning.* The sheer magnitude of these two subgroups—Learners and Would-Be Learners—is impressive. Expressed in percentage terms, 77 percent of adult Americans (aged eighteen to sixty) report interest in learning more about some subject or pursuing some skill; a remarkable 31 percent of the population is engaged in some form of adult learning; and 95 percent of the present Learners wish to continue their learning.

Table 1.

CHARACTERISTICS OF RESPONDENTS, LEARNERS, AND WOULD-BE LEARNERS

(Percentages for each characteristic may not add to 100% because of nonresponses.)

Characteristic	All Respondents $(N_w = 3910)$	Learners $(N_w = 1207)$	Would-Be Learners $(N_w = 3001)$
Sex:			
Male	48%	49%	46%
Female	52	51	54
Housewife	20	19	20
Non-housewife	27	29	30

* Item 17 of the questionnaire in Appendix A provided data on Learners, and Item 1 identified Would-Be Learners.

Table 1. (*cont.*)

Age:

18–24	18	22	20
25–29	14	18	15
30–34	12	12	12
35–44	22	20	21
45–54	23	20	22
55–60	12	8	9

Race:

White	87	90	88
Black	10	6	9

Marital status:

Single	12	18	14
Married	79	76	78
Widowed/divorced	7	5	7

Formal schooling:

1–8 years	14	5	10
9–11 years	19	12	18
12 years	38	38	38
Some postsecondary	13	21	15
4-year college graduate	11	21	13

Occupation:

Unskilled/semiskilled	25	16	22
Skilled	15	18	15
Sales/clerical	17	20	19
Small business	7	7	7
Prof/large business	8	16	10

Job status:

Full-time employed	55	57	55
Part-time employed	9	10	10
No job	34	31	33

Region:

Northeast	23	22	24
Northcentral	29	27	28
South	34	30	33
West	14	21	16

Type of community:

Urban	74	81	78
Rural	26	19	22

Table 1 compares the characteristics of Learners and Would-Be Learners with the total sample. As can be seen, neither sex is more oriented than the other toward continued learning; and among women, housewives differ little in orientation from single women or those working outside the home.

Learners tend to be somewhat younger than the general adult population in that 40 percent of them are under age thirty, compared to 32 percent of the total sample, while only 48 percent of the Learners are thirty-five or older, compared to 57 percent of all respondents. Both interest in and actual participation in learning activities begin to decline during the early thirties among both men and women and drop sharply after age fifty-five; yet even among respondents aged fifty-five to sixty more than half indicate continued interest in learning (Table 3). Comparing Blacks and whites, whites are somewhat better represented among Learners, with Blacks slightly underrepresented. And with regard to marital status, the high participation in learning by single people relates to the relatively young age of this subsample.

The two socioeconomic characteristics of education and occupation differentiate substantially the Learners from the Would-Be Learners as well as from the general population. Clearly, adults in America who engaged in learning activities in the past year tend to be people who are already relatively well educated: nearly twice as many of these Learners (42 percent) have had at least some postsecondary education as have all respondents (24 percent), and while 33 percent of the total sample did not graduate from secondary school, only 17 percent of the Learners never graduated. Similarly, with respect to occupational level, Learners are underrepresented among the unskilled occupations and particuarly well-represented among professionals and executives of large businesses.

In terms of geography, a disproportionately large number of Learners reside in the West rather than other regions and in urban areas rather than rural surroundings—due, to some extent, both to the generally higher level of formal education and wider postsecondary education opportunities in the West and in metropolitan areas.

Interests of Would-Be Learners

To learn in some detail the areas of knowledge and skill that American adults *wish* to study, Would-Be Learners were asked to indicate from a list of forty-eight topics *all* the subjects they would be interested in learning, and then the *one* subject they would most like to learn. Percentage responses for both questions are given in Table 2, where the forty-eight alternatives are combined into eight

Table 2.

Learning Interests of Would-be Learners
($N_w = 3001$).

Category and Topic	Percent Reporting Any Interest in Topic	Percent Reporting First Choice Interest in Topic
General education	48%	13%
Basic education	13	4
Biological sciences	8	1
Creative writing	13	1
English language	8	1
Great Books	11	0
Humanities	16	2
Languages	16	2
Physical sciences	6	0
Social sciences	9	1
Vocational subjects	78	43
Architecture	6	1
Business skills	26	9
Commercial art	12	2
Computer science	14	2
Cosmetology	10	2
Education	10	1
Engineering	9	2
Industrial trades	22	4
Journalism	4	0
Law	12	2

Table 2. (cont.)

Management skills	16	3
Medical technology	10	2
Medicine	5	1
Nursing	13	4
Salesmanship	7	1
Technical skills	19	5
Agriculture	11	3
Hobbies and recreation	63	13
Crafts	27	3
Fine and visual arts	16	2
Flight training	11	2
Performing arts	14	2
Safety	16	0
Sports and games	28	2
Travel	22	2
Home and family living	56	12
Child development	17	4
Gardening	26	2
Home repairs	25	2
Sewing, cooking	27	4
Personal development	54	7
Investment	29	4
Occult sciences	7	0
Personal psychology	15	2
Physical fitness	26	1
Public speaking	11	0
Religion	15	3
Public affairs	36	5
Citizenship	4	1
Community problems	14	1
Consumer education	15	1
Environmental studies	15	1
Public affairs	12	0
Other topic	3	1
No response	0	1

broad categories that approximate the typology developed by Johnstone and Rivera (1965) and where responses of "any interest" are indicated on the left and "first choice" are listed on the right.

PARTICULAR SUBJECTS

The two indices—"any interest" and "first choice"—yield similar but by no means identical results. Among the eight broad categories of subjects and skills for which American adults report *any* interest in learning, that of vocational subjects is the most popular, with hobbies and recreation second and the home and family living category and personal development not far behind.

Academic professionals will find it somewhat disheartening that adult Americans are so little interested in further study in traditional liberal arts subjects or, for that matter, in such public affairs topics as community and environmental problems. Most people seem mainly oriented toward improved adaptability for simple everyday living (investment, business skills, home repairs, sewing and cooking, gardening, physical fitness), together with a modicum of personal enjoyment and satisfaction (crafts, sports and games, travel). Of all forty-eight individual topics, investment and related financial matters have the greatest appeal, with 29 percent of the respondents reporting interest; followed very closely by sports and games, with 28 percent; then by crafts and by sewing and cooking, both with 27 percent; and by business skills, gardening, and physical fitness, all with 26 percent.

While these percentages shed light on the subjects American adults are interested in learning about, the "first choice" responses offer a sharper indication of what kind of learning they would actually engage in if and when they got down to it—and thus the immediate market for adult education. Here it is even clearer that vocational subjects are of greatest immediate interest, since the vocational category receives 43 percent of first choices and general education and hobbies and recreation tie for second place with only 13 percent each. Among the sixteen vocational subjects listed, business skills such as typing, accounting, and bookkeeping are by a sizable margin the most frequent first choice, at 9 percent. Technical skills such as auto mechanics, TV repair, and drafting rate second with 5 percent, followed equally at 4 percent by basic education (reading, basic math, writing), industrial trades, nursing, child development, sewing and cooking, and investment.

Comparing the "any interest" and "first choice" responses among the eight broad categories, at least half of all American adults report some interest in learning more about five of these eight general domains—but their first choice learning preferences clearly center on practical and often job-related topics: business, technical, and industrial skills, basic education, and homemaking activities. At the same time, especially large discrepancies exist between much professed general interest and little first choice priority for crafts, sports and games, gardening, and physical fitness.

CANDIDATES

Table 3 shows who among the Would-Be Learners is interested in learning what subjects by listing first-choice responses of various groups of respondents to the eight broad categories of knowledge, with these categories arranged from left to right in order of expressed interest. It also lists in column 9 the proportion of Would-Be Learners to all of the respondents of each type.

Comparing men and women, overall interest in learning *some* subject (column 9) is slightly more common among women (80 percent) than among men (74 percent). Among these male and female Would-Be Learners, the differences in interest in vocational, agricultural, and home and family courses could be expected, given the usual sex-role stereotypes in America; but for the other general categories—general education, hobbies and recreation, public affairs, and so forth—only negligible differences occur.

Blacks report substantially greater interest in vocational subjects than do whites (56 compared to 42 percent), somewhat higher interest in general education, and less interest in pursuing learning in the areas of hobbies and recreation. Although not shown in the table, the interests of Black men center on technical and business-related skills while those of Black women focus on basic education, business skills, and nursing. Among the Black respondents, only men indicate an interest in hobbies and recreation— apparently luxuries that Black women, unlike whites, cannot afford.

Table 3.

Fields of Learning of Interest to Would-be Learners, and Percent of First Choices of Would-be Learners ($N_w = 3001$)

Characteristic	1 Vocational Subjects	2 General Education	3 Hobbies, Recreation	4 Home and Family	5 Personal Development	6 Public Affairs	7 Agriculture	8 Religion	9 Would-be Learners as Percent of All Respondents ($N_{wb} = 3910$)
All would-be learners	43%	13%	13%	12%	7%	5%	3%	3%	77%
Sex:									
Male	46	12	13	5	8	6	6	2	74
Female	40	13	14	18	6	3	1	3	80
Housewife	36	9	15	25	6	4	0	5	77
Non-housewife	42	15	14	14	6	2	1	2	84
Age:									
18–24	47	12	16	9	4	3	4	2	87
25–34	44	13	10	13	8	5	3	2	83
35–54	43	12	13	12	7	5	2	3	74
55–60	30	16	17	13	8	4	6	7	58
Race:									
White	42	12	14	12	7	4	3	3	77
Black	56	18	5	9	2	3	3	3	70
Marital status:									
Single	40	13	24	5	5	3	4	2	87
Married	43	12	12	13	7	5	3	3	75
Widowed/divorced	50	10	10	14	6	4	2	3	75
Formal Schooling:									
1–8 years	36	29	5	14	2	0	5	7	55
9–11 years	48	10	13	16	2	6	2	3	75
12 years	47	8	11	12	7	4	4	3	77
Some postsecondary	44	12	18	9	7	6	0	3	89
4-year college graduate	32	16	22	9	12	5	2	1	91
Type of community:									
Urban	42	14	14	12	7	5	2	2	81
Rural	45	9	11	14	6	4	6	5	65

Note: Percentages may not total 100 percent due to rounding, "other topic," and no response—1 percent of all Would-be Learners made no first choice; 1 percent of all Would-be Learners marked "other topic" for first choice.

Single people show a relatively strong interest in hobbies and recreation, while widowed or divorced respondents, of whom 74 percent are women, are particularly oriented toward vocational subjects such as business and nursing, no doubt for purposes of economic self-sufficiency.

The strong relationship between educational attainment and the desire to engage in further learning appeared previously in Table 1. Table 3 indicates the greater interest in hobbies and recreation and personal development among those with more formal education—both in a sense being luxuries that can be afforded by the better educated and more affluent. In contrast, the relatively high interest in general education among Would-Be Learners with eight years or less of education is due to their need for basic literacy education.

In comparing urban residents with rural respondents, we see that urbanites are relatively more interested in general education and in hobbies and recreation while rural dwellers are naturally more interested in agriculture, and in religion. And although Table 3 does not report regional differences, hobbies and recreation and personal development appear to be of particularly wide interest in the western part of the country.

Subjects Taken By Learners

Turning from the knowledge and skills that adults say they would like to learn if they had the chance, and looking at the subjects in which adults have in fact received instruction other than as full-time students within the past twelve months, we find that the 31 percent of respondents who are classified as Learners studied subjects listed in Table 4 in the frequency shown there. Respondents could check as many fields as appropriate among sixteen listed in the questionnaire (item 17), and these alternative subjects have been organized in Table 4 into the eight broad categories used in the earlier Johnstone and Rivera study. The first column of this table shows the frequency with which these subjects were studied among the total sample, which approximates the adult American population. The second column lists the corresponding percentages for the Learners themselves.

Table 4.

PERCENT OF ADULTS STUDYING VARIOUS TOPICS

Category and Topic	Percent of All Respondents ($N_w = 3910$)	Percent of Learners ($N_w = 1207$)
General education	8%	25%
Adult basic education	1	4
High school level courses	2	7
College level courses	3	11
Graduate level courses	2	5
Vocational subjects	11	35
Technical and vocational skills	6	18
Managerial skills	3	10
Professional skills	3	9
Agriculture	1	3
Hobbies and recreation	13	42
Safety	3	10
Hobbies and handicrafts	8	25
Sports and recreation	4	13
Home and family living	4	13
Personal development	4	11
Religion	4	14
Public affairs	2	6
Citizenship	1	3
Civics and public affairs	1	4
Other topic	2	7

Note: Percentages for the topics within most of the broad categories total more than the percentage for the category itself because some individuals reported studying more than one of the subfields. For example, some respondents checked both the hobbies and handicrafts *and* the sports and recreation topics in the hobbies and recreation category.

Of all sixteen subjects, hobbies and handicrafts such as photography, weaving, and music, were the most popular by a sizable margin among respondents, being studied by 8 percent of the total sample (and thus by approximately 8 percent of the general population) and by one fourth of the Learners. Next most frequent were technical and vocational skills like typing and auto mechanics, studied by 6 percent of all respondents and by 18 percent of the Learners, followed not far behind by religion, home and family living, and sports and recreation courses.

Comparing the eight broad categories of subjects, that of hobbies and recreation (including safety) is most popular, with vocational training in various technical, managerial and professional skills a close second and general academic subjects, including basic education, in third place. The remaining five general content areas drew relatively small percentages of students, ranging from religion and home and family living through personal development and public affairs down to agriculture. If courses in first aid, water safety, and the like were excluded from the hobbies and recreation category, vocational subjects would be roughly equal to this remaining avocational category, with one-third of the Learners engaged in studying each of them.

Changes that have taken place in the content of adult learning activities during the last ten years, since the Johnstone and Rivera survey, can be gauged by comparing these data with those of Johnstone and Rivera. Unfortunately the comparison is approximate at best: the questions and alternative response categories were not identical in the two studies.

The proportion of Learners among the American adult population appears to have increased in the last decade. Johnstone and Rivera found that, in the year preceding June 1962, approximately one in five adults was engaged in some kind of learning outside of full-time schooling. In the current survey, close to one in three adults (31 percent) reported part-time learning activities in the year preceding early summer 1972.

One reasonably clear trend is for greater involvement in

hobbies and recreation learning. A decade ago an estimated 24 percent of adults engaged in instruction were studying hobbies and recreation topics, compared with 42 percent of the present sample who were studying these subjects. (The two categories are not entirely comparable in that the Johnstone and Rivera study did not include the alternative safety courses, chosen by 10 percent of the current Learners.) This avocational trend is consistent with increasing leisure for many adults in American society. In contrast, study of vocational subjects seems to have declined slightly, from 39 percent to 35 percent of participants.

While the general education category is particularly difficult to compare because of the different formats of the two surveys (Johnstone and Rivera's, for example, having not included basic education within general education), the study of general academic subjects may have increased somewhat in the past decade—from 15 percent in 1962 to 25 percent in 1972. Similarly studies related to personal development have increased somewhat (from 7 to 11 percent), while religious study has declined slightly (from 17 to 14 percent). Learning in the remaining categories of home and family living, agriculture, and public affairs has not essentially changed, shifting by only one or two percentage points.

LEARNERS AND THEIR SUBJECTS

Comparing subgroups of Learners in terms of the subject of their learning, Table 5 arranges the eight broad categories of content from left to right in order of participation.

As could be expected, men and women differ substantially in the subjects they study. Many more women than men reported studying topics in the general fields of hobbies and recreation (notably handicrafts), religion, home and family, and personal development, while almost twice as many men as women (46 percent to 24 percent) engaged in vocational learning and three men to every woman participated in the vocational field of management training.

Among women, non-housewives more often studied vocational and general education subjects, while housewives more commonly pursued avocational, home and family, and religious learning.

Table 5.

Fields of Learning Studied by Learners, Percent of Learners of Each Type
(N_w = 1207)

Characteristic	1 Hobbies, Recreation	2 Vocational Subjects	3 General Education	4 Religion	5 Home and Family	6 Personal Development	7 Public Affairs	8 Agriculture	9 Learners as Percent of All Respondents (N_w = 3910)
All Learners	42%	35%	25%	14%	13%	11%	6%	3%	31%
Sex:									
Male	36	46	27	8	9	7	7	5	32
Female	48	24	24	20	17	15	6	2	30
Housewife	55	7	12	31	22	17	3	0	29
Non-housewife	44	34	31	13	14	14	8	3	33
Age:									
18–24	41	40	43	6	15	14	10	7	38
25–34	45	34	24	13	16	13	3	2	36
35–54	40	34	20	18	10	10	8	2	28
55–60	45	26	12	14	13	7	1	4	22
Race:									
White	44	36	22	15	14	13	5	4	32
Black	13	37	74	2	9	0	12	0	1ᵃ
Marital status:									
Single	45	32	41	6	14	13	9	8	45
Married	42	35	22	16	12	11	6	2	30
Widowed/divorced	36	43	12	13	28	11	5	3	22
Formal schooling:									
1–8 years	35	38	20	5	21	0	0	10	10
9–11 years	32	19	35	9	15	11	13	3	20
12 years	46	33	19	17	15	12	6	5	31
Some postsecondary	46	42	29	14	10	16	4	1	48
4-year college graduate	37	40	28	12	12	10	6	2	57
Type of community:									
Urban	44	33	28	14	13	12	7	3	34
Rural	35	44	12	11	14	10	3	4	23

Note: Entries in each row for columns 1–8 total more than 100% because some respondents studied multiple subjects.

Among all Learners, the study of religion increases with age until the highest age bracket, while the study of home and family topics drops during middle age and general education declines markedly throughout aging. Among the vocational fields not detailed in Table 5, although technical and vocational training declines with age the reverse holds true, as could be expected, for managerial training.

With regard to race, the differential in participation between Blacks and whites is most marked in the areas of hobbies and recreation, religion, and personal development, where whites proportionally far outnumber Blacks. On the other hand, Black Learners greatly exceed whites in the general education fields of basic education and high school-level courses, and enroll proportionally more often in public affairs education.

In terms of marital status, single people are not only more interested in new learning, as reported earlier; they more often actually receive instruction than married, divorced, or widowed respondents. They enrolled in general education courses—particularly high school-level courses—much more often, while divorced or widowed Learners more often studied vocational subjects, probably for economic self-sufficiency, and also home and family subjects, possibly to learn how to run a household or raise a family without a partner.

In terms of educational attainment, although far more highly educated respondents participate in continued education than less educated ones, patterns of participation by field are inconsistent. The study of home and family subjects does decline consistently with formal education, however, while the study of personal development and public affairs is totally nonexistent among Learners with an eighth-grade education or less.

Among urban-rural differences, the percentage of urban Learners is more than twice that of rural Learners in general academic subjects and appreciably higher in hobbies and recreation, while rural Learners are disproportionately enrolled in vocational training. Finally, although regional differences are not shown in Table 5, three are worthy of note: A disproportionately high number of Western Learners studied hobbies and handicrafts, personal development, and undergraduate and graduate level courses; a small proportion of Southern Learners studied handicrafts and hobbies; and, for some reason, an equally small proportion of North-easterners studied religion.

Methods

PREFERRED METHODS

One of the key principles of non-traditional study is that people should be free to learn in new and different ways. Critically important, then, to planners of non-traditional programs is evidence about how people feel about these unconventional methods. In item 5 of the questionnaire, Would-Be Learners checked the one method out of eleven options that they would most like to use in learning. Table 6 lists their preferences in rank order.

Interestingly enough, the most widely preferred method, chosen by 28 percent of the Would-Be Learners, is lectures or classes. On-the-job training or internship follows with 21 percent, and short-term conferences, institutes, and workshops rank third with 13 percent. It seems clear that there is little existing interest in less conventional modes: only two percent or less chose travel-study programs, television or video tape cassettes, or records and audio cassettes.

Several differences in preference among different groups of Would-Be Learners deserve mention. Interest in on-the-job training declines with age and with educational and occupational level—the least interest in it being shown by college graduates—while interest in lectures and formal classes rises. Blacks and particularly Black women prefer on-the-job training, and Blacks more often favor group learning while whites are proportionally more interested in individualized approaches, including independent study, private individual lessons, and correspondence courses. And perhaps naturally, twice as many rural Would-Be Learners prefer self-study without formal instruction than do their urban counterparts.

METHODS USED BY LEARNERS

The Learners among the sample were asked to report the instructional methods employed in their studies, using the same list

Table 6.

METHODS FOR LEARNING

Method	Percent of Would-be Learners Preferring the Method	Percent of Learners Using the Method
Lectures or classes	28%	35%
On-the-job training, internship	21	14
Short-term conferences, institutes, or workshops	13	8
Individual lessons from a private teacher	8	6
Discussion groups, informal book club or study group	8	4
Study on my own, no formal instruction	7	17
Correspondence course	3	5
Group action project	3	2
Travel-study program	2	*
TV or video cassettes	1	*
Radio, records, or audio cassettes	1	*
Other method	*	2
No response	4	8
Total	100%	100%

* Less than 1 percent.
Note: Percentages rounded.

of eleven methods as the Would-Be Learners; and their responses appear in the second column of Table 6. Among them, 35 percent participated in lectures and classes, 17 percent studied on their own with no formal instruction, and 14 percent engaged in on-the-job training or internship, while at the other extreme less than one percent studied by means of tours, radio, records, or television.

Of the 35 percent who participated in lectures and classes,

most were from twenty-five to fifty-four years old, high school graduates, and urbanites. High school dropouts studied on their own more than respondents of other educational levels. On-the-job training was more popular with men than with women and generally with Learners under thirty-five, although not usually the most highly educated people. Three times as many unskilled workers as professionals and large businessmen, and rural more than urban Learners, used on-the-job training. Professionals and businessmen used conferences and workshops more than the general population; disproportionate numbers of respondents fifty-five to sixty also preferred conferences, workshops, and group-centered activities. Individual lessons were favored by more women than men and by more urban than rural people. Correspondence courses, on the other hand, were used more by men than by women and by rural Learners more than by urban Learners.

Both Would-Be Learners and Learners chose lectures and classes most frequently. This method and self-study are a little more frequently used by the Learners than desired by the Would-Be Learners, whereas on-the-job training is less frequently used than desired. These differences may be due to the lack of availability of desired subjects or desired methods, but it is significant that "innovative" methods have not had much impact on either Would-Be Learners or actual Learners.

In 1962 Johnstone and Rivera also asked about methods of instruction used. As now, class attendance, independent study, and lectures and talks (considered to be a method separate from classes) were most frequently used. On-the-job training is now more widely used than in 1962, while use of discussion groups (including group action projects) seems to have declined in relative popularity. Both the 1962 and 1972 surveys indicate that few American adults consciously seek to *learn* by television. In 1962, 59 out of 4624 Learners (1 percent) reported learning by educational television; in 1972, only three individuals out of 621 (unweighted sample) said they learned by television or videocassettes.

In both the 1962 and 1972 surveys more men than women used on-the-job training and correspondence courses, while more women learned through private instruction (individual lessons) and group discussions. In both surveys disproportionate numbers of young adults learned on the job, and the oldest age groups (fifty-five to over seventy in 1962, fifty-five to sixty in 1972) were least likely to attend classes and lectures.

Locations

Another concept central to non-traditional study is that education can occur in settings other than the school or college campus. In item 6 of the survey, Would-Be Learners chose their preferred location for learning from among seventeen alternatives, and item 19 asked Learners the location of their studies.

Table 7 ranks these seventeen alternatives in order of preference, and the following analysis emphasizes differences among four major types of location: (1) Home, preferred by 10 percent of Would-Be Learners and used by 17 percent of Learners; (2) Employer, preferred by 5 percent of the Would-Be Learners and used by 13 percent of Learners; (3) Educational System—the conventional instructional institutions of public high school, two-year college, private vocational-business school, four-year college, and graduate school—preferred by 45 percent of Would-Be Learners and used by 26 percent of Learners; and (4) Less Conventional Settings—a variety of less conventional locations represented by the remaining ten options (community free school, business or industrial site, individual instructor, correspondence school, community or social organization, art studio, library, religious group, government agency, recreational group)—preferred by 36 percent of Would-Be Learners and used by the same proportion of Learners.

PREFERRED LOCATION

As Table 7 shows, no single option is overwhelmingly popular among Would-Be Learners. The most popular choice is the public high school with 16 percent; followed by home, two-year college, or technical institute, and community free school, each with 10 percent; and four-year college and private business school with 8 percent each. No other option attracts more than 5 percent. In terms of general categories, 45 percent of the Would-Be Learners prefer to study in institutions comprising the educational system,

Table 7.
LOCATIONS FOR LEARNING

Location	Percent of Would-be Learners Preferring the Location	Percent of Learners Using the Location
Public high school, day or evening	16%	9%
Home	10	17
Public two-year college or technical institute	10	6
Community-run "free school"	10	3
Four-year college or university	8	6
Private vocational, trade, or business school	8	3
Employer	5	13
Business or industrial site	5	5
Individual instructor	5	4
Correspondence school	4	2
Community or social organization, such as YMCA	3	6
Graduate school	3	2
Fine or performing arts or crafts studio	3	*
Religious institution or group	2	6
Government agency (federal, state, or local)	2	5
Library or other cultural institution, such as museum	1	2
Recreational or sports group	1	2
Other location	1	2
No response	5	5
Total	100%	100%

* Less than 1 percent.
Note: Percentages rounded.

36 percent prefer other less conventional locations, 10 percent choose home study, and 5 percent favor their place of employment.

Among the 45 percent who prefer educational institutions are a few more women than men (especially in preference for public high schools), more Blacks than whites, and more urban than rural Would-Be Learners. Would-Be Learners with at least a high school diploma want to learn through a greater variety of educational institutions than do those without diplomas, who opt for either public high schools or home study more than any other choices. The group with some college but no degree shows the most interest in four-year colleges—three times the interest of respondents in general. Twice as many adults with college experience or a college degree want to learn at a four-year college or graduate school, compared with the less educated adults. Similarly among the occupations, people in the highest level jobs are the most interested in graduate schools, and white-collar workers express relatively greater interest in four-year colleges than blue-collar workers do.

LOCATIONS USED BY LEARNERS

Table 7 shows that no one location predominated as a site for the Learners either. Study at home (17 percent) led the list, followed by employer (13 percent) and high school (9 percent).

Study at home was a location reported by more housewives (20 percent) than non-housewives (11 percent), more high school dropouts (31 percent) than persons with greater (or less) education, and 10 percent more Learners in the Northeast than in other regions of the country. An employer was used by more men (16 percent) than women (10 percent), more Learners under thirty-five than over thirty-five, more Blacks (18 percent) than whites (13 percent), and more Learners with eight or fewer years of formal education than those at higher educational levels.

Use of educational institutions declines with age, whereas use of unconventional locations increases with age; twice as many of the Learners fifty-five to sixty, compared to those under twenty-five, used unconventional locations, most notably a local social organization or individual instructor. Blacks used the educational system much more than whites; high school was the only educational institution used more by whites than Blacks. Single Learners (37 percent) used educational institutions, especially colleges, more than married Learners (24 percent) or widowed and divorced Learners (17 percent). Use of the formal educational system increases with educational level among the Learners; Learners at each educational level tended to use the next educational level for learning. Urban residents used the educational system, particularly four-year colleges or graduate schools, slightly more than people in rural areas. Rural more than urban Learners were likely to use a variety of locations, especially government agencies. People in the West (who generally have more education) tended to use the educational system, especially the two-year colleges.

Would-Be Learners indicated a greater preference for the educational system and less interest in home and employer as learning sites, compared with the sites actually used by Learners. Much of the discrepancy may be a result of different areas of learning involved, the wider involvement in hobbies and recreation on the part of the Learners, or either a lack of facilities or a lack of awareness of facilities. That 45 percent of the Would-Be Learners express a preference for educational institutions while only 26 percent of the Learners use these sites may indicate that facilities do not supply the needs of those who want to learn.

Finally it is worth drawing attention again to the relatively small numbers of adults who wish to learn in a college or university setting. Only 14 percent of the Learners pursued their studies on college campuses; only 21 percent of the Would-Be Learners report wanting to study at a college or university. While the absolute numbers may seem large, the fact that the overwhelming majority of adult Learners will wish to study elsewhere than on a college campus is a sobering finding which needs to be recognized by higher education planners.

Credit

A continuing issue in adult education centers on formal acknowledgment of learning, through credits or other forms of recognition. Credit implies evaluation of students by some standard, which can markedly affect their educational experience.

PREFERRED CREDIT

Would-Be Learners were asked to check one of seven options regarding their preference for various types of credit. The left column in Table 8 shows that nearly two-thirds (63 percent) of the Would-Be Learners would like to receive some form of recognition for their learning. One-fifth would be satisfied with a certificate

Table 8.

CREDIT

Type of Credit	Percent of Would-be Learners Preferring Credit	Percent of Learners Receiving Credit
No formal credit	32%	61%
Certificate of satisfactory completion	21	15
Skill certificate	20	7
High school diploma	5	4
Two-year college degree	4	2
Four-year college degree	8	3
Advanced college degree	5	2
Other type of credit	1	2
No response	4	4
Total	100%	100%

of satisfactory completion; another fifth are interested in skill certification; and 22 percent want educational credit: a high school diploma (5 percent) or college degree (17 percent).

Men and women have fairly similar preferences for credit, although more men (29 percent) than women (21 percent) are interested in skill certification and an advanced degree, while more women (23 percent) than men (19 percent) want a certificate of satisfactory completion. Desires for college credit are similar for men (18 percent) and single or working women (20 percent), while housewives are somewhat less interested in a college degree.

Interest in some form of credit decreases with age, ranging from 76 percent for individuals between age eighteen and twenty-four to 37 percent among people over fifty-five. Interest in college credit also declines with age, with more Would-Be Learners aged twenty-five to thirty-four expressing interest (26 percent), especially for four-year and advanced degrees, than any other age group. Adults between age eighteen and twenty-four are most interested in a high school diploma; almost a third want a skill certificate, with more interest shown by young men (37 percent) than women (25 percent). More Blacks are interested in credit than whites, with many Black men interested in high school credit and skill certification, and two-year college credit of interest much more frequently to Black women than to Black men.

In terms of educational level, most college graduates (53 percent) have no interest in more credits, while Would-Be Learners with eight or fewer years of schooling are the most likely to prefer a certificate of satisfactory completion. The level of credit desired naturally varies with educational (and occupational) level: The widest interest in advanced degree credit is reported by college graduates (and by professionals and executives of large businesses), while interest in four-year college degree credit occurs predominantly among respondents with only some postsecondary education. Desire for credit toward high school diplomas is high, as expected, among people who have none, and skill certification is wanted most by high school graduates with no college experience (27 percent) and blue-collar workers in contrast to only 5 percent of the college graduates who want such certification.

Several patterns emerge when interest in credit is analyzed according to the preferred field of study, as shown in the top half of Table 9. Would-Be Learners of vocational subjects most often want some form of credit for their work, while people interested in religious studies and hobbies and recreation are the least interested in credits. *College* credit is most widely desired by people interested in such vocational subjects as education or teacher training (83 percent), law (80 percent), medicine or dentistry (70 percent), management skills (49 percent), engineering (43 percent), and architecture (40 percent). Desire for college credit is

Table 9.
CREDIT BY FIELD OF LEARNING

	No formal credit (975)	Certificate satisfactory completion (625)	Skill certificate (600)	High school diploma (152)	College degree (510)
All Would-Be Learners (3001)	32%	21%	20%	5%	17%
WOULD-BE LEARNERS					
Preferred Field of Learning					
General education (377)	39	15	8	13	20
Vocational subjects (1291)	16	23	29	5	24
Agriculture (86)	47	13	31	0	7
Hobbies, recreation (403)	50	19	15	3	8
Home and family (360)	46	26	9	6	5
Personal development (204)	43	21	14	1	19
Religion (89)	50	25	7	5	3
Public affairs (136)	47	17	17	0	14
All Learners (1207)	(734)	(183)	**LEARNERS** (81)	(52)	(94)
	61%	15%	7%	4%	7%
Participation in Field of Learning					
General education (304)	33	12	5	16	28
Vocational subjects (422)	51	21	14	3	6
Agriculture (41)	77	0	13	0	0
Hobbies, recreation (505)	72	15	6	2	3
Home and family (161)	81	4	5	0	3
Personal development (138)	77	6	7	5	4
Religion (167)	72	11	5	4	3
Public affairs (77)	61	13	9	0	13

also frequently reported by people interested in general education (notably in the humanities—literature, philosophy, and art or music appreciation) and in personal development (particularly personal psychology—encounter groups or study of the "psychology of everyday life").

High school diplomas are most wanted by respondents interested in general education—especially in basic education (reading, basic math, and writing) and in English language training. Adults oriented toward agriculture and vocational subjects—cosmetology, medical technology, medicine or dentistry, nursing, engineering, industrial trades, and computer science—are most interested in skill certification. Interest in a certificate of satisfactory completion cuts across all content fields; at least 13 percent of the respondents interested in any field of learning would be satisfied with this kind of credit, while the most interest in such a certificate occurs among people who want to study English, gardening, environmental subjects such as ecology and conservation, safety, or physical fitness and self-defense.

CREDIT EARNED BY LEARNERS

As indicated in the right-hand column of Table 8, one-third of the actual Learners who studied one or more subjects in the last year received some form of recognition: 15 percent, a certificate of satisfactory completion; 7 percent, skill certification; and 11 percent, academic credit. Only about one in fourteen received credit toward a college degree.

Among Learners, proportionally a few more men had earned credit in the preceding year than women; more young people (particularly those between eighteen and twenty-four) than old; and many more Blacks (three-fourths) than whites (one-third). The level of the credits they earned naturally corresponded to their level of educational attainment: Learners with less than twelve years of schooling most often received credit toward a high school diploma, while those with four or more years of college more often received advanced degree credit. Occupational level followed roughly the same pattern, with credit toward a skill certificate earned mainly by Learners with blue-collar jobs, and credit toward advanced degrees most often received by professionals and businessmen.

Table 9 makes clear that those Learners taking general education courses primarily received credit: six out of ten of them received some kind of recognition, compared to only three out of ten in the total sample of Learners. Roughly half of the respondents who took high school or general education college level courses preceding the survey received high school or college credit for their work. In only two fields other than general education—vocational subjects and public affairs—did as many as a third of the Learners receive credit.

Comparing Learners with Would-Be Learners, while the highest percentages of both groups prefer no credit or only a certificate of satisfactory completion, the Would-Be Learners twice as often express a desire for credit than Learners actually receive it; thus while only one-third of the Learners obtained credit for a learning activity, nearly two-thirds of the Would-Be Learners were interested in credit for their first-choice learning activity. And three times as many Would-Be Learners were interested in skill certification as Learners who received such certification. Comparing these 1972 data with the 1962 data by Johnstone and Rivera, we find that learning for credit appears to have become more widespread in that decade. Only one-sixth of the courses taken in 1962 were for some type of credit, while one-third (15 percent, certificate of satisfactory completion; 18 percent, skill certification or educational credit) of recent Learners obtained some form of recognition for their learning activities.

To estimate the extent to which the present adult population aspires to some formal certification, particularly a degree, in the future, both Would-Be Learners and Learners were asked to indicate all the certificates or degrees ranging from "none" to "doctoral degree" they would like to obtain in the next ten years. Among the total sample, 39 percent indicated no interest in formal recognition; 22 percent would like to receive a certificate or license; 16 percent, a high school diploma; 12 percent, a B.A. degree; 9 percent, an A.A. degree; 8 percent, an M.A. degree; and 4 percent, a doctorate. Thus while noncredited learning will continue to be sought by many adults, the majority may seek learning opportunities that lead cumulatively to formal recognition.

Reasons for Learning

In items 9 and 25 (Appendix A) Would-Be Learners and Learners indicated the importance to them of twenty alternative reasons for learning. This list incorporates seven factors developed by Burgess (1971) and two additional factors not delineated in the Burgess factors but judged to be important—desire for personal fulfillment and desire for cultural knowledge.

REASONS OF WOULD-BE LEARNERS

Would-Be Learners checked whether each of the twenty reasons in item 9 was "very important," "somewhat important," or "not at all important" to them. The left-hand column of figures in Table 10 shows the percent who reported the reasons as "very important." Knowledge and personal fulfillment are the most frequently cited reasons for learning indicated by Would-Be Learners. Personal (economic) goals—getting a new job or working toward a certificate or license—are also relatively common reasons for learning.

Some subgroups report "no reason" as "very important" frequently; for example, twice as many respondents between fifty-five and sixty indicate no reason as those from eighteen to twenty-four; and thus the subgroup over fifty-five indicates an average of 2.8 reasons as very important, while the total sample of Would-Be Learners reports an average of 4.6 reasons. Similarly Blacks generally cite more reasons as very important—indicating an average of 6.3 compared to an average of 4.4 reasons for whites, while about twice as many whites as Blacks consider no one of the reasons to be very important.

Comparisons of percentages of subgroups must thus hold this caveat in mind. Nevertheless, men (especially aged twenty-five to fifty-four) report "job advancement" more often than women; women (especially in childbearing years) cite "be a better parent or spouse" more often than men. Knowledge reasons are cited

Table 10.

Reasons for Learning

Reasons	Percent of Would-be Learners Checking "Very Important"	Percent of Learners Checking Why They Participated
Knowledge Goals		
Become better informed	56%	55%
Satisfy curiosity	35	32
Personal Goals		
Get new job	25	18
Advance in present job	17	25
Get certificate or license	27	14
Attain degree	21	9
Community Goals		
Understand community problems	17	9
Become better citizen	26	11
Work for solutions to problems	16	9
Religious Goals		
Serve church	12	10
Further spiritual well-being	19	13
Social Goals		
Meet new people	19	18
Feel sense of belonging	20	9
Escape Goals		
Get away from routine	19	19
Get away from personal problems	11	7
Obligation Fulfillment		
Meet educational standards	13	4
Satisfy employer	24	27
Personal Fulfillment		
Be better parent, spouse	30	19
Become happier person	37	26
Cultural Knowledge— study own culture	14	8
Other reasons	4	2
No response or other response	14	3

Note: Columns do not total 100 because respondents gave multiple reasons. These data supercede those reported in *Diversity by Design* and *The External Degree,* which were based on preliminary analyses.

especially often by young women, while young men aspire particularly to new jobs and degrees.

Learning for reasons of knowledge does not decline appreciably with age, but learning for a degree, certification or licensing, or a new job does decline, especially after age thirty-four. Escape reasons and feeling a sense of belonging are most important to respondents under twenty-five. Personal fulfillment is also relatively more important to younger adults. Serving the church as a motivation shows little variation with age, and improving spiritual well-being is indicated least often by the respondents from thirty-five to sixty.

In terms of educational level, college graduates cite knowledge reasons most often and job reasons least often. Interest in complying with requirements generally declines with the level of formal education; only 3 percent of the college graduates, compared to 23 percent of those with elementary schooling only, want to learn in order to meet requirements for an educational program. Religious reasons appear to be relatively important for the groups with the least formal education. Patterns of response according to occupation are similar to the educational patterns: respondents in the top occupations are the ones who most frequently cite knowledge reasons and least often indicate job reasons.

Differences in the reasons of urban and rural Would-Be Learners are generally small, although religious reasons are reported more often by people living in rural areas and in the South than elsewhere.

REASONS OF LEARNERS

Instead of indicating the degree of importance for each reason as did Would-Be Learners, Learners indicated in item 25 all the reasons why they had engaged in their studies. The right-hand column of Table 10 gives the percentages of Learners who checked each reason.

For Learners, as for Would-Be Learners, the most important reasons center around knowledge for its sake, with personal fulfillment reasons and job-related reasons next in importance.

Differences between the sexes in reasons for learning are

more pronounced among Learners than Would-Be Learners. Men more often reported job advancement and the requirements of employer or other authority, while women (especially housewives) more frequently mentioned personal fulfillment, especially being a better parent or spouse, curiosity, getting away from the routine of daily living, and religious reasons.

As with the Would-Be Learners, Learners citing a new job, certification or licensing, or degree are most frequently in the youngest age group. Being a better parent or spouse was most often reported by Learners between twenty-five and fifty-four. Learning for curiosity increases with age, with the age group from fifty-five to sixty nearly twice as likely as the group under thirty-five to cite curiosity as a reason for their studies.

Black Learners much more frequently than whites mentioned certification or licensing, a degree, new job, "learning about my own background and culture" and community goals, such as the reduction of discrimination and pollution, while white Learners were more concerned than Blacks with job advancement, getting away from the routine of daily living, and knowledge for its own sake.

In terms of educational level, individuals with at least some high school experience most frequently reported social goals and community goals as reasons, and were somewhat more likely to learn for knowledge reasons than those with only an elementary education. As with Would-Be Learners, Learners in the top occupations most frequently mentioned becoming better informed as their reason for studying. Learners in the unskilled and semiskilled jobs were the most likely to learn to become a happier person and for escape reasons. Learners who were fully employed learned for the purposes of job advancement and to meet requirements of employer or authority more frequently than those not fully employed (most of whom are women), who more often gave religious, escape, and personal fulfillment reasons than did Learners with full-time employment.

Comparing the reasons cited by the Learners in the present study with those cited by Learners in 1962, Johnstone and Rivera (1965) dealt with eight reasons, six of which correspond to reasons used in the present survey. They asked Learners the purposes they had in mind when they enrolled for adult education courses: "In which of the following ways had you hoped the course would be helpful to you?" The two reasons which have no specific counterparts in the present study are "spend my spare time more enjoyably" and "carry out everyday tasks and duties away from home." In 1972, as in 1962, the most frequently mentioned reason for learning was that of becoming better informed. A much larger proportion (55 percent) of today's Learners mentioned this reason, however, than did the 37 percent of Learners in the Johnstone-Rivera study. Job reasons appear to be somewhat less important to Learners today. For example, a new job was mentioned by 36 percent in 1962, but by only 18 percent in 1972. Along with the decrease in job-related reasons is an increased concern with the problem of routine. About twice as many Learners today—19 percent—report they learn to get away from the daily routine (compared with 10 percent in 1962). Thus the Learner of today perhaps has more opportunity to learn for personal development and to escape routine instead of for job reasons.

Several similarities exist among the various subgroups of Learners in both 1962 and 1972. Job-related considerations were more important to men than women; home-centered reasons were generally of more importance to women than to men in both surveys. In both 1962 and 1972 young adults tended to learn more for job reasons than did older respondents, who wanted to learn for less practical reasons—in 1972, notably for curiosity; in 1962, to become a better informed person.

Barriers

Since the non-traditional movement seeks to facilitate adult learning through the use of maximally effective delivery systems for diverse populations, it is important for planners of non-traditional programs to know why people do not engage in further learning. The Would-Be Learners were asked to indicate all the reasons, from a list of twenty-four, that they felt were important in keeping them from learning what they want to learn (item 11, Appendix A). Table 11 shows the percentages that checked each of the barriers.

Table 11.

BARRIERS TO LEARNING

Barriers	Percent of Would-be Learners
Cost, including books, learning materials, child care, transportation, as well as tuition	53%
Not enough time	46
Don't want to go to school full-time	35
Home responsibilities	32
Job responsibilities	28
Amount of time required to complete program	21
Afraid that I'm too old to begin	17
Courses aren't scheduled when I can attend	16
No information about places or people offering what I want	16
Strict attendance requirements	15
Low grades in past, not confident of my ability	12
Courses I want don't seem to be available	12
No child care	11
Too much red tape in getting enrolled	10
Not enough energy and stamina	9
Don't enjoy studying	9
No transportation	8
No place to study or practice	7
Don't meet requirements to begin program	6
Tired of school, tired of classrooms	6
No way to get credit for a degree	5
Don't know what to learn or what it would lead to	5
Hesitate to seem too ambitious	3
Friends or family don't like the idea	3
Other barrier	2
No response	3

Note: Percentages do not total 100 because of multiple responses.

Financial cost was the most widely reported potential obstacle, cited by slightly more than half of all Would-Be Learners. Second was "not enough time," reported by 46 percent of the sample, followed by not wanting to go to school full-time, home responsibilities, job responsibilities, and the amount of time required to complete the program, each indicated by at least one-fifth of the group.

Twice as many men as women mention job responsibilities; the opposite occurs with home responsibilities; and almost ten times as many women as men cite lack of child care as a barrier to learning. Women who are single or working outside the home echo the men's concern with job responsibilities as well as lack of time, and women in general feel more constrained by cost (available finances) than men. Interestingly, men more often report not enough time and the amount of time needed to complete a program as problems; women (both housewives and non-housewives) more frequently mention not enough energy; and they disproportionately report "I'm afraid I'm too old to begin."

Several of the barriers vary markedly with age. Cost is a deterrent particularly for adults under thirty-five, with nearly three-fourths of the young women and more than half of the young men indicating some kind of financial burden regarding tuition, books, materials, transportation, or child care. The youngest respondents most often indicate not wanting to go to school full-time and being tired of school and classrooms. Low grades in the past, as expected, is of special concern to the group with the most recent experience with grades; three times as many adults under twenty-five, compared with the older respondents, consider this an obstacle to further learning. Barriers of relative significance to people in the middle age groups include not enough time (mentioned particularly by men) and responsibilities of the home and care of children (cited nearly twice as frequently by women as by men). Feelings of being too old and not having enough energy naturally increase with age, especially among women.

Whites mention not enough time and home responsibilities twice as frequently as Blacks, and more commonly cite job responsibilities, not wanting to go to school full time, and not enjoying studying. Proportionately twice as many Blacks as whites mention low grades in the past and not meeting requirements to begin the program, with cost, child care, and lack of transportation and study facilities being relatively widespread deterrents for Blacks, and cost and child care of particular concern to Black women.

Understandably, people of limited education feel that low grades in the past are an important barrier; three times as many adults with an elementary education as high school graduates mention this problem, while no college graduate in the sample considers poor past performance a barrier. The importance of requirements to begin programs and enjoyment of studying also declines with increased formal schooling. In addition, disproportionate numbers of respondents with no college experience are troubled by financial considerations and fears of being too old to begin learning. The more highly educated respondents tend to report time problems—job responsibilties, not enough time, the amount of time required to complete program, and courses not being conveniently scheduled.

All in all, the greatest barriers for Would-Be Learners, aside from cost, seem to relate to the factor of time. Not enough time, full-time attendance, job responsibilities, and home responsibilities all seem to be ways for respondents to indicate that their present situation does not leave enough free time for learning. While one cannot say whether this is a realistic appraisal or a rationalized barrier, available time is certainly widely *reported* as a deterrent to acting on learning desires.

Pertinent to cost and time as major barriers to continuing education is the amount of money and time people are willing to spend to further their learning. Would-Be Learners were asked in item 10 the amount of money they would be willing to spend for studying their subject of interest. From among alternatives ranging from "nothing" to "more than two hundred dollars," 23 percent indicated an unwillingness to pay anything, and 30 percent would pay no more than fifty dollars, but a surprisingly large 42 percent reported willingness to pay between fifty and two hundred dollars. Item 24 asked Learners how they financed their studies; 31 percent reported that the course or activity was free, 39 percent said they or their family paid for it, and 18 percent said that costs were assumed by their employer. Roughly two out of five adult learning activities, then, take place at direct financial cost to the learner himself.

Concerning the amount of time they would be willing to spend on a learning activity, Would-Be Learners were asked in item 8 to select one of seven options, ranging from "less than one month" to "more than two years." Somewhat surprisingly, there is little interest in the shortest option; "less than one month" is cited by only 2 percent of the respondents. Over half say they would prefer to spend at least nine months. Thus, while lack of time is reported as a widespread obstacle to adult education, nonetheless many Would-Be Learners say they are willing to spend substantial amounts of time at it—a fourth of them being willing to meet two or more evenings a week, as item 7 in Appendix A shows.

Learners were asked in item 22 how long their course or learning activity ran; 37 percent reported it lasted three months or less, while 30 percent reported it extended over nine months or more. As might be expected then, the actual length of time spent on learning is somewhat shorter than the time anticipated by the Would-Be Learners; but it is impressive that the majority of Learners devoted at least four months to their most recent studies. As another index, item 21 asked Learners how much time each week they spent on their learning activity; 33 percent said they used two to four hours a week, and 44 percent reported five or more hours a week. At a minimum, these patterns show that many adults are truly serious about continued learning.

Implications for Planning

The likelihood that over three-quarters of American adults are interested in some form of new learning, and almost a third of them participated in some kind of formal or informal learning within the past year, based on a national probability sample of almost 1900 respondents, has major implications for planners of non-traditional programs. Translated into numbers, some eighty million Americans between the ages of eighteen and sixty who are not studying full-time are probably interested in continuing their learning, and some thirty-two million adults have most likely recently engaged in learning.

Of particular import for the planners of adult education are both the wide range of learning interests expressed by adults and the generally pragmatic and nonacademic nature of these interests. Vocational subjects rank as first choices for 43 percent of potential learners, followed by general education (13 percent), hobbies and recreation (13 percent), and home and family living (12 percent). Investing, sports and games, crafts, sewing and cooking, business skills, gardening, and physical fitness are all of some interest to at least one-fourth of these adults—more than any academic discipline. Only 17 percent of these Would-Be Learners want college credit, and over 50 percent would be satisfied either with no credit or with a certificate of satisfactory completion. Only one in five feels that "work toward a degree" is a very important reason for learning.

The learning activities of the 31 percent of the respondents who had participated in educational activities within the past year further accentuate the nonacademic nature of much adult learning. These Learners tend to be relatively young, well-educated, and of high occupational level. Yet postsecondary institutions were used by no more than one-sixth of them. Forty-two percent of them pursued hobbies and recreational subjects, 35 percent improved vocational skills, and only 25 percent studied general academic subjects. Only 7 percent of the Learners received college credit, while 61 percent received no formal credit, and 15 percent obtained only certificates of satisfactory completion. Learners, too, seem more concerned with content or participation per se than with academic recognition.

It thus appears that the adult education programs of public secondary schools and community colleges may come closer to meeting the desires of the bulk of American adults than non-traditional programs that emphasize credit and degrees. While interest in college credit and degrees obviously exists, this interest is most characteristic of individuals who already have some postsecondary education and are relatively high on the economic ladder. Focusing on credit and degrees will continue to exclude from the learning process those who until now have been excluded.

The barriers of cost (mentioned by 53 percent of potential learners) and time (46 percent) present a challenge to the development of new delivery systems. Not only must the content of programs be appropriate, but to maximize adult participation its delivery must be inexpensive and convenient. In particular, we suspect from this survey that the time required to travel to and from a learning site is a serious factor in preventing much adult learning. Yet despite this problem of travel, prospective learners express surprisingly low interest in television—a fact that highlights the difficulties of creating broad acceptance for new delivery systems. Most likely, study by television is perceived by many respondents as a relatively solitary activity. Hence while televised instruction may be adequate to provide information, home viewing does not meet the interest of many Would-Be Learners in social interaction. Three-fourths of them prefer to learn in group settings such as classes, discussion groups, conferences, workshops, group action projects, and on the job. Developing television and other technological delivery systems that meet these social needs of Learners might markedly increase their popularity and use.

Another fact that institutional planners should keep in mind from these data is that adults differ substantially in their learning interests and activities according to sex, age, previous education, occupation, race, size of community, and even region of the country. Consequently, national statistics on the overall market for further education should be interpreted in light of local conditions and the distinctive constituencies of individual institutions and agencies.

Nonetheless, the survey data presented above illustrate the breadth and depth of the current market for adult education in America and, in particular, the possible dimensions of the emerging non-traditional thrust in adult learning. From them planners may better be able to delineate policy alternatives and design and implement programs tailored to adult interests in a nation and an era committed to life-long learning.

References

BURGESS, P. "Reasons for Adult Participation in Group Educational Activities." *Adult Education,* 1971, *22*(1), 3–29.

Commission on Non-Traditional Study. *Diversity by Design.* San Francisco: Jossey-Bass, 1973.

HOULE, C. O. *The External Degree*. San Francisco: Jossey-Bass, 1973.

JOHNSTONE, J. W. C., and RIVERA, R. J. *Volunteers for Learning*. Chicago: Aldine, 1965.

Non-Traditional Opportunities
and Programs

JANET RUYLE
LUCY ANN GEISELMAN

ๅๅๅๅๅๅๅๅๅๅๅๅๅๅๅ๕๕๕๕๕๕๕๕๕๕๕๕๕๕๕

Many of the ideas behind the non-traditional study movement are rooted in earlier practices of British and American higher education, including advanced placement, tutorial study, informal education for adults, and time-shortened and external degrees, to name only a few. But these practices are now taking on new dimensions as a wave of interest in them has swept the country. Colleges and universities are increasingly awarding academic credit for knowledge and experience formerly unaccreditable; they are creating more programs for adults beyond the typical "collegiate" age of eighteen to twenty-one; and they are offering more and more programs off campus and by new media.

When the Commission on Non-Traditional Study agreed that up-to-date information about present offerings as well as pro-

Assistance in this study by K. Patricia Cross, Leland L. Medsker, JB Lon Hefferlin, Mel Bloom, Kathryn Hill, and Ann Kirton is gratefully acknowledged.

53

posals and plans for new programs was an urgent need, the Center for Research and Development in Higher Education at Berkeley was asked to undertake this basic inventory.

Design of the Study

To describe the characteristics of non-traditional opportunities and programs currently provided or planned by American colleges and universities, in 1972 the Center surveyed the entire population of American colleges and universities and their branches listed in the *Education Directory* of the U. S. Office of Education except for the eleven institutions located in territories beyond the fifty states, and some two hundred professional schools—such as optometric or theological schools or maritime academies and the like, which offer specialized professional training rather than general programs. Because the institutions listed in the *Education Directory* are all accredited or approved colleges and universities, some new and widely publicized non-traditional institutions such as Empire State College and Minnesota Metropolitan State College were not surveyed because they were awaiting accreditation or approval of some agency. In the spring of 1972, the 2670 eligible institutions— the nation's traditional colleges and universities—received the questionnaire reproduced in Appendix B. Later, nonrespondents received a return postcard, asking whether they offered any non-traditional programs even if they were unable to provide information about them on the questionnaire. By the deadline for the study, some 72 percent of the institutions had responded. Of these, 1207 returned the questionnaire—1185 of which were deemed usable for this report. An additional 724 institutions provided limited information about their programs through postcard or materials, and 739 did not respond. The 1185 institutions did not differ greatly from others, when compared by institutional type, although slightly more of the large senior colleges and universities and slightly fewer of the small two-year colleges are represented among them than in the total population.

Further analyses of respondents and nonrespondents on other variables led to the conclusion that the 1185 may be assumed to be generally representative of American colleges and universities at

large, with three exceptions: First, because comparatively fewer
two-year institutions responded, extrapolations to the population of
two-year colleges at large may be less reliable than for universities
or senior colleges. Second, and for the same reason, wherever major
differences occur between universities and two-year colleges on any
particular variable, the total percentages are skewed in the direction
of the universities. Nevertheless, in spite of their lower rate of response, the two-year colleges constitute 34 percent of the total
responses of all institutions, while only 19 percent of the responses
are from universities. Thus the majority of institutions responding
in the survey are public two-year colleges and private four- or five-
year colleges. Third and most important, the 1185 institutions
whose responses form the basis of this report may be more involved
in non-traditional study than are colleges and universities in
general. One item of evidence leads to this conclusion: 47 percent
of them reported offering programs they consider to be non-traditional, while only 37 percent of the other 724 institutions that responded by card reported such programs. Thus caution should be
exercised in extrapolating the following data on the number of non-
traditional programs and opportunities to the total population of
institutions. For example, if all 739 nonrespondent institutions are
as conventional as the 724 that responded by card, probably only
between 35 and 40 percent of American colleges and universities
can claim to offer any non-traditional programs, instead of the 47
percent described in later pages. (Readers who wish further details
about these issues or the tabulations by type of institution for the
following data may obtain them from Wesley W. Walton, Project
Manager, Non-Traditional Study Research Program, Educational
Testing Service, Princeton, New Jersey 08540.)

Opportunities for Adult and Part-Time Students

The findings of Carp, Peterson, and Roelfs in Chapter Two
demonstrate beyond question the desire of adult Americans for
continued education. The present survey of the supply of opportunities to meet this demand reveals that adults are welcomed in
all but about one-sixth of the colleges and universities of the nation.
Only 17 percent of the responding institutions state that adults over

twenty-five are not actively encouraged or recruited to attend. Nineteen out of every twenty community colleges report seeking adult students—more than any other type of institution. And although proportionally fewer universities than colleges are interested in adults as undergraduate students, nonetheless nearly two out of three encourage them to enroll.

The overwhelming majority of colleges and universities expect their adult students to enroll in regular programs along with younger students. Only 5 percent admit most adults into special part-time programs.

Unfortunately adults cannot easily know if institutions are interested in them. Some colleges that admit adults do not have active recruitment programs for them. Ten percent do not publicize their interest in adults in any way, and another 10 percent merely make literature available to adults on inquiry. A little more than half of those interested in enrolling adults place newspaper or radio and television advertisements to this effect, and less than half maintain occupational contacts with professional societies, military services, industrial corporations, or other sources of potential students. A fourth of them spread the word through community agencies and organizations, such as welfare offices and churches. Only one in five provides special facilitating services for adults, such as low fees or special counselors. All in all, it appears that four out of five colleges do make some special attempt to recruit older students, but many still rely primarily on word of mouth. Even among community colleges, nearly one-fourth do not advertise their interest in adults through the mass media, possibly deeming advertisements an unnecessary expense or assuming that adults are familiar with local opportunities.

PART-TIME OPPORTUNITIES

In three out of four American colleges and universities students can earn their undergraduate degree entirely by part-time attendance, although some short-term intensive campus residence may be required. Another 15 percent permit students to take at least some of their work—up to 75 percent of it—on a part-time basis. Less than 10 percent require students to complete their degree only by full-time attendance.

While different types of institutions have different regulations about part-time enrollment, two generalizations are clear: First, more two-year colleges grant degrees on the basis of part-time attendance than do four-year colleges, and more four-year colleges do so than universities. Second, more publicly supported institutions grant degrees by part-time study than do private institutions. Thus more community and state colleges grant degrees earned part-time than do religious or independent colleges. Putting these two facts together shows that students can earn a degree on a part-time basis more often from a public community college—from nine out of ten of them—than from any other type of college or university. Although fewer independent and religious universities than other institutions permit part-time study leading to degrees, over half grant undergraduate degrees for part-time work.

Since adults and part-time students may have family, economic, and educational problems different from those of traditional undergraduates, they may need different opportunities and services than other students. Institutions can facilitate the attendance of non-traditional students in these ways:

Tuition. Only occasionally—at 3 percent of the institutions—do tuition rates discriminate against part-time students by requiring them to pay the same tuition fees as full-time students. In all other institutions, part-time students pay on a per-credit or per-unit basis or at some other reduced rate. Sometimes the aggregate cost of their courses may be higher to them in the long run than to full-time students, but at least they are not required to pay full-time rates for part-time attendance.

Financial aid. Part-time students are eligible for at least some kind of financial assistance in more than half of the institutions that permit them to earn degrees entirely by part-time study—at six out of ten senior colleges and universities and at seven out of ten two-year institutions. Among the two-year colleges that provide financial aid to these students, 59 percent make scholarships or other non-repayable grants available to them; 49 percent provide work-study jobs; and about 45 percent reserve NDEA loans, federally insured loans, or other loan funds for them. Among senior colleges and universities that provide aid, half offer one or another type of loan, 47 percent provide scholarships and grants, and 42 percent have work-study jobs. But since a third of the institutions make no financial provisions for part-time students, such students who need aid should inquire about its availability before deciding which college to enter.

Child care. At seven out of ten institutions, parents should be prepared to find and pay for child care on their own if they want to enroll, since most colleges and universities do not provide child care or assist in locating child-care facilities. Nevertheless, one in every six institutions will at least assist in locating such facilities, and one in ten will offer these services itself. Among the 10 percent that offer child care, the majority charge for the service; only 3 percent of all institutions provide care for the children of students during class without extra charge. More of the institutions that allow students to earn degrees entirely on a part-time basis are responsive to needs for child care than others, and among all types of institutions, public universities are taking the lead in locating and providing these services.

Special counseling. The broader experience of adults, their motivation for learning, and their freedom from compulsory schooling not only distinguish them from younger students but, together with the distinctive educational problems of adults, may call for specialized guidance and counseling. Yet there are separate counseling and advisement services for adults in less than 10 percent of the surveyed institutions. Conditions vary within another 8 percent for which data exist, but in slightly more than 80 percent of the institutions the counseling staff and services are the same for adults as for younger students.

Far more two-year colleges keep their counseling offices open before and after classes for evening and weekend students than do senior colleges and universities: 85 percent of the two-year colleges that grant degrees for part-time study provide counseling at a time convenient to part-time students in contrast to only 52 percent of the senior institutions.

Other services. In three out of four institutions, the part-time student who attends class on evenings or weekends will not have to take time off from work during weekdays to use the library, student lounges, and study areas. Laboratories, bookstores, and cafeterias are similarly open before and after their classes in at least half of the institutions; but access to most other services is limited, with the proportion open at convenient times for part-time students declining from 39 percent for physical education and recreation facilities and less for computer terminals or centers, business office, financial aids office, and placement offices, down to only 22 percent for health services. By and large services are available before and after evening and weekend classes at more of the two-year colleges than at senior colleges and universities.

OPPORTUNITIES FOR "STOPPING OUT"

In the past, undergraduates have been allowed to interrupt their education in most institutions only by taking a leave of absence, and continuous registration was expected. Recently more students have felt the need to interrupt their undergraduate study for various reasons. While only 4 percent of the institutions now actually encourage intermittent or interruptible study by undergraduates, nearly half report that they facilitate the process but do not encourage it. Another quarter neither encourage nor discourage the idea, and only 17 percent continue to expect their students to complete their programs by continuous registration. No large differences among major types of institutions exist on this issue, although somewhat more private institutions than public ones report that they facilitate the process of "stopping out" even if they do not actively encourage it.

Opportunities to Earn Credit for Nonclassroom Learning

For years, with interest coming in cycles, educators have wrestled with the question of whether to grant credit to students who have acquired independently of the institution a skill or a body of knowledge within the purview of the institutional curriculum. Standardized examinations to test such skills and knowledge have come to be widely accepted, but the use of the results of the examinations is not at all standardized; some institutions accept the results only for placement or to waive required courses while others grant extensive credit for them toward a degree. Credit by examination remains controversial in some institutions because of disagreements over which examinations to use, what scores are acceptable for credit, how much credit should be allowed, and whether credit will be accepted by another institution.

Even more controversial than credit by examination for traditional subject matter is credit for experiences not directly related to traditional courses. Many people may agree that experience is more relevant to education than courses, lectures, and reading assignments; but question how educational experiences can be evaluated and equated to credit hours without an examination. And some question whether "learning" experiences related to personal development or to employable skills should be eligible for credit if they are unrelated to a college education as traditionally conceived.

These issues fundamentally affect the roles and the purposes of colleges and universities—particularly those of teaching and granting degrees. Does a degree certify simply that a student has mastered a body of knowledge or also that he has spent a certain amount of time in college? It did not seem necessary to draw this distinction in the past since the two went together. Today, however, many institutions are rethinking the criteria for their degrees because of the demand for greater academic flexibility and opportunities.

PAST WORK EXPERIENCES

Most institutions currently will not grant credit for work experience—such as teaching in the Peace Corps, VISTA service, or other volunteer or professional experience—unless the student passes an examination as well. Respondents were asked to indicate whether any of the following four students would ordinarily receive credit for their experience without having to take a special examination: A 25-year-old student with two years of teaching experience in the Peace Corps or VISTA; an older man with ten years of investment counseling experience; a middle-aged wife with five years of volunteer social work experience; or a sophomore who dropped out of another college after his freshman year and worked in a newspaper office for a year. At present, no more than 8 percent of the responding institutions grant credit for the most acceptable of these four experiences—Peace Corps or VISTA service—and only 5 percent grant credit for the least accepted—volunteer social work.

A few more independent colleges and universities than either the public or the religious institutions will allow such credit. But even institutions that are liberal in granting credit by examination are not likely to accept these experiences without an examination; only 18 percent of them report that without a test they grant credit.

COURSES TAKEN ELSEWHERE

Students can more often receive credit for previous education than for work experiences. Servicemen will receive credit for military courses recommended by the Committee on Accreditation of Service Experience of the American Council on Education in 50 percent of the institutions that report giving credit for out-of-class work, but in only 35 percent of all institutions surveyed. Students who transfer from unaccredited colleges will receive some transfer credit from over a fourth of the institutions. One in every six institutions give credit for study abroad sponsored by groups other than educational institutions, and one in seven will do so far for completing formal courses of instruction in business, industry, or government agencies. But many of these institutions will grant these credits only after an examination.

NON-COURSE WORK

At over half of the institutions students may gain credit toward their degree for work like that listed below:

Cooperative work experience	35%
Volunteer work in community agency	28
A completed work (book, sculpture, patent, etc.)	17
Participant in local community theater, orchestra, or civic activity	14
Student body officer or active participant in institutional governance	10

Sensitivity training or encounter group experience	7
Classes at local free university or local experimental college	6
Unsupervised foreign travel	6
Other	8

Among the "other" experiences that institutions credit are apprenticeships, tutoring, political campaigning, service to the institution, varsity athletics, choir, band, and other experiences that faculty sponsors accept as leading to demonstrated proficiency.

While different types of institutions accept different out-of-class experiences in different proportions, in general more community colleges and senior colleges grant credit for these experiences than do universities.

EXAMINATIONS

At two-thirds of the surveyed institutions, students can now earn some credit toward a degree, and reduce the length of their program, by scoring acceptably on one or another examination. At some of the remaining institutions, students may be excused from some requirements by examinations but cannot reduce their period of residence. In no more than 20 percent are students still unable to earn any credit through examinations, and this number is likely to continue to dwindle.

While New York and New Jersey have recently created means for students to earn degrees entirely by examination, a few long established institutions have never prohibited their students from earning degrees simply by passing examinations. As one nationally-famous institute of technology reported, a student could in theory satisfy all its graduation requirements by examinations— except that none has ever done so. Other colleges and universities report that students may challenge any course by passing either the final examination or a specially created test, but none indicated that students have earned their degrees completely by this means. Almost all four-year colleges and universities that permit unlimited credit by examination continue to require students to remain in residence for at least a minimum period. In short, the much-discussed "external degree" awarded by institutions on the basis of examinations alone is far from being widespread in practice.

Unlimited credit by examination is rare among the surveyed institutions, but one-fourth of them place the limit at no more than one full year of credit. An additional one-fifth indicate that they will grant *more* than a year of credit, but will not grant the total degree by examination. These and other policies are listed below, together with the percentages of the 1083 institutions which reported them.

No credit awarded for examination alone	13%
Less than one quarter or semester of full-time credit	7
Not more than one quarter or semester of full-time credit	10
Not more than one year of full-time credit	27
More than one year of credit but some course attendance is required and degree cannot be earned by examination alone	21
Other, including no limits and no specific policy	22
TOTAL	100%

The 22 percent classified as "other" report no set policy, variable limits as set by each department, or limits determined by a specific number of courses, and includes the 7 percent that specify no limit in theory.

Although many institutions report their policy on credit by examination to be liberal, a variety of restrictions may prove obstacles in practice—for example, limitations placed on eligibility for examinations, special fees charged for the tests, and, in some cases, entering on transcripts every test that is failed. In sum, credit by examination is a widespread possibility, but without data on the numbers of students actually earning credit by this method and the extent of credit earned, it cannot be said that it is commonly used in practice. At present, it is more likely that examinations are used to waive specific course requirements, such as those in foreign language or mathematics, than to amass many credits toward a degree. As a result, college programs may not be much shorter, but they can be more flexible and tailor-made.

A somewhat greater proportion of public institutions than private ones are willing to grant credit by examination. For example, 38 percent of the public universities will grant more than one year of credit in this way compared to only 15 percent of the independent universities. All but about 8 percent of the community colleges will grant at least some credit by examination, compared to about 25 percent of the private two-year colleges.

Kinds of examinations. The many examinations open to students can be grouped into two general categories: standardized examinations available nationally and institutional examinations prepared within the individual institutions.

Fully 89 percent of the institutions report using at least one of the following standardized tests, and in these proportions:

Advanced Placement Program tests	64%
College-Level Examination Program (CLEP) tests	64
USAFI Subject Standardized Tests	38
CEEB or ACT achievement tests	27
Cooperative Test Service (ETS) or Cooperative Foreign Language Tests	14
Testing programs in the professions (nursing, office management, etc.)	14
College Proficiency Examination Program (CPEP) of New York State	11

In addition, 54 percent of the institutions report that they accept for transfer the credits that other colleges and universities award for passing such standardized tests as these. However, by implication up to one-third of the colleges—the difference between this 54 percent and the total 89 percent that use these tests themselves—may not transfer the credit earned by examination from other institutions.

Senior institutions somewhat more commonly grant credit for these standardized tests than do two-year institutions. For example, three-fourths of them accept Advanced Placement Program scores, compared to only half of the two-year colleges; and 71 percent accept CLEP tests in contrast to 58 percent.

In comparison to the nearly nine-tenths of all responding institutions that use standardized tests, approximately three-fourths (74 percent) report granting credit on the basis of special examinations that they themselves prepare, and in the following proportions:

Institutional proficiency or equivalency examinations	51%
Special departmental tests	46
End-of-course tests without course enrollment	24
Oral examinations or interviews	18

Considering both the standardized and institutional examinations together, fully 93 percent of colleges and universities report using one or another kind of test for granting credit or waiving course requirements: 70 percent of them employ *both* external and internal examinations; 19 percent use only *standardized exams;* 4 percent use only *institutional exams;* and 7 percent report *no* use of either type of test.

Encouragement of credit by examination. Although most institutions are willing to grant credit for examinations, at least 40 percent surveyed report no real encouragement of students to earn credit by this means. Only 26 percent widely publicize the availability of the opportunity, although 39 percent administer the examinations on campus for the convenience of students. Sixteen percent contact students individually and encourage them to take examinations, and 2 percent either waive or pay the examination fees for students.

Even among the 175 senior colleges and universities that are most liberal in the amount of credit they will accept by examination—permitting more than one full year of credit—28 percent report no real encouragement for the practice; 56 percent actually administer examinations on their own campuses, 45 percent circulate wide publicity, and only 26 percent report that students are contacted individually.

Earning credit by examination thus depends as much on student initiative as on institutional encouragement and support. In at least one in every ten cases, institutions in effect discourage credit by examination by charging the same fee for these credits as for those earned by class attendance.

Reduced length of time toward a degree. Credit by examination plays a large role in time-shortened degree programs, but only 63 percent of the 1185 institutions report this opportunity to reduce the length of time. Heavier than usual course loads (69 percent) and year-round attendance (74 percent) are more common methods. Only 3 percent of the institutions have reduced the number of credits required for a degree by revising their curricula— for example, to 90 or 96 credits from the traditional 120. Similar proportions of senior and junior institutions allow less time to earn a degree by heavier student loads and credit by examination, but more of the senior than junior institutions have revised a curriculum or report year-round attendance as a means.

While many colleges and universities permit students to earn a degree in a reduced length of time, only 20 percent of the 785 senior colleges and universities publicize it; in another 31 percent a time-shortened degree is being considered.

INTERRELATIONSHIP OF LIBERAL POLICIES

Some colleges and universities are more oriented toward serving non-traditional students than others. They are systematically more liberal in offering opportunities to adult or part-time students and for non-classroom credit. Not every institution fits a consistent pattern, but correlation among non-traditional opportunities is high. For example, only 20 percent of the colleges and universities that demand full-time attendance toward a degree encourage adults over twenty-five to enroll, whereas 87 percent of the senior institutions and 96 percent of the two-year colleges that grant degrees entirely for part-time study encourage adult enrollment. The same pattern holds true for most other opportunities. The colleges and universities that grant degrees for part-time study are also more likely than others to grant credit by examination, to allow students to graduate in a shorter time, to offer specially designed programs for non-traditional students, and to publicize these opportunities more widely.

Similarly, the institutions that grant credit by examination also tend to grant credit for non-classroom work and prior work experience, and those that grant the most amount of credit by examinations tend to recognize a variety of standardized tests.

The only major exception to the systematic liberal pattern involves credit for previous work experience, such as in the Peace Corps or social work. Only a small proportion of institutions give credit for such experience without an examination, but the proportions accepting prior work experience are about the same for the institutions most liberal toward part-time attendance and those that demand full-time student attendance.

Non-Traditional Programs

Postsecondary education is clearly relaxing its former rigidities through new experiments in time, place, evaluation, and content of programs. The limitations of the survey data do not preclude a general estimate that during 1972 between a fourth and a third of American colleges were not merely providing unconventional opportunities for students but were actually offering non-traditional degree-credit programs.

The survey instrument described non-traditional programs as "any specially designed programs based on new or unconventional forms of education free of the time or place limitations of traditional classroom instruction." They may be unconventional in any of the following ways:

The *type of student* enrolled—such as working adults, housewives, young and older adults motivated to study independently, or others who cannot easily come to the campus or do not wish to devote full time to classroom work.

The *location* of learning experience—such as regional center offerings, field work, home study, or other off-campus programs.

The *method* of instruction—such as nonlecture or nonclass-room teaching and learning methods, distinctive from those common in higher education.

The *content* of the program may either be different from or the same as conventional courses or programs; but in either case it must be a program offered for *nontypical students* or at an *unusual location* or in a *novel way*.

Institutions were asked not to report programs of these three types:

Noncredit programs—such as one-shot weekend workshops and non-credit lecture or concert series.

Conventional programs for regular students—such as inter-disciplinary majors, cluster colleges, independent study for full-time students, January intersessions, and remedial or compensatory education.

Professional programs at the graduate level—such as medical school innovations or continuing education for the bar.

Of the 1185 respondent institutions, 560 or 47 percent reported offering at least one non-traditional program, but some listed programs that were outside the specified definition of non-traditional offerings, such as conventional interdisciplinary majors, cluster colleges, remedial programs, and typical short-term adult educational offerings such as single courses in underwater photography, flower arranging, or sewing with stretch fabrics. When the survey staff eliminated these programs from further analysis, there remained 386, or 33 percent, of the respondent institutions offering 641 programs deemed adequately non-traditional.

These non-traditional programs range across almost every conceivable topic, from training in biological parks management at the local zoo to courses on board ships plying the Great Lakes; from three-year bachelor's degree programs for exceptional students to special research programs open only to retirees and people over sixty-five; and from highly structured programs that prepare juvenile court aides to student-initiated and student-designed off-campus majors.

Some institutions conduct their programs in nearby industrial plants, in prisons, or on military bases. Some report new programs for the physically handicapped, the unemployed, or the disadvantaged. A few, such as Evergreen State and Friends World, regard their entire curriculum as non-traditional.

Among the accepted on-campus programs are those using individualized or programed methods of instruction or designed for atypical students such as housewives or for new occupational groups such as teachers' aides and health paraprofessionals. The off-campus non-traditional programs include field study, internships, practicums, cooperative work experience, off-campus experimental colleges or divisions, and individualized majors, contracts, and self-designed programs if taken in large part off campus. Non-traditional programs also include extension offerings for credit and accelerated degree programs.

To determine if institutions offer fewer or more non-traditional programs than those reported in this survey, the staff conducted a spot check by telephone to twelve California institutions—in most cases to officials other than those who had completed the questionnaire. At ten of the institutions, the reported programs were the major ones in existence. At the remaining two institutions the original respondents failed to report degree programs offered by their extension division or division of continuing education, both of which would have been accepted.

Thus, assuming that the 641 programs do not overrepresent the number of existing programs in the 1185 institutions, and assuming that the 1485 institutions which did not complete the survey offer even as many as half the number of programs conducted by respondents, the survey staff estimates that between one thousand and fourteen hundred such programs were conducted by American colleges and universities in 1972.

Over a third of the 641 programs are offered in public two-year colleges; public universities and independent and religious senior colleges provide about 45 percent of the programs in about equal numbers. However, these percentages reflect to some extent the large number of community colleges and private senior colleges in the survey. Although few in number, of the 54 independent universities, half offer one or more programs. Of the public universities and the community colleges, about 40 percent of each offer programs; and in all three types of institutions, half of those that conduct non-traditional programs provide more than one. Less than a quarter of the religious institutions that were surveyed provide one or more of these programs. Large institutions are more likely to have at least one program: 53 percent of the 137 colleges and universities enrolling over ten thousand students compared to only 21 percent of 136 institutions with less than five hundred students reported a non-traditional program.

Geographically, more of the institutions in the West and Mideast offer programs than do those in other regions of the country, as the following proportions of responding institutions with accepted programs in each area shows:

Rocky Mountain States	41%	Great Lakes	30%
Far West	40	New England	29
Mideast	39	Plains States	28
Southwest	30	Southeast	28

The majority of the programs have small enrollments—one hundred or fewer students, but a quarter of them enroll up to five hundred students, and 10 percent of them have even larger enrollments. All in all, judging by estimates based on the extremes of the intervals of the enrollment categories in the questionnaire, the 641 programs enrolled from seventy-seven thousand to one hundred eighty thousand or more students in 1972.

Not all of these students desire a baccalaureate degree. Many want to improve a special skill or qualify for a better job. Others, less concerned about a degree or certificate, are looking for self-development or enrichment studies and have the leisure to pursue such interests. Thus programs vary in length of time for completion and consequent recognition. Over half of the programs generally take two years or less to complete. Of programs up to one year in length, over half are offered by universities and senior colleges rather than by two-year colleges. The following lists shows the percentages of the 641 programs that give various types of recognition upon completion:

Not a certificate or degree program	12%	Associate or bachelor's degree and graduate or professional degree	3%
Certificate less than degree level	11	Other combinations (primarily certificate and associate or graduate degree)	10
Associate degree only	21		
Bachelor's degree only	25		
Graduate or professional degree only	8	Other recognition (primarily credits applicable toward a degree)	6
Certificate or associate degree and bachelor's degree	4		

The emphasis on certificates and associate degrees in these programs conforms to the educational goals of adults as reported by Carp, Peterson, and Roelfs in Chapter Two.

CHARACTERISTICS

Of the four major characteristics that define unconventional programs, non-traditional types of student and location are more common than non-traditional method or content. Of the 641 programs, 70 percent are designed for non-traditional students; 67 percent are carried out at non-traditional locations; 57 percent use non-traditional methods; and 48 percent offer non-traditional content. It appears that these 641 non-traditional programs more often constitute new ways of teaching old subjects to new students rather than new subjects as such.

Only 20 percent of these programs are considered by their institutions to be distinctive in all four ways. An additional 18 percent—the next largest group—are distinguished by their unconventional students and location. And 21 percent are considered to be distinctive in only one of these four ways, so the majority have two or more of the four distinctive features.

Among the 127 most common programs which have all four major non-traditional characteristics are the affiliates of University Without Walls and many of the external degree programs, such as certain ones in Oklahoma, Florida, and New York, which offer a bachelor of liberal or general studies degree, and those that offer a regular baccalaureate degree for studies beyond the traditional course offerings. Other less general programs include a Wyoming community college program for training plant maintenance apprentices off the main campus, a farm mechanics program in Texas, an Alaskan on-site teacher education program that offers undergraduate and graduate degrees and relies heavily for instruction on tape cassettes and closed-circuit television as well as on correspondence, an Indiana university program conducted in cooperation with six other state institutions to provide statewide television instruction at sixteen locations, and a Massachusetts community college cooperative regional program serving students in sixteen cities and towns.

The second most common programs which are designed for atypical students in unusual locations but using conventional methods and content include generally, traditional continuing education or extension programs conducted at regional centers and specifically, a program to teach Alaskan teacher aides, a public service career program, a program for training teachers of the deaf, a graduate program for a special occupational group with instruction in the evening at a business site, a program at a community center to train black adults working in a nursery school, and a program for corectional counselors taught in the correctional institution by a Minnesota community college.

Nine percent of the programs are distinguished by location, method, and content—but not students—and frequently include the University Year for Action, field internships, or cooperative work study. Another 9 percent of the programs are distinguished only by serving unconventional students, are primarily continuing education or extension programs offered on campus, some of which are designed especially for women.

Programs that have a traditional content but serve new students in unusual locations with new methods of instruction—7 percent of the 641—include a program in Detroit for career mobility in allied health fields using programed instruction and field work, a program in Alabama using tutorial and field-work experience for teachers at the graduate level, an external degree program in Michigan with mainly home study for adults over twenty-five, and a special program in Arizona at regional centers for unemployed migrant workers which uses programed instruction, tutorials, tape cassettes, and closed-circuit television, and can lead to an associate degree.

As Table 12 shows, 1 percent of the 641 programs remain traditional in content, location, and clientele and are non-traditional only because of their instructional methods. Only 6 percent merely provide a traditional curriculum on campus to non-traditional students. The rest are distinctive in several ways from traditional college programs. Half the programs are designed exclusively for non-traditional students such as housewives, working adults, and special occupational groups. Of these programs, seven out of ten are taught primarily off campus and only one in ten is simply a traditional curriculum taught on campus. Only 14 percent of the programs are designed exclusively for traditional students—the same age as those in conventional programs. While slightly over half of these programs are held off campus, they are non-traditional mainly because of their instructional methods and their unusual content.

Excluding the programs designed only for traditional students, 546 programs are designed for non-traditional students. The following list shows the percentages of each type of non-traditional student in the 546 programs. The percentages do not add to a hundred because some of the programs are designed for more than one group of students, and 42 percent allow traditional students to enroll as well.

Housewives and working adults	53%	People confined or beyond commuting distance	21%
Special occupational group	48	Military personnel	16
Independent learners of all ages	35	Other non-traditional students (handicapped, elderly, etc.)	6
Unemployed and economically disadvantaged	30		

Programs for housewives and working adults are most common, especially among the programs offered in independent institutions and public colleges. Nearly as common are programs for special occupational groups, such as firemen, health workers, and

Table 12.

PERCENTAGE OF NON-TRADITIONAL PROGRAMS BY LOCATION, STUDENTS, AND CONTENT

Content	Primarily On Campus			Primarily Off Campus			Totals
	Exclusively traditional students	Both traditional and non-traditional students	Exclusively non-traditional students	Exclusively traditional students	Both traditional and non-traditional students	Exclusively non-traditional students	
Exclusively traditional	1%	1%	5%	1%	3%	4%	15%
More than one focus, one of which is traditional	1	7	2	2	6	9	27
Exclusively occupation or career-oriented	1	2	3	1	6	11	24
Exclusively general or liberal studies	1	1	1	+	1	2	6
Exclusively social problems	+	–	+	2	1	+	3
Occupation or career-oriented and general or liberal studies or social problems, or all three	1	2	2	1	3	6	15
More than one focus, not including any of the above	1	1	2	1	2	3	10
Totals	6%	14%	15%	8%	22%	35%	100%

government employees, and they are more likely to be found in public institutions than in private ones. The third most common programs among those offered by the universities and the private four-year and five-year colleges are for independent learners of any age. In contrast, among public four-year and five-year colleges and community colleges programs for the unemployed and economically disadvantaged students are the third most common.

Of the 546 programs, only slightly more than one-fourth are aimed at one kind of non-traditional student: four in ten of these are for special occupational groups, two in ten are for housewives and employed adults, and the rest serve other groups. Nearly one-third serve three or more groups of non-traditional students, and more than half of these serve traditional students as well.

CONTENT

Nearly half of the 641 programs have one major focus: 24 percent are devoted only to occupational preparation, 15 percent to the same content as the traditional curriculum, 6 percent to general or liberal studies, and 3 percent to social problems. The other half have multiple non-traditional emphases, half of which involve a traditional curriculum and half a combination of non-traditional course offerings.

Programs involving occupational and traditional emphases are most common; 62 percent of the programs include occupational and career preparation as part of the curriculum if not the only focus, and at least a majority of the programs are occupationally oriented at every type of institution except for those in the independent universities and the religious two-year colleges. Most of the occupational preparation programs are short-term off-campus course sequences leading to certificates or to associate or graduate degrees. These opportunities coincide with the expressed interests of adults, about three-quarters of whom (Chapter Two) would like to study in areas related to vocations.

Almost half—42 percent—of the programs include or consist of the same content as the traditional curricula of the institutions; 38 percent include general or liberal studies; 28 percent provide study of social problems. Only 9 percent involve recreational or leisure activities, a small percentage of program opportunities compared to the large proportion (63 percent) of adults who expressed interest in the area of hobbies and recreation.

Of the programs with an occupational emphasis, 56 percent are designed for special occupational groups and only 30 percent for the unemployed and economically disadvantaged; but of the programs designed for special occupational groups 83 percent have an occupational focus, and of the programs designed for the unemployed or economically disadvantaged 73 percent have an occupational focus.

But although the majority of programs with each focus are designed for certain groups of students, some serve other students as well, and there are programs of every type of curricular content serving every type of student. Half or more of the programs with a traditional, a general or liberal studies, or a social problems emphasis are designed for housewives and working adults and fewer for other kinds of non-traditional students. Sixty-three percent of the social problems programs serve traditional students. Of the 55 programs with a recreation emphasis 62 percent serve traditional students, 60 percent serve independent learners, and 71 percent serve housewives and workers as well.

LOCATION

While the principal location of instruction is on the main campus for 35 percent of the programs, the off-campus programs are offered principally at regional centers, in the field, or at locations other than business or industrial sites, community centers, or at home, as the final column in Table 13 shows. Ten percent of the programs are scattered among military bases, correctional institutions, hospitals, high schools, and "wherever the student wants." Multiple locations (11 percent) primarily combine the use of the main campus with a regional center, community center or field work. Most of the off-campus programs use the main campus to some extent, just as some of the on-campus programs involve off-campus instruction, usually in the field and less commonly at a business site. There is virtually no difference in the proportion of

Table 13.
PRINCIPAL LOCATION OF NON-TRADITIONAL PROGRAMS FOR SPECIAL STUDENT TYPES

Principal Location	Traditional Students (323)	Housewives and Workers (291)	Special Occupational Groups (264)	Independent Learners of All Ages (193)	Unemployed and Economically Dis-advantaged (166)	Confined or Beyond Commuting Distance (116)	Military Personnel (89)	All Programs (641)
Main campus	40%	35%	26%	36%	41%	9%	22%	35%
In the field	15	11	14	11	15	14	12	13
Regional learning center	10	13	14	7	11	15	17	13
Business or industrial site	6	4	13	6	2	2	6	7
Community center, agency, library	4	8	8	6	7	9	5	6
Home	3	9	1	11	4	16	9	5
Multiple principal locations	15	14	14	18	15	15	12	9
Other location	7	6	10	5	5	20	17	12
Total	100%	100%	100%	100%	100%	100%	100%	100%

on-campus programs and off-campus programs that make some use of home study or public libraries.

Table 13 also shows the relationship of the principal location of programs to their clientele. Naturally, for example, nearly all the programs for people confined or beyond commuting distance are offered off campus, with a large proportion at home or in other special locations and extremely few in business sites. Most of the 9 percent of such programs mainly located on the campus use off-campus locations to some extent, and some involve periodic intensive seminars on campus.

Specially Selected Programs

To provide more detailed information about particularly important programs, the respondents in each institution were asked to select the one undergraduate program that seems likely to receive the greatest resources and support by the institution in the near future. A comparison of the basic characteristics of the 351 selected programs to those of the 641 programs shows that, overall, the institutions are not planning to emphasize programs of any one type; the selected programs from all institutions are so remarkably representative of the total group that the magnitude of the differences in characteristics is no greater than 5 percent. Slightly fewer of the selected programs are occupationally oriented. A few more are larger in enrolment than the proportion of all programs, but even in their expected enrolment for 1973—where differences might be expected to be great because of the emphasis placed on the selected program—they do not differ greatly: 61 percent of all programs are expected to increase in enrollment compared to 60 percent of the selected programs.

Nearly two out of three programs use some form of technological teaching aid, and one in ten uses programed learning or tape cassettes as its principal form of instruction. A total of 38 percent use one or two of these aids, and 26 percent use three or more. The following proportions of 332 programs for which detailed information exists about teaching methods do not indicate the general use of technological aids on campuses, merely their use in non-traditional programs:

No use of technological aids listed below	36%	Computer-assisted instruction	14%
Tape cassettes	48	Closed-circuit live talkback television	11
Programed instruction	46	Broadcast radio or television	11
Closed-circuit television or videotapes with no immediate feedback	21	Talkback telephone instruction	8

Tape cassettes and programed instruction not only are more commonly used than the others, but are also frequently used in conjunction with each other, especially in community colleges. While 35 percent of the 332 use both cassettes and programed instruction, only 8 percent use tapes alone and only 7 percent use programed instruction alone. Of the fifteen programs that use five or more technological teaching aids, most have a general or liberal studies emphasis, often in conjunction with a traditional curriculum; only half offer a curriculum with any occupational focus. Although all but three involve some use of a business site, only one of them—run by a technical institute associated with the University Without Walls program—is conducted mainly at a business or industrial site. Five of them rely heavily on their technological aids rather than on traditional classroom lectures and field work, including a "College of the Air" television program from a technical college, a university-based undergraduate and graduate external degree program that relies mainly on talkback telephone and correspondence, and a community college program for the unemployed and economically disadvantaged based primarily on programed instruction.

Three options are more common in programs that use technology in instruction than in those that do not: (1) pacing of the program is determined by the student; (2) students may begin the program at any time (as opposed to only at the start of term); and (3) learning contracts are devised between students and faculty members. The use of tape cassettes is associated with particularly wide options to students. In general, as the number of technologies used increases, the greater is the proportion of programs with these options.

Four out of five programs designed for the unemployed and economically disadvantaged involve some technological teaching aids, compared to three of five of the programs designed for military personnel and special occupational groups, and to two out of three of those for traditional students, housewives, and workers. More of the programs for the military than for other students, however, use a variety of teaching aids, including closed-circuit television with and without immediate feedback, broadcast radio and television, and talkback telephone arrangements. Programs for people confined or beyond commuting distance and for independent learners also use technological aids. Somewhat more of the programs with only a general or liberal studies focus use programed instruction and tape cassettes than the other more occupationally oriented programs.

FLEXIBILITY

Although some academics and laymen may believe that non-traditional programs consist only of individually designed and tailor-made plans of study, like those of the University Without Walls programs, in 44 percent of the selected programs, most or all of the curriculum is structured or prescribed, and in only 31 percent do students design their own curricula. Even among student-designed programs, one in four requires concentration or distribution among courses, as do most conventional programs.

What is particularly distinctive about these selected programs is flexibility not of curriculum but of time and place for student needs. Nearly three out of five allow students to complete the program entirely on a part-time basis; half leave the pacing of the program to the student; one out of three allows course work at several different campuses; almost one in three allows students to start the program at any time rather than at the beginning of a term only; and almost one in three uses learning contracts devised between students and faculty.

The diversity among programs is apparent. For example, of the programs involving learning contracts, only half are student-designed programs (although that is twice the proportion in other programs without the contract option), and two out of three are student paced (again, more than for other programs), but the two options are certainly not common to all learning contract programs.

SCHEDULING

While 12 percent of the programs offer instruction only during the day, 44 percent offer classes both during the day and at other times. Three out of five schedule some instruction in the late afternoon and evening; weekend classes are available in nearly one-fourth of the programs; and periodic blocks of several days are involved in one out of five programs. One in six of all programs has no scheduled instruction or involves a unique period of time, such as whenever the student and faculty member agree to meet or scheduled resident periods during the year.

ADMINISTRATIVE AND FINANCIAL CHARACTERISTICS

The offices governing traditional college programs are directly responsible for the majority of non-traditional programs as well. Almost twice as many (46 percent) of the 351 non-traditional programs are administered by the usual academic administrators of the institution as are administered by special divisions such as extension, continuing education or evening divisions, and special offices or organizations, such as a division of liberal studies (28 percent). Another 20 percent are directly responsible to an executive officer. While continuing and adult education programs traditionally have been housed in separate divisions, these non-traditional programs do not generally fall in that pattern.

Only two in five of the programs involve another organization: half of them with another educational institution and half with noneducational institutions, such as business and industrial firms or hospitals. Far more of the on-campus programs—79 percent—operate without a cooperative arrangement than do the 49 percent off-campus programs that operate independently. Cooperative programs among educational institutions appear to rely on the use of technologies, since four out of five of them employ some form of technological aid, while less than half of those involving noneducational institutions use any technological methods.

Funding programs is a current major problem in education, causing concern for the support of non-traditional programs. Programs will usually be subsidized in the early stages of development, but in time they they are generally expected to be self-sustaining. Only two out of the 351 selected programs are primarily self-sustaining on the basis of student fees and grants, and the proportion of self-sustaining is only slightly larger among those in existence for more than five years and those less than three years (48 percent and 43 percent, respectively). Most receive substantial subsidy: 25 percent from the institution itself, 14 percent from foundations or outside grants, and 13 percent from other sources, such as state and federal appropriations, industrial and employer support, and community contributions.

As might be expected, private institutions offer a greater proportion of self-sustaining programs than do public institutions. Proportionally more of the programs designed for special occupational groups and for the unemployed and economically disadvantaged are maintained by outside grants than are programs for the military, housewives and workers, and independent learners, which are more often self-sustained through student fees and grants.

Information on costs is not available in over 20 percent of non-traditional programs. Of those that could respond, however, half report that the cost of conducting the program is generally the same as for conventional programs. Of the other half, slightly more indicate lower costs than higher costs. Programs primarily located in community centers and those using more than one principal location for instruction tend to report higher costs, while home study programs most often report lower costs. Of the more costly programs, 75 percent use some kind of technological teaching aid, compared to 56 percent of the less costly programs. More of the programs designed exclusively for traditional students and for the unemployed and economically disadvantaged cost more than programs for other kinds of students.

FACULTY INVOLVEMENT

In four out of five programs, regular faculty committees are involved to some extent in policy decisions; in three out of five, their extent of participation is the same as or greater than in conventional programs. Nearly all of the programs are taught by faculty members who teach in conventional programs as well; in three out of five, they constitute the majority of the teaching staff. Over half of the programs employ special instructors from the community, professions, business, industry, or the arts; but in only one out of six do the special instructors constitute the majority of the faculty, particularly in the off-campus programs designed for special occupational groups, for military personnel, and for the unemployed and economically disadvantaged. In on-campus programs special or separate faculties are less common; they are used in less than a third of the programs and comprise the majority in only one-fifth of these programs.

A significant role of faculty members in non-traditional programs is that of counselor. In two out of three programs they are the only advisors, and slightly more often they advise in cooperation with counseling or administrative staff. In only one out of six programs do administrators or counseling staff exclusively advise students. Counseling staff advise alone or in combination with faculty or administrators in considerably more of the public than private institutions.

Non-traditional programs offer frequent academic and educational advising and counseling. Nearly half (47 percent) offer intensive and continual advisement throughout their length, while only 19 percent concentrate the advisement primarily at enrollment and registration period. Intensive counseling is more common in programs located on campus, at home, or in the field than in those meeting in other locations, and it is more common among programs designed for traditional students, military personnel, the unemployed and economically disadvantaged, and independent learners of all ages, than for other groups of students.

Trends

Wide diversity abounds in the programs, regardless of the length of time they have been in operation. In general, there are one or more programs of every age category with every characteristic surveyed. The *proportions* vary, however, among old or new programs with specific characteristics.

Of the 638 programs for which respondents reported the length of time in operation, the majority were fairly new in May 1972, as the following shows:

Less than one year	26%	Six to ten years	7%
One to two years	36	More than ten years	7
Three to five years	24		

Although past programs that have already been terminated were beyond the scope of this study, this distribution and other evidence beyond this survey suggest that nontraditional programs are on the increase. However, the 337 programs that were selected by the institutions as the most promising for the future, and for which age of program was reported, are almost identical in age distribution to the total number of programs, indicating no dramatic shift in support toward the newest programs.

A program of every age category is offered in nearly every type of college or university. However, a greater proportion of the older programs are offered by public or independent universities and by independent four-year or five-year colleges, in contrast with the younger programs, more of which are offered by community colleges.

The following differences, indicating a trend among the newest programs compared with the oldest, involve at least twenty percentage points unless otherwise noted; and there is a linear relationship between the extremes.

No major trend is evident toward designing more of the newer programs for any particular group of adults, although somewhat more of the older programs are designed for special occupational groups and military personnel. A trend is evident toward creating more non-traditional programs for younger students, as well as for adults. More than half the newer ones also enroll students the same age as traditional college students, compared with only a third of the older programs.

Older programs enroll more students than do newer ones. In programs more than ten years old, the median enrollment is more than a thousand students. In programs six to ten years old, median enrollment ranges from one hundred to five hundred students, and in programs up to five years old the median enrollment is between twenty-five and one hundred students. Nearly one-third of the newest programs enroll fewer than twenty-five students. Their small enrollments may be due to their developmental or pilot nature, since projected enrollments, like those of older programs, are much larger.

No trends are apparent in the proportions of programs that offer different kinds of degrees, or in the length of time required to complete them. But programs over ten years old less commonly award certificates or degrees (particularly the associate degree), fewer require two years or less to complete the program, and fewer of those that provided information report that all or nearly all of their students complete the programs, in comparison to newer programs. The older programs tend to schedule instruction more in the late afternoon and evening, while more of the newer programs offer day time programs.

Older programs more commonly use traditional content and methods of instruction, while newer programs more often use unconventional methods of instruction, revised curricula, or more liberal student options, particularly learning contracts (36 percent of the newest compared with 12 percent of the oldest programs.) A traditional curriculum is involved in 59 percent of the oldest programs, compared with 34 percent of the newest ones. Occupational and career-oriented curricula are increasingly typical of the newer programs—as are social problems, although the study of social problems is only a part of 28 percent of the newest programs. Many more of the new programs than old programs involve field work or cooperative work-study. Although there is only a 15 percent difference between the newest and oldest programs, more of the newer programs use programed instruction or tape cassettes than do older programs, but otherwise there appears to be no trend in the new programs for greater use of other technological aids such as computer-assisted instruction and closed-circuit television.

No trend toward off-campus instruction is apparent—unconventional locations are common to roughly two-thirds of all programs. But differences exist in the off-campus locations of programs. Nearly a fourth of the programs over ten years old are taught mainly in regional learning centers, compared to 6 percent of those under one year old, which more commonly use business and industrial sites and public libraries as supplemental locations.

More of the oldest programs are offered by an extension division; none of them report directly to an executive office, as do more than 20 percent of the other programs. Somewhat more of the newer programs cooperate with noneducational agencies, and somewhat more of the older programs use special instructors from the community, business, industry, or the arts, but otherwise no trends appear in faculty involvement or composition. Far fewer of the oldest programs provide intensive and continual advising and far more of them involve administrators in academic advising than do the new programs.

New progams more often receive foundation and grant support than old programs. Few of the programs more than five years old, and none over ten years old, are funded primarily by foundations or other outside grants. Information on the operating costs of the oldest programs reveals that, for a large proportion, costs are generally less than in conventional programs; a small percentage report costs to be similar, and none of them report their costs to be more, while the newer programs do sometimes cost more than traditional programs.

In summary, more of the newer programs compared to older programs are designed for college students as well as for adults; have an occupational or career focus rather than a traditional academic focus; have small enrollments and high completion rates; involve learning contrasts between students and faculty; use field work or cooperative work study; schedule instruction during the daytime; use business or industrial sites and public libraries rather than regional learning centers as instruction sites; provide intensive and continual counseling by nonadministrators.

While other differences exist between newer and older programs, they are not consistent. Among them, *no* apparent trend is evident toward off-campus instead of on-campus learning sites, toward an increase or decrease in programs for the unemployed or economically disadvantaged, toward technological teaching aids or home study, toward more interinstitutional cooperation, or toward

greater involvement of regular faculty in policymaking and instruction.

Problems

Of seventeen problems that have posed difficulties or obstacles for institutions in developing non-traditional programs, opportunities for non-traditional students, or new policies on the award
and acceptance of credit, the two most commonly reported are lack
of funds and difficulty in assessing nonclassroom learning. The
following list shows the percentages of the 1184 institutions that
encountered difficulties:

Lack of funds	41%	No evident demand or need for such developments	15%
Difficulty in assessing nonclassroom learning	40	Recruitment of appropriate faculty	13
Concern about academic standards	34	Recruitment of students	12
Faculty resistance	32	Inadequate preparation of students	12
Budget based on FTE units	25	Lack of interest among constituency	12
Lack of interest within the institution	21	Accreditation	10
Suspicion of passing fad	20	Licensing and certification	9
Lack of approved examination or other assessment techniques	19	Employers' concerns about graduates' qualifications	7
Acceptance of graduates into advanced education or graduate schools	18	Other	6
		No response [no problems?]	15

The four most commonly mentioned problems—shortage of
funds, assessment of nonclassroom learning, concern about academic
standards, and faculty resistance—were reported by a greater
proportion of universities than colleges. Lack of funds appears to be
a particular problem at public universities and religious colleges.

The fifth most common problem—budget difficulties because of FTE formulas—concerns more community colleges than any other type of institution and affects as many of them as does the lack of funds.

Among the "other" problems identified by 6 percent of the 1184 institutions are the need for independent study resources, faculty preparation, cost to students and to the institution, limitations on time needed for implementation, state government requirements, curriculum limitations, transfer problems, and "foot draggers."

Apart from inadequate funds, all of the most frequently mentioned problems are basically internal rather than imposed from outside. They can be resolved—indeed, *must* ultimately be resolved—within colleges and universities themselves by faculty and administration. External restrictions do not appear to be frequent; the problem least mentioned among the seventeen is employers' concern about graduates' qualifications.

The colleges and universities that have developed the most non-traditional opportunities for their students tend to report different types of problems than the other institutions, probably because they have actually encountered them, while the others can only anticipate them. For example, almost half of those that award degrees for part-time study alone or that grant credit for examinations report difficulty in assessing non-classroom learning, compared to one-third of those that do not award such degrees or credits. Similarly, institutions with the most opportunities more frequently consider lack of funds and faculty resistance as problems, while the institutions offering the fewest opportunities more frequently report the lack of demand for such opportunities as inhibiting or a statement of fact. Institutions with the most non-traditional opportunities also report their concern about maintaining academic standards and about employers' concerns about the qualifications of graduates somewhat more frequently than other institutions do.

Anticipated Changes

Of the 1185 institutions surveyed, 843 reported no immediate plans in non-traditional studies. The plans of the 342 others are as follows:

Initiate program in 1972–1973 that appears to meet survey criteria for non-traditional programs 71%

Initiate program in 1972–1973 that does not appear to be non-traditional 61

Expand existing program 46

Grant credit for non-classroom experience by examination 28%

without examination 5

Offer a shortened degree program (three years or early admission) 18

Design and develop program or new opportunity during 1972–1973 that may or may not be non-traditional as defined here 113

Slightly more public universities and independent two-year colleges anticipate some changes but are still planning them. More of the religious universities do not anticipate any changes, and those that do are planning programs that are apparently conventional by the definition used in this survey. While 24 percent of the institutions with existing non-traditional programs are planning to initiate new ones or enlarge their non-traditional opportunities (with an additional 10 percent planning to expand their existing programs), only 19 percent of the institutions with no non-traditional programs are planning them.

Among the new non-traditional programs planned for the 1972-to-1973 term, twenty-one of the seventy-one institutions were organizing external degrees through credit for life experiences and special curricular arrangements for adults and special occupational groups. These plans include external programs offering a certificate program for city clerks, a B.A. in counseling to be offered at an off-campus center, a college of continuing education, division of extended learning with four pilot programs for part-time under-graduates in mathematics, biological sciences, agriculture, economics, and English.

Other plans are set for more technological teaching, either on campus or through off-campus networks and systems of closed-circuit television; for programs of continuing education that do not necessarily lead to a degree; for individual studies majors in which students design their curricula with faculty counsel; for greater field work and internship activities; for credit by examination, and participation in CLEP; for a reconstruction of the academic administration of non-traditional students and supplementing regular faculty advisors with a core of special advisors; for shortened programs leading to a degree—either a three-year baccalaureate or a four-year combined bachelor's and master's degree program; and for greater community participation.

Thirty-two of the seventy-one respondents indicate that the programs will be for traditional-age students, and thirty report programs for adults. Forty note that the programs will be held on campus, and fourteen indicate that their programs will use community centers and field work.

The majority of programs that will still be in the planning stages are external or non-traditional degree programs. Among the 113 institutions, twenty-four expressly stated that they were working on external degrees and eighteen reported they were studying the possibility of an external degree. Seventeen mentioned individualized study majors; another seventeen mentioned changes in credit, such as awarding crdit on the basis of examination; eleven mentioned continuing education programs; five noted more technological teaching; four identified the shortened degree; two indicated plans for greater flexibility for students; two others mentioned honors programs; and two mentioned community programs. Forty-eight of these respondents indicated that the programs were for students the same age as traditional undergraduates, while forty-four reported their programs would be for adults.

Among the forty-six institutions planning to expand existing programs, ten were concerned with individualized study programs, nine with existing external degree programs, seven with occupational and continuing education, four with more field work, three with greater facilities for non-traditional students, and three with more technological teaching. Twenty-three of the forty-six reported the student group to be same age as traditional students; nineteen indicated that their students were occupationally oriented. Another eighteen described their students as independent learners of all ages. Thirty of the forty-six described their programs as primarily on campus, while twenty reported use of community centers and field work.

Implications

If it were necessary to sum up the findings of this national survey in one sentence, it might be: "There is something for everyone somewhere in the accredited colleges and universities across the United States." For every activity surveyed by the questionnaire, it was striking that there were at least a few institutions that reported that they allowed or fostered one or another non-traditional educational opportunity.

The survey also substantiated a widely held suspicion (especially by students): Certain policies of an institution may not be reflected by implementation. Most institutions encourage adult students to enroll, and three out of four allow students to earn a degree entirely on a part-time basis or with short-term residencies. We do not know how many students avail themselves of this opportunity, but the data show that while many institutions actively recruit adult or other potential students, only a little more than half publicize the possible opportunities. And in many institutions that claim to welcome the part-time or adult student, the special needs of these potential students are not being met—needs for lower fees, special counselors, counseling, financial aids, business and job placement, offices open at times when the student is on campus, child care, grants, work-study jobs. More community colleges than other institutions try to provide for the needs of part-time and adult students.

Although very few institutions grant credit for a student's work experience prior to college, nearly all grant credit or at least waive courses on the basis of a passed examination. But encouragement of credit by examination is not widespread. Four out of ten institutions report no encouragement and only a fourth publicize that they award credit by examination. Possibilities for students to earn credit are limited: One out of every ten institutions allows no credit by examination whatsoever; two out of ten allow no more than the equivalent of up to one semester's worth of credits; another three out of ten allow no more than a year of credit; and only two out of ten allow more than a year of credits. (Two more out of ten have no set policy, no limits, or limits that vary by department.) In the absence of information about the numbers of students who actually take advantage of these opportunities or the amount of credit actually awarded, the evidence only suggests a disparity between the opportunities expressed in the policies and the extent to which students take advantage of them. The disparity may not be created by the institutions; it may be due to the limitations or disinterest of students. But even for students who have the abilities and interest to earn considerable credit by examination, relatively few institutions actively encourage it.

Although nearly half of the institutions surveyed do offer non-traditional programs, by our definition only one in three provide specifically non-traditional programs. Even so, at least one such program exists in each of the fifty states and the District of Columbia; the greater the population in a state, the more institutions with non-traditional programs. But in some states that are not heavily populated, non-traditional programs are extremely rare; the same is true in some states that rank in the middle third by population. Thus, while there may be something for everyone somewhere, it may not be offered close to his home or even within his own state. Moreover, the primary location of learning activity is rarely the student's home.

Many of the programs do not offer students freedom of time and space. Although the scheduling of classes seems to be convenient for adult and part-time students, in only a quarter of the programs are students allowed to begin their study at any time convenient to them. Only half the programs allow students to determine the pacing of their studies individually. Fewer programs allow freedom of space. Traditional classroom lectures are basic to most programs —even those off campus. The technological teaching aids employed are primarily tape cassettes and programed instruction, and rarely do these methods constitute the major method of instruction.

Finally, as might be expected, institutions encounter difficulties in developing non-traditional studies and providing more options to students. But, apart from funding, the issues that pose difficulties are internal rather than external—problems of assessing nonclassroom learning, concern of the institution about its academic standards, and resistance of the faculty. These are not insurmountable problems. Institutions with experience in non-traditional study can help newer institutions to move toward solutions.

In several areas, further research would be fruitful. This survey reveals much information about rules and regulations regarding the award of credit, the granting of degrees, and provision for special student services; but comparable data about the numbers of students actually using these opportunities or, even better, likely to need and want them, would be useful for educational policymakers. The need for further clarification of policies and practices seems both basic and indispensable.

Even where there is great determination to provide non-traditional programs, information about relative costs to the students and the institutions is fundamental to institutional planning. Our findings have shown that most non-traditional programs cost the same as conventional programs, but the reasons why some cost more and some cost less need to be assessed.

More of the newer non-traditional programs involve traditional students as well as non-traditional students. Will this result in greater flexibilities of options, revised or enlarged curricula, and methods of instruction, or will the participation of traditional students change the non-traditional nature of the programs toward more traditional approaches? The frequently expressed conviction that the education of adults calls for different approaches than those used in the traditional education of eighteen to twenty-two-year-olds does not appear to be put into practice by many programs. Is there indeed a difference in student performance and completion rates in programs with different approaches designed for adults?

But, while more research might be useful, action can proceed before further research is undertaken. The data gathered by the Commission, together with the recommendations of the Commission and the assistance of more experienced institutions, can assist more colleges and universities to join the non-traditional movement. While the costs may be too great and the needs too few for every institution to provide "something for everyone," these opportunities may be easily accessible elsewhere—institutions and educational systems should consider how they and other concerned agencies together can best provide enough opportunities to satisfy the varied needs of students and potential students. Institutions planning to initiate their own non-traditional programs can learn from the experience of older programs. Institutions which do not contemplate beginning non-traditional programs can still adapt elements of non-traditional education to their traditional programs. Greater communication and broader cooperative efforts can help all institutions to find the path most appropriate to their own institutional goals and to the needs of the public they serve.

New Paths for
Adult Learning

WESLEY W. WALTON

☆☆☆☆☆☆☆☆☆☆☆☆☆☆☆☆☆☆☆☆☆☆☆☆☆☆☆

*A*dults have numerous needs to be met in education. Conditions of careers and occupations are changing rapidly: prerequisites to employment, requisites of continued employment, refresher-study and retraining to keep up, even the concept of gainful employment itself. Engineers, executives, and professors have to prepare for new occupations in midcareer; women, to have a proportionate share of the available jobs, even on college campuses, must prepare in larger numbers to compete on equal terms with the men. Constructive use of leisure time too becomes more important and for more years, as life-span creeps upward. Learning in the society at large is a way of life, all through life, and will become more so. Continuing adaptation to ever-evolving conditions is increasingly necessary.

Adults interested in learning have a hard time of it. Only infrequently do they find what they want, where they can go to get it, at times they are free to do so. This need not be. Their search

I acknowledge the substantial assistance of Jane Quigley and Climene Lubrano in typing the manuscript.

is made difficult on two counts. The interested adult learner can turn to either the core source of non-traditional studies—the colleges and universities—or to the periphery made up of numerous correspondence and other proprietary schools and knowledge industries. Despite the welcome increase in the number of non-traditional programs offered by the higher institutions, when viewed in the context of eighty million would-be learners, these programs fall far short of meeting the need. Wanted programs offered by colleges are out of reach of much of the market.

Going the other route, to the private sector, makes it desirable, even necessary in some cases, for the "buyer to beware." Our Research Program on Non-Traditional Studies (Walton, 1972), for example, turned up a distressingly widespread practice. High-pressure salesmen signed returning servicemen to high-cost, long-term courses; the would-be learner often lacked the background to complete them but was obligated to pay for them even after losing VA benefits because of noncompletion. Primary attention to the needs of the learners would forestall such practices. Both the colleges and the proprietary schools should keep in sharp focus the interests and needs of the would-be learners. Making the way easy for those adults interested in learning will hasten the arrival of that learning society which trends in non-traditional education seem to foretell.

When the needs and interests of the adult learner are put first, and institutional interests are subordinated, it becomes unmistakably clear that telecommunications technologies have become essential components for the delivery of instruction. Without them, it is impossible to deliver instruction to the adults who want and need it. And the technologies beneficial in a diversity of styles of adult learning are now in being. There is no need to wait for further technological development, or until the resolution of issues that the technologies impose. To wait means that critical needs for adult learning are largely left unmet; timely opportunities for the colleges to develop learning activities that adults need and want will be left to slip away by default, only to be picked up by those less qualified to develop high quality learning packages—people more than willing to fill the vacuum for the "gold in them thar hills."

A delivery system without technologies cannot offer instruction that adults need, *where* they can give it their attention, and at times *when* they are free to do so. These key elements have been virtually ignored in much of the current effort toward non-traditional studies by the colleges and universities. While about a quarter million students are enrolled in non-traditional programs (see Chapter Three) many of the programs are of short duration (less than six months), are designed primarily for college students, and have unconventional features dealing more with the "what" and "how" of instruction than with the "where" and "when."

The non-traditional programs I have seen are offered pretty much at the convenience of the college, rather than in ways that make it convenient for the would-be learner to gain their advantages. Furthermore, Ruyle and others (Chapter Three) have said "it appears that these programs more often constitute new ways of teaching *old* subjects to new students, rather than *new* subjects as such.

With particular reference to the "where" of non-traditional studies, the surface data show that special accommodations for the location of instruction are made by 67 percent of the 641 institutions whose non-traditional studies met the criteria for analysis in the Ruyle study (Chapter Three). In most cases, though, this takes the form of off-campus offerings at regional, field, or community centers. In a few cases, radio and television studios are the venue, as at Mesa Community College in Arizona, or a microwave television tower is the source from which instruction emanates, as at the University of California at Davis. But unfortunately, only 5 percent of the programs regard the learner's home to be a primary learning site (see Chapter Three).

The 351 programs of non-traditional study that are thought by their institutions to be particularly important reflect the same limited flexibility. In 65 percent of the cases, *no use* is made of homes or local public libraries as locations for learning activities, and in only 10 percent of the programs is "much use" made of the home. Instead, 63 percent of the programs place heavy dependence upon the campus and regional learning centers. And one of the most confounding findings is that among the total of 1185 institutions responding, seven out of ten still impose a minimum residency requirement of a year or more. In only 4 percent of the institutions is there none. More of the instruction made available to adults should reach them *where they are.*

The "when" of non-traditional studies shows more promise than the "where." In 351 programs deemed most likely to receive the greatest support, 28 percent permit students to start at any time, and students are allowed to earn degrees or complete programs entirely on a part-time basis in almost three programs out of five. Even dropping out and dropping back in is facilitated (though not encouraged) in almost half the programs. Moreover, 62 percent time their instructional offerings during late afternoon and evening, and weekend classes are available in nearly one-fourth of the cases.

The only major "when" shortcoming in these more or less exemplary programs is that in very few of them is it possible to choose when to study fully on a self-determined basis, at the discretion of the learner. Another complicating factor combines the elements of "where" and "when." In 70 percent of the total sample of 1185 respondent institutions, there are no provisions for child care or for assistance in the location of such care. So young mothers, even if they could fix a schedule and get to a place at a time with children in hand, would be prevented from doing more.

Much more of the instruction available to adults can reach them when they want it, rather than when it is plausible for the professor to appear to deliver it in person. Present technologies may be combined into viable delivery systems. College faculties and others interested in advancing the cause of lifelong learning can cooperate in putting these technologies effectively in the service of adults who want to learn. These delivery systems need to be not only technologically effective but also sufficiently enriched with the human elements of the learning process—mentors, teachers, counselors, and guides.

Videocassettes

The videocassette (packaged videotape) is a device which shows great promise for making non-traditional study independent of time and place. A course of instruction by videocassette would

be accompanied by reading lists, textbooks, workbooks, a schedule
for meeting a mentor, and packaged programs to play through the
learner's television set or through one at a nearby learning center
or public library (*Vid News*, 1972a). Cost effectiveness could be
assured by putting as much of the instruction as possible in the
videocassette. The videocassette is at least as good as (or no worse
than) an in-person lecture (Carpenter and Greenhill, 1958). The
videocassette would probably be even better than a class situation
at enhancing visual or aural stimuli (with two-track sound), or
where audiovisual impact is most effective. Anything that can be
delivered on a television screen, in black and white or color, using
stereo or monaural sound, or in a different language on each of the
two sound tracks, can be packaged in videocassette.

A learner using a videocassette, cassette player, and television
set is free to put in the videocassette whenever he pleases, look at
his lesson material from start to finish, stop partway through to
return to it later, stop the action to look at a detail, back it up to
see a segment over again, repeat an intriguing segment a half
dozen times, or refer back to something early in the tape and
quickly return to the point of interruption. The videocassette leaves
the user free to determine when he chooses to give the recorded
material his attention, for how many repetitions, and for how long
a sitting—the epitome of independent study!

Although the videocassette is new and not yet available for
the average American home, it will be soon. During the remaining
years of the 1970s the videocassette industry and its growth will
likely bear the same relationship to television as long-playing
records and magnetic tape have borne to radio in the past (*Vid
News*, 1972b). Users of cassette audiotape recorders will know the
ease and speed with which tape can be transported through the
machine in either direction and the ease with which a given segment
on a given sound recording can be located. The same features
characterize the videocassette, and in addition some features—such
as stop action—are unique.

The videocassette is now an increasingly common feature in
learning centers, education or training programs of industry (for
example, Anheuser-Busch, Coca-Cola, Hewlett Packard, Pepsi
Cola, and Ford Motor, which is now installing a network of video-

cassette centers for information and training at four thousand dealerships in the United States and Canada), business (for example, CUNA Mutual Insurance Society, Employers Insurance of Wausau, Kemper Insurance, Morgan Guarantee & Trust), and government (for example, the National Audio-visual Center and the U. S. Army, with its first six hundred videocassette machines running eighteen hours a day, according to *Vid News*, 1972a). With the new videocassette industry placing high priority on the education market, the medium seems assured of finding its way into widespread use in schools, colleges, and libraries. By 1975, experts expect that it will not be unusual to see a videocassette player standing alongside the television set in the typical house. Some of these machines have capabilities both for playing pre-recorded tapes and for recording program material off the air or from other video or sound sources, even in some cases while a different television program is on (*Videocassette Industry Guide*, 1972). The incompatibility among videocassette systems continues to be a major issue to resolve, but recent improvements suggest optimism for this problem area.

The software side of the videocassette story reflects even more activity than the hardware. By June 1972, a hundred video-cassette libraries had been identified; packagers of program material were at work in over sixty educational subject areas. Among learning material in videocassette form are series on accounting, alcoholism, anthropology, art appreciation, Black culture, business, careers, ceramics, chemistry, child psychology, community affairs, cooking, crafts and hobbies of various kinds, ecology, economics, family life, finance, gardening, geriatrics, government, health, history, human behavior, marketing, management, music, nutrition, religion, physics, sex education, science, travel, and woodworking (*Videocassette Industry Guide*, 1972; *Video Play Program Catalog*, 1972). Although titles in videocassette formats now number in the thousands, the vast majority of program materials is copied from motion picture films on the basis of videocassette distribution rights. A few substantial efforts are now underway to produce original TV programing for videocassette distribution, and the need for them is certain to be real and urgent in a short time.

By turning to the videocassette as a medium for non-traditional study, the educator will be enabled to draw upon invaluable resources for learning—Shakespearean drama magnificently staged, film classics, records of the critical events of history and of the works of famous men, operas and symphonies and plays, microscopic and telescopic views, moon shots and moon walks, documentaries on the rise and fall and ebb and flow of nations and their power, Clark's *Civilisation* and Tolstoy's *War and Peace*. These resources can be made integral parts of videocassette study programs.

The videocassette brings a major challenge to colleges and universities too. If higher education institutions organize their resources and attract additional resources to the task, by their power to lead they could assure that the videocassette becomes a medium for turning television from the wasteland it so frequently has been into the oasis of learning, culture, and enduring values it is capable of becoming (Carnegie Commission, 1972). There has never been a greater opportunity for the exercise of educational leadership in the advancement of the social good.

Community Antenna Television (CATV)

Although its early years have been frustrated, cable television also holds great promise for making non-traditional study independent of time and place. The Sloan Commission on Cable Communications has recently finished its year-and-a-half study on the problems and possibilities of the cable. The Commission concluded (1971, pp. 173–178) that the growth of cable television is in the public interest, and that by the end of the seventies cable television systems will be serving 40 to 60 percent of all American television homes. The cable is seen to bring "the television of abundance." Recent rulings of the Federal Communications Commission (fcc) point in that direction too: Twenty channels are now the required minimum and forty channels are already technically feasible. Public access channels are mandatory, as are provisions for at least digital two-way capabilities. The favorable ruling by fcc on the importation of distant signals into the top hundred markets has cleared away the one remaining major stumbling block at the national level (*Federal Register,* 1972). State governments are trying to bring some order out of the recent chaotic state of franchising, and cable franchises granted by local governing bodies may be expected within the near future to be in the *public* interest.

CATV was once called community antenna television, for its most common form was just that: a hilltop installation that captured signals of television stations broadcasting over the air and cabled them down to the valley and into the homes of those living there. Recently though, CATV more broadly designates cable television, a system that focuses more on the cable that carries the signals than on the hilltop antenna that captures them.

Two features of CATV make it attractive even in metropolitan areas well served by over-the-air television. The cable delivers a wide selection of over-the-air television programing from sources otherwise denied the subscriber, at least as quality reception. And the large capacity of the cable opens a variety and diversity of television programs and other electronically sophisticated services that could not possibly be supplied to television viewers who receive programs through the familiar housetop antenna.

CATV is possible because of a kind of coaxial cable that consists of an inner conductor of copper wire surrounded by a mass of plastic foam. Surrounding the foam is an outer conductor of knit aluminum webbing, and the whole cable is covered with weatherproof sheathing. This enables the cable to carry all the many separate signals used in television transmission on various channels each in a different frequency band within the range of forty to three hundred megacycles per second. The signal from each television station requires a band width of only six megacycles per second; thus a coaxial cable can carry forty channels or more within bands in this portion of the electromagnetic spectrum.

A wired town is a treelike system of coaxial cables starting at the head end (root), where studios, electronic gear, and the antenna are located. At least one trunk goes out from the head end through feeder cables and then droplines into the antenna leads of the home television set. Amplifiers along the way compensate for weakening signals.

At the head end, signals can come from local over-the-air television stations, from more distant stations, from the CATV studio, where live programing can originate or where use may be made of reel-to-reel videotape, videocassette, or film. Transmissions can be cabled or microwaved to the cable live or recorded on videotape for later cablecasting, or both. (See Sloan, 1971, and "A Short Course in Cable," 1972, for further nontechnical explanations of the cable system.)

In a statistical study done for the Sloan Commission by McGowan, Noll, and Peck (1971) a sample of thirty-one CATV systems was subjected to least squares regression analysis, in which three combinations of offerings were hypothesized. The basic finding was that a cable system which provided its subscribers three network affiliates—all local VHF independents receivable off-the-air, a public broadcasting station, plus four other imported independents would be subscribed to by over three-fifths of all homes if they were offered the service, and it would attract nearly half the households to which the service could be offered. The addition of a fourth national net-worklike option in place of one of the imported independents would increase penetration percentages. Conclusions from this impressive analysis mean that the top one hundred television markets could be virtually completely wired (except New York and Los Angeles, where there now are wide offerings off-the-air, including three independents). The overall result: CATV going by the front door of from 73 to 78 percent of the households in the United States.

Growth in CATV seems assured, but part of the modest en-couragement CATV needs to continue growing should come from the educational community. The television of abundance is not likely to come about without a very significant component of educational, and public service programing. CATV affords the opportunity to devote numbers of channels to educational purposes, to repeat programs, to cablecast instruction in prime time rather than at sunrise, to tailor instructional programs for relatively small and even specialized audiences, and even to enable two-way communi-cation between students and instructor.

Issues in CATV and Videocassettes

Especially the educators interested in lifelong education and in study opportunity divorced from the constraints of time and place should be actively involved with revisions of the long-obsolete

Copyright Law and the establishment of related policy by which royalties rightfully due originators or owners of program materials are handled on an equitable and routine basis, as is the case now with recorded music. Educators must also concern themselves with the current incompatibility of equipment and software. The critically urgent need for standards and standardization and for the removal of obstacles of incompatibility imposed by manufacturers (usually for indefensible reasons) must be impressed upon the industry with all the force the community of education can muster.

A third, seemingly less urgent issue for educators to deal with is the special protection clause included in the FCC ruling, which excludes from authorized importation nonsyndicated programing which has been copyrighted for exclusive local showing. The active participation of interested educators will assure the development of CATV and the videocassette in directions that will enable extensive and diversified delivery of lifelong learning experiences.

Program Approach

Other technological means for providing instructional materials without place and time constraints reinforce the need for a program approach to bring study and learning within reach of all—where, when, and however they want it. One such approach is the Modes-of-Learning Model (Valley, 1972) defined as a model in which "a degree-granting and instructional institution or agency establishes a new degree pattern of learning and teaching that seeks to adjust to the capacities, circumstances, and interests of a different clientele from that which it customarily serves." In this model "the student works at home, but is required to have certain minimal contacts with his advisor. . . . special curricula have been developed by the participating colleges. . . , student learning packages are to be developed to include cassette-recorded lectures, tape-slide presentations, videotapes and movies. . . , substantial use is made of independent study . . . , a broad mix of resources—including regular courses, . . . telelectures, videotapes, programed learning. . . is to be used, there is no fixed curriculum and no fixed time for the award of a degree" (Valley, 1972, pp. 100–109).

Since only 18 percent of adults who want to learn are

interested in credit toward degrees (see Chapter Two), focus on degree patterns seems overly restrictive. With this in mind, television-oriented technologies can be put to work in the context of Valley's Modes of Learning Model.

While the use of educational technology in continuing education by college faculties, even by individual faculty members, is now an out-of-the-ordinary, relatively rare involvement, and resistance by faculties is the number one problem standing in the way of forward progress, the systematic introduction of instructional television into college courses can now encounter much less faculty resistance than in the recent past, if the major use is in the context of lifelong learning. The college campuses have internal needs for dramatic change in the nature of learning activities; the economic plight of hard pressed colleges provides further motivation for improving the quality of instruction. Once faculty members learn what the needs are for learning materials among adults and how the technologies can be used in systems for their delivery, a new energy-source will be ready to satisfy the needs.

One of the walls that will need to come crumbling down early is the one that has separated continuing education from college education. Education is a matter of wanting or needing to learn something not known; this lack may be recognized and need to be satisfied at any age. College education, until recently, might have been defined as for young people from seventeen through twenty-one; it must now become synonymous with continuing education—lifelong.

Cooperative approaches to the development of educational materials for lifelong learning should be planned. It is plausible for faculties from several colleges to join forces perhaps with other agencies developing the content and methodology for needed systems of lifelong learning (*The Futurist*, 1972). The Carnegie Commission on Higher Education predicts that by the year 2000 informational technology will have penetrated farthest into off-campus instruction at postsecondary levels. What would it take to realize this result which in the Carnegie Commission's view "better than ever before can bring education to the sick, the handicapped, the aged, the prisoners, the members of the armed forces, persons in remote areas, and to the many adults . . . who will find instruction at home more convenient?" (1972) It would take a major effort

(a) to plan, produce, evaluate, and package fully transportable "mediated"* instructional units, (b) to combine the packaged units with other segments of direct and personal teacher-student interaction, and (c) to develop this packaged and personalized instruction into courses of six months duration or more. Considerable progress would at the same time be made to improve the quality of instruction on campus; developing transportable course materials will lead faculty members to raise the communicating power of their materials in traditional classrooms.

An effort to provide for the numerous needs of lifelong education would necessitate the systems approach (Churchman, 1968)—objectives defined, programs devised, alternatives explored, developments pursued, results evaluated, objectives redefined, programs revised, and so on. Several alternative delivery systems might be considered; flexibility from the learner's standpoint—known at the outset to be a keystone in the design—might be achieved along a dependence-independence dimension. Under some circumstances, the adult learner would have to study independently—entirely on his own. Under others adult learners might best be served through engagement in teacher-dependent study as the traditional college student does. Between these extremes, there can be options for varying amounts of teacher-student interaction, access to the help of a mentor, counselor, advisor, or guide, and varying amounts of classroom-laboratory instruction on campus, at regional and community centers, or at the public library. The goal might be to see each learner engage in the maximum amount of independent study commensurate with his behavioral style. As much instruction as possible would be made available in the instructional materials the learner has with him. For those learners opting an independent mode, most learning units should fit into an attache case or a posted parcel.

Lifelong Learning Materials Service Center

A lifelong learning materials service center can provide a base for cooperative program development. The center would be

---

* *Mediated* denotes use of appropriate media, especially audiovisual support, in packaging instruction.

a major cooperative effort at technological learning materials development and revision and evaluation in order to raise individual competence, to increase adaptability to change, and to enhance productivity and performance in careers among all interested adults. "Educators find the fast-moving developments of technology baffling and use their puzzlement as both a reason and an excuse for not making the capital investment needed to take advantage of what exists (Commission on Non-Traditional Study, 1973, p. 96), but the evidence by the Research Program on Non-Traditional Studies should give educators the full confidence they need to make the necessary moves.

A lifelong learning materials service center would help all those who are interested, both substantively and procedurally, to create new educational patterns fitting the times, to find imaginative ways to use all available instructional resources to build these patterns into programs, and in doing these things, to hold the needs of the students as paramount over the convenience of institutions.

The center would provide coordination, assist in development, gauge research requirements, organize research projects, and provide other services that the individual institutions might require with specific programs of non-traditional studies. The center would seek out and utilize the talents and capabilities of faculty members from the colleges, behavioral scientists, specialists in learning, media experts, information specialists, librarians, and so on. There might be, for example, one set of activities by which to delineate instructional units, packages and courses which would have wide appeal in specified subgroups of the potential student population—personal psychology for people trying to understand themselves, human development for young mothers, sociology for Blacks, ecology for urban dwellers, civic-social responsibility for young marrieds, business for small business owners. By such analyses, institutions interested in developing course packages could be guided to tailor their efforts to confirmed demand. A major component would work on matters related to areas of learning, including the pertinent market research. Planning would have to be a major function in the scheme for instructional systems development at the service center. Both the planning and the execution need a team approach.

Lessons and courses too can be developed at the service

center; appropriate parts of them would involve television production. Efforts at the service center would be undergirded by an ongoing research program. Of fundamental importance, the model is expected to be largely "do it yourself." Centers now operating produce program materials for teachers and institutions to use, but the service center would work with the faculties and colleges to plan and produce the instructional materials they want, mainly for use in their own programs and secondly for use by others who find the materials desirable.

With or without the colleges, the television set will be the key instrument for telecommunications and for purveying knowledge in the foreseeable future. Other technologies, such as the computer, will serve education in longer time frames as subsystems. The prospect of television as a prime medium for instruction and learning—as it is certain to be soon—immediately raises the question of quality. One reasonable criterion of quality is the established quality of traditionally delivered instruction. The no-significant-difference findings of Carpenter and Greenhill in 1958 continue, in the main, to be sustained in recent research efforts: instruction by television has been found no better than conventional instruction—nor has it been proven any worse. According to Oettinger (1972, p. 6) learning as we are presently able to measure it is largely independent of the detail of means or method; the dominance of no-significant-difference findings opens promising "alternatives to the accepted ways of schooling." Neither the content of learning nor the fruits of learning-research necessarily swing the choice among the available media of instruction.

Materials planned for taping and for ultimate presentation over television would, by the nature of the preparation, be well suited to use in any instructional setting, including the conventional classroom. Motion pictures fitting the course objectives would be previewed and chosen; 35mm slides would supply visual support when selected and ordered in the best sequence. Overhead projection transparencies would be designed, executed, and fitted into the lesson. Film clips too would be fitted in. Notes for narration, discussion, and lecture sequences would be sharpened. A given lesson would materialize on a story board and become a scripted "production."

Interplay between the videotaped segments and the portions of study involving books and other printed materials would be planned, as would the orienting-explaining sequences. The television support would thus contain major portions of course content, including the instructions, counsel, and guidance by the professor and other members of the instructional staff—the same sort of counterpoint to class instruction as the informal help students get from the professor at the end of class on campus. The systems approach would also require a hard look at the needs and opportunities for direct student-teacher interaction. An optimum mix of the human element and technological elements could be timed and placed in accordance with the constraints of the learner.

Why the focus on television? First, instructional units that are planned well for television are more communicative than they would be even when put on in the lecture hall or classroom. Putting them on videotape just makes them more cost effective. Learning material thus is available to a person interested in learning, rather than holding a student captive for purposes of accruing credit. Second, when the television production is run in the studio, it is right then put on videotape; it can at the same time be run live over-the-air on educational television or on wire over closed-circuit television. Third, the videotape would become part of a library of instructional material for television, available for later use. Fourth, CATV can use the same videotape as program material over the channels devoted to educational purposes. Fifth, as soon as a videocassette standard is decided upon or a videocassette configuration is selected, it would then be possible to make duplicates of the videotapes and to package them into videocassettes. All the parts of the program produced by television would then be fully transportable—a course in an attache case.

The prime goal of the service center is to amass a widely diversified collection of high quality course offerings employing varied mixes of educational technology. Several different kinds of people can participate. In curriculum development, a departmental or interdepartmental faculty from a college may decide to launch an extramural program; or a curriculum development group might arise from the professional membership of an organization such as the American Psychological Association. Another might involve an intercollegiate, interdisciplinary task force representing interests of several colleges in course development with broad cross-disciplinary focus. Another combination might be a team of professors from the academic community and editors from the publishing industry.

For any of these groups, the service center is the setting within which lesson outlines and lecture notes could evolve into packaged instructional units and where, lesson by lesson, a systematically developed course outline at the end of a given effort would evolve into a viable and fully transportable program of study. In each instance, the cooperative venture would have the advantage of full and ready access to technical know-how on instructional systems development and to those aspects of the supporting educational technology most likely to make up the best combination of delivery means for that particular piece of instruction.

OBJECTIVES

As an ongoing organization, the service center would perhaps set objectives such as the following:

(1) Carry out surveys and studies to determine (a) societal, business, occupational, and personal needs for courses of study designed for motivated adults and (b) changes in needs as they occur.

(2) Provide the organizational components and the technological means to enable a coordinated, cooperative approach to developing up-to-date learning materials.

(3) Revise resulting courses of study as needs change.

(4) Offer the widest possible variety of proved communications systems options for use in instructional units and add to and delete from the offerings as further technological development and obsolescence suggest.

(5) Exploit to the fullest extent possible the economy-of-scale advantages that will characterize wide-ranging involvement by a number of faculties and institutions and the consequent sharing of the latest technological means.

(6) Supply guidelines to help developers of instructional

materials devise measurements for evaluating student performance and achievement and for evaluating program quality and effectiveness.

(7) Evolve the best possible techniques for promoting and advertising instructional offerings to would-be learners and assist participating institutions to make effective use of the media in attracting students.

(8) Develop a communications network to keep institutions and publishers informed of specific programs of instructional materials—completed, in progress, and planned—and to make them aware of instructional materials for which there are unfilled needs.

(9) Execute development projects and supporting research programs related to how people learn, learning styles and strategies, occupational training requirements, characteristics of optimum learning systems, technical specifications for educational communications systems, field tests for program verification, and the like.

STUDENT OPTIONS

The person wishing to learn with materials produced at the service center would be able to choose the format and delivery systems most suited to his own style of learning and living. He could seek and find advice on paths thought to offer the best odds that he will complete the program. Avoidance of permanent drop-out would be part of the design.

The student could have programed materials transportable to and usable at the place where he spends most of his study time. The materials would include a textbook, workbook exercises, lab instructions, and other printed materials, audiotapes, videotapes, and audio, visual, or audiovisual materials. Access to certain supporting equipment may then be necessary, perhaps an audio-cassette player, videocassette player, television set, cable hookup, or cartridge film projector. These items would either be the student's own possessions or equipment that he could borrow, subscribe for, or rent from a nearby school or public library, college campus, businessman, or shopkeeper.

Surrounding these course offerings that would be completely independent of time and place, the student would find options available within the constraints of his calendar, clock, transportation, and geography for direct interaction with staff and faculty. Among such personal contact offerings are key lectures on campus, in regional centers, and in local libraries; weekend seminars and workshops in a classroom setting; two or three weeks of on-campus summer sessions for concentrated study; late afternoon-evening discussions of instructional program content; guidance and counseling sessions on group and individual bases; return of written work with constructively critical marginal comments; and telephone conference hours for group and individual discussion.

A lifelong learning materials service center with all these capabilities would be the materialization of a flexible paradigm for learning that would enable institutions to offer instruction that adults need, where they can give it their attention, at times they are free to do so.

Learning specialists are needed at the center, specialists who know the behavioral sciences, the psychology of learning, the foundations of pedagogy, the productive applications of communications and measurement theory, and the findings of instructional research about communications media. The major functions of these specialists at the center are to apply the systems approach to course development—to help the subject matter specialists define objectives, plot learning strategies, and structure evaluational procedures to be used in measuring effects. They also would be concerned with research design and with the formulation of hypotheses to serve as the bases of course verification and validation.

Media specialists, who know the capabilities and limitations of technological applications for multimedia course production, would be able to suggest alternative prospects for packaging course materials for delivery, for fitting audiovisual support systems to the instructional content, for building the lesson outlines into scripts for production, and for executing the production itself. Both audiovisual generalists and technologically trained specialists would need to be available—the former to advise on the technology useful in increasing the communicability and potential impact of an instructional unit, the latter to deal with the specifics of television or film production, computer systems design, computer programing, and so on.

Information specialists know sources of "off-the-shelf" materials that can be used for a given piece of instruction. The specialists will be able to locate materials in print, on film, on tape, or in other formats available from the Library of Congress, National Audiovisual Center, public television and educational television suppliers, university-based audiovisual centers, or commercial sources. The major functions of information specialists are to identify, locate, and secure for the center any available resources appropriate in an instructional package.

Graphic arts specialists, who have command of visual communications and the means for their design and execution would be able to prepare tailored visual support materials on paper, film, or tape that will enable the television production to minimize the time during a given program when "the talking face" is featured on the screen. Graphic artists would be the masters of the medium— the experts to whom the cooperating team would turn for matters related to the scale of the screen (size of lettering for readability, for example), visual effect of colors, black and white, graphic displays, and other visual communications.

This small task force of specialists could without great difficulty develop preliminary plans and prepare detailed proposals for organizing and financing the first lifelong learning materials service center.

All of these capabilities need not be on call at all times, nor for that matter, accessible at the same place. A lifelong learning materials service center is more the organization and functioning of a set of specialists and other resources toward a common set of goals than it is a common venue and time block where and when these resources could be engaged.

As many as seven such centers for meshing technology and lifelong learning through course development are needed (Carnegie Commission, 1972), each to serve a defined region. But one such service center should be established, funded, organized, and operating as quickly as possible.

The center should keep systematic track of the output of instructional materials development nationally and internationally.

It should have provisions for evaluating the effectiveness, cost, adoptability, and practical success of the programs in non-traditional studies before they become entrenched in a "non-traditional tradition." This combines tracking (an operating information system) and research (perhaps a research-development-evaluation-dissemination-diffusion model as that used by the National Institute of Education). Both functions could be performed with effectiveness and distinction by a nonprofit educational organization with diversified professional staff and large computer capability.

References

Carnegie Commission on Higher Education. *The Fourth Revolution: Instructional Technology in Higher Education.* New York: McGraw-Hill, 1972.

CARPENTER, C. R., and GREENHILL, L. P. *Instructional Television Research.* University Park, Penn.: Pennsylvania State University, 1958.

CHURCHMAN, C. W. *The Systems Approach.* New York: Delacorte Press, 1968.

Commission on Non-Traditional Study. *Diversity by Design.* San Francisco: Jossey-Bass, 1973.

Federal Register, February 12, 1972, *37* (30), 3261-2–3264-6.

The Futurist, August 1972, *4* (4).

MC GOWAN, J. J., NOLL, R. G., and PECK, M. J. "Prospects and Policies for CATV." In Sloan Commission on Cable Communications, *On the Cable: The Television of Abundance.* New York: McGraw-Hill, 1971, Appendix B.

OETTINGER, A. G., and ZAPOL, N. *Will Information Technologies Help Learning? An Analysis of Some Policy Issues.* Berkeley, Calif.: Carnegie Commission on Higher Education, 1972.

"A Short Course in Cable," New York: Office of Communication, United Church of Christ, 1972.

Sloan Commission on Cable Communications. *On the Cable: The Television of Abundance.* New York: McGraw-Hill, 1971.

VALLEY, J. R. "External Degree Programs." In S. B. GOULD and K. P. CROSS (Eds.) *Explorations in Non-Traditional Study.* San Francisco: Jossey-Bass, 1972.

Videocassette Industry Guide, June 1972, *1* (1).

Video Play Program Catalog. Ridgefield, Conn.: C. S. Tepfer, 1972.

Vid News, July 24, 1972a, 2 (10).

Vid News, September 4, 1972b, 2 (13).

WALTON, W. W. *Interviews with Non-Traditionalists Outside Education.* Princeton: Educational Testing Service, 1972.

Awarding Credit

Jonathan R. Warren

🙟🙟🙟🙟🙟🙟🙟🙟🙟🙟🙟🙟🙟🙝🙝🙝🙝🙝🙝🙝🙝🙝🙝🙝🙝🙝

*T*he assignment of credits for college courses is so entrenched in American higher education that a system of earning a degree without accumulating semester hours or quarter hours or some other set of units is hard to imagine. Yet the credit-hour system is scarcely a hundred years old and was not a completely accepted part of higher education until the beginning of the present century. It arose when the elective system, which had been sputtering for forty years, began to be widely adopted in the last quarter of the nineteenth century. Before that time students received their degrees on completing a four-year curriculum that was fixed for all students and that varied little from college to college.

The colleges that initiated the four-year degree in the American colonies were vastly different from the colleges and universities of today. In contrast to the thousands of courses offered to undergraduates by today's institutions, with students scattering among a multitude of classes during the day, not only did every student in the colonial colleges study every part of the curriculum, but each entering class proceeded through the prescribed curriculum by attending every class in a body. Instruction until well into the nineteenth century consisted not in lecturing but in assigning lessons to be studied outside class and hearing recitations during class time. Professors were primarily examiners, checking on whether the students could recite their lessons. What teaching occurred was done by tutors who drilled the students to recite properly in class. With learning occurring almost entirely outside class and professors serving as examiners, American colleges during their first two centuries were more like examining centers certifying out-of-class accomplishment than like today's higher education institutions. Attendance in class with proper decorum through four years led to a bachelor's degree. Receipt of the degree entitled the graduate to engage in public debate and conferred on him some measure of status, but certified no professional capabilities.

The prescription of four years instead of some other period of time stemmed, as illustrated by the Statutes of the College of William and Mary, from the practice of "the two famous universities in England" (Hofstadter and Smith, 1961). Curiously, the four-year curriculum remains almost unquestioned to this day. Present proposals to shorten that period, for example by the Carnegie Commission among others, merely rearrange blocks of time, keeping the presumed substance of the four-year curriculum and reducing the number of class hours only negligibly if at all. Any shortening of the four years is accomplished either by extending the academic calendar, permitting capable students to take course overloads, or providing for college study during the last year of high school (Carnegie Commission on Higher Education, 1972). None of these procedures is new—more than a third of the Harvard class of 1906 graduated in three years for example—but they have never become widespread, among other reasons because college was an enjoyable enough experience that most students were reluctant to terminate early (Rudolph, 1962). More important, as President Bok of Harvard has pointed out, none of these procedures is based on an examination of what the college curriculum is to accomplish —that is, of the purposes of undergraduate education, with the period of study set at whatever is necessary for the desired purpose (Bok, 1972).

The influence of the German universities and the development of graduate schools in the United States in the latter part of the nineteenth century led to curricular diversification and election in the undergraduate colleges, the formation of academic departments, and the organization of each student's studies around a specialized major field of concentration. Because of conscious efforts to fit the four-year degree tradition, many present four-year programs are coherent educational experiences that could not be accomplished in a shorter period. But whether four years is an optimal period for most college programs has not often been examined. That every major field in present undergraduate colleges should find its optimal organization in a four-year time span seems absurd.

Despite the limitations, in hindsight, of equating a college degree with any particular number of years, American higher education has continued to use the academic year and its various subdivisions as the basic building block for its degree structure. The diversification of courses late in the nineteenth century and the practice of allowing students to choose among them in fashioning a degree program created a need for some system to determine equivalence among these courses and programs, all of which led to a common degree. The accounting procedure most commonly adopted was to divide the typical four-year program into units small enough to represent individual courses, assign several units to each course according to the amount of time it required, and aggregate these units or "credits" into a full college program. (Courses could as well have been designated fractionally as one-fortieth or one-thirtieth or one-sixtieth of a degree, but probably the attraction of whole numbers, such as three or four credits per course, made the present credit and course system preferable.) Thus credits have derived their meaning entirely from the degree. Once the qualifications for a degree are established, the definition and use of credits are arbitrary procedures for the purposes of permitting educational activities to be quantified for management and accounting reasons and for indicating the progress each student has made toward a degree.

Uses of Credit

A credit is currently defined as three hours per week of instruction or study, in or out of class, for whatever number of weeks constitutes a term, although deviations from that standard

are common (Lorimer, 1962). Credits from different institutions
are equated by weighting them according to the number of weeks in
a term—commonly ten for quarter systems and fifteen for semesters
—at the institution awarding the credit. With students permitted a
wide range of choices among courses that satisfy the requirements
for a degree, determinations of both quantitative and qualitative
comparability among courses are necessary. Assigning some number
of credits to each course permits quantitative comparisons of different courses. The qualitative comparability of two courses in, say,
philosophy and literature in satisfying a requirement for some level
of accomplishment in the humanities is simply a matter of judgment
by institutional authority, either an individual staff member or a
committee. Within the same institution the comparability of different courses is seldom a problem. When students transfer to other
institutions, judgments of the suitability of courses at the first
institution for meeting requirements of the second are more difficult,
but the wide agreement on the definition of a credit permits assignment of quantitative comparability, while course catalogs permit
judgments of qualitative comparability. Determining credit for
experiences outside the classroom—travel, work, or community
service, for example—requires still more difficult judgments. But
ultimately the basis for any of these judgments of comparability—
within an institution, between institutions, or between nonacademic
and academic experiences—is the way the degree-granting college
or university defines its degree.

The use of credits as markers on the path to a degree is
gaining importance as students increasingly withdraw and reenter
college—interspersing other activities between periods of college
attendance—and transfer between institutions. The year of college
enrollment is correspondingly declining in importance. Sophomore,
junior, and senior standing are becoming less useful terms than
statements of numbers of credits completed, as is evident in the
following statement from the bulletin of a major university: "At
the close of each quarter, the courses, units, grades, and grade-points
earned are added onto the student's cumulative University record.
From this record, he may determine his progress toward a degree."
If the degree is implicitly the educational goal of college students,
then credits are the immediate means of charting their progress,

In addition to their use as indicators of progress toward a degree, credits serve value as rewards or tokens of accomplishment. Their receipt each ten to fifteen weeks probably plays an important role in maintaining student interest and involvement in a long-term enterprise toward a goal too distant to provide its own satisfaction. The intrinsic enjoyment associated with intellectual stimulation and learning plays some role in keeping students involved in the academic enterprise. But intellectual curiosity and excitement alone may lead students in erratic paths that can change direction with any chance encounter. Pursuit of course credits requires students to direct their energies down more orderly disciplinary paths.

Credits serve students' purposes as well. Just as a baccalaureate degree makes its holder eligible to apply for admission to graduate and professional schools or to a variety of jobs not open to persons without degrees, so credits short of a degree confer similar kinds of qualifications. Not only admission to advanced courses in the student's institution and admission with advanced standing at a new institution but also qualification for application to some jobs and for some occupational licenses is now based on the accumulation of specified numbers of credits less than those needed for a degree. Educational requirements for an increasing number of jobs are being set higher than a high school diploma but lower than a bachelor's degree. The most common subbaccalaureate requirement is for credits equal to two years of college—a practice growing rapidly with the burgeoning junior colleges—but a number of occupational certificates can be earned with credits representing one to three years of college. Thus although the degree still dominates higher education, credits—established initially as an accounting device to keep track of the degree progress of students— are beginning to be used as a continuous measure of educational accomplishment independent of the degree. The continuing education unit, indicating ten hours of participation in an organized educational program not creditable toward a degree, has been adopted by a number of colleges and universities to credit non-degree activities (*The Continuing Education Unit,* 1970).

Beyond their utility for students and for institutional recording of student progress, course credits are now used in a wide range of institutional, governmental, and societal accounting functions, probably the most important being to link education to monetary measures. Student credit hours per one thousand dollars of educational and general expenditure, for example, has been called by the Carnegie Commission on Higher Education (1972) the best measure of the output of institutions of higher education. Student enrollments are reported and appropriations often made in terms of Full-Time Equivalents (FTEs) based on the total number of credit hours for which students are enrolled. Tuition charges are often based on costs per credit hour. And comparisons of costs across departments within institutions and between departments in different institutions are based on numbers of student credit hours they "produce." All these practices have arisen largely through convenience. The course credit, initially established as a unit for educational accounting, has now been appropriated for fiscal accounting.

Current Practices

CORRESPONDENCE STUDY

If *non-traditional* study refers to ways of earning credit that do not consist of faculty-directed classroom exercises on a college campus, the oldest American collegiate non-traditional form is correspondence study. It originated in Boston about the time the elective system became popular—about 1870 (Mathieson, 1971)—as a way for institutions to bring higher education to people unable because of distance or employment to attend college in residence. Late in the nineteenth century, colleges offered degrees entirely by correspondence, but concern over standards and fear of the possible debasement of residential degrees led college and university authorities to abandon the practice not long after the beginning of the present century. Then as now, however, standards for degrees taken in residence were not defined except in terms of the length of time passed under instruction. Today, most colleges and universities permit a limited number of credits for correspondence study pursued in their own programs, at another accredited institution, or at an institution of known reputation such as the United States Armed Forces Institute (USAFI) to count toward their regular degrees.

College credit for work experience has a fairly long history in limited form (Auld, 1971). The University of Cincinnati in 1906 started a program in which engineering students alternated periods of study with periods of employment in industry; other schools of engineering followed; and in 1921 Antioch College started a similar program for its liberal arts students. Today over two hundred institutions offer programs alternating work and study, and as of 1970, about one-third of them gave credit for the work experience that could be substituted for classroom credit (Wilson 1971). In the rest, the periods of employment simply stretch out the time required to earn enough classroom credits to graduate.

Undergraduate professional programs have long given credit for supervised field experience, as in student teaching, nursing practicums, and other internships. Recently a few colleges, but not yet enough to constitute a major trend, have begun to incorporate similar work experiences into selected liberal arts programs. Metropolitan State College in Denver, for example, has political science majors serving as interns with the Denver City Council. The University of California at Irvine has students receiving credit for work in various mental health, law enforcement, and judicial agencies. California State College at Dominguez Hills and the State University of New York at Albany have similar programs. As of the fall of 1972, in the University Year for Action supported by the federal government, twenty-eight institutions had full-time community service programs for about twelve hundred students. Usually each student earns a full year of credits in courses appropriate to the activity. Working in a day-care center, for example, or caring for mentally-retarded children, may earn credits in child development, education, or psychology, depending on the student's major field and on supplementary work planned with and supervised by a faculty adviser.

In each of these cases, credit is determined in advance, as with any regular course, and the experience is supervised and evaluated by regular faculty members. Credit is based not so much on evaluating the learning after it has occurred but on planning the experience so that the fact of engaging in it will necessarily be educationally productive—essentially the same way credit is handled in regular campus courses. Few if any students who enter a course or internship adequately prepared and willing to engage themselves in it fail to be awarded its full credit. Whether in traditional or non-traditional study, given adequate planning and preparation, evidence that the experience has been honestly undertaken has universally been sufficient for the award of credit. Almost any experience reasonably indicative of intellectual competence can now be recognized for credit somewhere. As Ruyle and Geiselman report in Chapter Three, these creditable activities range from completing a patent, work of art, or other product to participating in a local theater, orchestra, or other civic activity; or even in sensitivity training or encounter groups.

PRIOR EXPERIENCE

In contrast to the widely-accepted policy of giving credit for cooperative or supervised work experience while the student is enrolled in college, far fewer institutions give newly enrolled students credit and advanced standing on the basis of experience acquired before enrolling in the institution. Only 7 percent of the institutions in the study reported in Chapter Three give credit without an examination for prior work experience such as VISTA or Peace Corps service; and of these, the number having a formal program for doing so is probably tiny. Yet, changes are occurring in the way credit is awarded for prior experience. "Life" experiences other than employment are being accepted by an increasing number of institutions, and possibly in recognition of the fact that non-academic experiences are by definition different from those of the usual college or university course, attempts to equate prior experiences to specific courses seem to be declining. Thus most programs for adults credit prior experience only indirectly. Special seminars, independent study, and credit by examination are established that presume adults' experiences make them capable of reaching the degree through a different and shorter path than regular students. Yet the particular experiences adults may bring are often neither examined nor credited. Instead, a faculty member or administrator makes a judgment that an applicant's prior experiences are worth some number of credits, and the applicant is thereby placed at some position beyond the usual starting point on the path toward a degree. But those judgments rest on no clearly established principle. They are often pulled from the air with all the inconsistency and unconsidered implications that characterize any unsystematic decision.

Yet judgments need not be inherently unsystematic, inconsistent, or invalid. All academic credits rest ultimately on subjective judgments of accomplishment, and the difficulty in judging the suitability for credit of prior nonacademic experiences is that existing definitions of a college degree all rest on the amount of time students spend in a traditional academic setting. Relating specific accomplishments to degree requirements naturally presents problems in the absence of an adequate definition of a degree.

EXAMINATION OR EVALUATION

Any form of off-campus learning experience—previous employment, independent study, travel, or other unsupervised study—can be used to gain formal college credit if it can be validated through taking a standardized examination. Limitations on credit by examination vary widely, depending on the institution, the content of the experience, and the number of credits the applicant has already earned; but it is now possible to earn a bachelor's degree entirely through examinations. The Regents External Degree in New York, which is available nationwide, and the degrees of Thomas A. Edison College in New Jersey can be awarded for satisfactory performance on examinations regardless of how the competency for satisfactory performance was acquired. Despite the reluctance of most existing institutions to award more than a limited amount of credit by examination, the external degree by examination has thus become a reality.

Among the nearly thirty institutions participating in the University Without Walls program of the Union for Experimenting Colleges and Universities (1972), several are moving away from the traditional time-oriented degree to the competence- or achievement-oriented degree exemplified by the Regents and Thomas A. Edison external degrees. They are awarding credits not on the time spent in an activity, but on the accomplishment of specified criteria. At Skidmore College, for example, a student may pick her field, examine degree requirements for that field in several other college catalogs, determine in light of her past experience what more she needs to do to reach a point equivalent to these degrees, and then get a committee of knowledgeable people to approve her plan and her achievement of it.

In spite of some misgivings—financial as well as educational —by traditional educators, the award of college degrees by examination and evaluation of competence is likely to become as widely accepted by the end of this century as the award of course credit had become by its beginning.

Problems in Measurement of Performance

The present system of credits—resulting from grafting the elective system a hundred years ago onto an earlier tradition of a four-year baccalaureate degree—rests entirely on what a student is presumed to learn in four years of full-time instruction. Even though arbitrary, this basis for the credit system is not indefensible for the measurement of education. Physical units of measurement are no less arbitrary except for those, like days and years, which have an inherent relationship with recurring patterns of light, temperature, and climate. But unlike a platinum bar in Paris or the frequency of radiation emitted by excited krypton atoms, the standard on which credits are based—the degree—is not only variable but inadequately defined. It is an archaic standard for supporting the structure of postsecondary education.

Our nineteenth-century degree-credit system is maintained the same way that monetary systems and other measurement systems are maintained—through public confidence and use. As long as degrees are accepted as prerequisites for further education or for employment, they will be valued, as will the credits that lead to them. But several indications suggest that the degree is losing at least some of its value. One is the rising frequency of challenges to the degree as a selection criterion for employment (Berg, 1971; Miller, 1972), including the developing stance of the courts against employers requiring a degree as a condition of employment or licensure unless it is demonstrably related to occupational competence. Other indicators of decline are the cooling of public enthusiasm for higher education as its costs rise more rapidly than the economy as a whole. As the numbers of college graduates have grown more rapidly than the population as a whole, as degrees have come to be required for entry into occupations that previously had lower educational requirements, and yet as possession of a degree has no longer assured entry into jobs for which it was previously adequate, the inflation of educational requirements has brought with it lessened confidence in the present system of educational credentials based on the degree (Milner, 1972). In the future, qualifications for advanced education as well as for employment may rest more heavily on indicators of specific competencies and accomplishment than on degrees. Such a development will require a substantial reformation of the present credit system.

TRADITIONAL PROCEDURES

Even without the particular problems created by non-traditional programs, inadequacies in the credit system are apparent in conventional programs. For example, under the present system, satisfactory completion of a course results in the award of a fixed number of credits regardless of the student's level of performance. Grades vary with performance; credits do not. While proposals have occasionally been made to adjust the amount of credit received in a course to the student's level of performance in it (Elton, 1968), they have not been widely considered. They raise serious doubt, nonetheless, about the desirability of a system in which students performing at a minimally acceptable level earn the maximum number of credits a course offers.

Discrepancies among different instructors in their expectations of satisfactory performance in a course have been criticized so frequently that this perennial problem of individual idiosyncrasy needs no elaboration. But other problems in the award of credit are less well known. In traditional college courses, credit is awarded to students who complete the assigned tasks—writing papers, working problem sets, completing laboratory or field assignments—and who pass the prescribed tests. Both these bases for credit rest on the assumption that the experiences of the course will necessarily produce the desired learning in any adequately prepared student who applies himself. The student papers, reports, and other products are evaluated only to assign grades, not to determine credit. Rarely will credit be denied a student who has completed all the assigned tasks, whatever the quality of his products, if he has passed the tests at an acceptable level. But the tests, too, primarily indicate the student's engagement with the activities of the course. Most course examinations are limited to those particular aspects of learning that lend themselves readily to measurement. They are insensitive to many course outcomes faculty members consider important, such as the integration of details into a higher order of understanding or the application of general principles to new situations (McKeachie, 1970). Their importance lies in the assumption that any student who gives enough attention to the course activities to pass the examinations will also have acquired the competencies the course is intended to produce but that are not measured in the tests. This assumption is virtually never examined and is often unwarranted. Thus much of the learning expected to occur in traditional college classes is not measured directly but only assumed to follow from engagement in the prescribed activities. In this respect, traditional learning differs little from the non-traditional.

Another problem in assessing traditional learning appears when attention is focused on the award of credit rather than the assignment of grades. Most classroom tests indicate relative levels of student accomplishment rather than the degree to which the students have accomplished the requirements of the course. With capable students, the lowest score on a test may accompany acceptable performance. Similarly, if the test was poorly constructed or opportunities to learn were not adequate, the highest score may be associated with inadequate accomplishment. Thus credit may be assigned capriciously, depending on such extraneous elements as the capabilities of the other students in the class. The award of credit in traditional college programs is no less vulnerable to criticism than the award of non-traditional credit. It is only more familiar.

PROBLEMS IN NON-TRADITIONAL STUDY

These existing problems in the evaluation of conventional classroom study have not seriously hampered conventional instruction, but similar problems in the measurement of performance and the award of credit may be major deterrents to creating programs of non-traditional study. Among the institutions surveyed for the Commission on Non-Traditional Study, as Ruyle and Geiselman indicate in Chapter Three, 40 percent cited the assessment of non-classroom learning as an obstacle to the introduction of non-traditional programs, putting it in a virtual tie with lack of money as the most frequently cited deterrent. About half the institutions reported a general resistance to non-traditional study, citing faculty resistance, lack of interest, no apparent need, or the belief that non-traditional study is a passing fad. Almost as many, however, cited problems that involved the award and recognition of credit, such as concern for standards, for accreditation, for licensing and certification, and for acceptance of graduates by employers and graduate schools. While these problems ought to be as important for traditional as for non-traditional programs, they clearly indicate the major inhibiting influence of questions of credit on non-traditional study.

In principle, the measurement of learning is unaffected by the process through which the learning is acquired. Thus the measurement of non-classroom learning ought to be no more difficult than the measurement of classroom learning. The widespread belief that the difficulty of measuring nonclassroom learning hinders the adoption of non-traditional educational practices therefore needs further examination. Three factors appear to contribute to this wariness over the assessment of non-traditional study: unfamiliarity with out-of-class learning, the possibility of fraud and error, and uncertainties over both purposes and procedures.

Unfamiliarity. In assessing classroom learning, the assessor is usually the same person who has directed the learning. He can supplement his formal assessment with informal judgments and make whatever adjustments he considers necessary. Because he has directed the student's learning he also is reasonably confident that everyone given credit has learned enough to merit it. But in most forms of non-traditional learning, validation of the formal measurement by informal observations is not possible, leading to the fear that some students will receive unmerited credit through error in the measurement process. As Milton (1972, pp. 8, 32) has pointed out, faculty members value and guard their surveillance role in directing student learning. Faculty members are much more cautious about giving credit for someone else's teaching or for an unfamiliar kind of learning experience than giving credit for learning they direct themselves.

For example, suppose a student wants his experience of working for three months on the campaign of a congressional candidate to count for the three credits he could earn in a course titled "Organization and Functions of Political Parties." How is his experience to be assessed? The course experiences are well-known to the faculty member who teaches it and who certifies credit for it, but the learning experiences associated with the campaign are not. Credit for the campaign experiences will probably not be awarded until the nature of the experiences and their relation either to the content and objectives of the course or to the requirements for a degree in political science have been carefully considered and the student's accomplishment examined in elaborate detail. Then after a number of students have been through political campaign experiences and have demonstrated their effectiveness in producing desired results, credit can be assigned to later students for similar experiences without the need for the same intensity or complexity of assessment. By then, the non-traditional experiences will have been validated; until then they are suspect. But the same cautious approach is just as justifiable for conventional course experiences. Familiarity alone is an insufficient basis for assuming that existing course procedures accomplish the desired learning outcomes. Yet that is all that supports most present practices.

Familiar teaching procedures are believed to be "tried and true," producing the desired learning even when test scores are low —a result more likely to be attributed to error in the testing than to ineffective instruction. The same confidence is absent with respect to unfamiliar instructional procedures, yet the limited justification for this confidence in familiar procedures does nothing to ease faculty members' reluctance to accept the unfamiliar (Milton, 1972, pp. 11–15). College instruction has a long history, and traditional procedures are older than the instructors applying them. It is thus natural for instructors to assume that someone at some time determined that these procedures work; but the assumption is usually wrong. Since the measurement of learning is not sensitive to the nature of the learning process, pinning the distrust of non-traditional study on distrust in procedures for awarding credit reveals a parochial view of education. One's own procedures and judgments are to be respected. Those of others are to be questioned.

Error and fraud. A more valid problem in crediting a student's competencies is protecting against fraudulent or erroneous claims of competence. Hiring a substitute to take an examination, falsifying an employment record, buying papers or artwork or other products to present as one's own, and presenting documents that falsely testify to previous activities are some of these fraudulent practices, and erroneous decisions can stem from honest overestimates of an applicant's competencies.

No crediting procedure can be entirely free of the possibility of either error or fraud, whether applied to traditional instructional procedures or to new and unfamiliar practices. Cheating on examinations, plagiarism, and the organized marketing of term papers are activities that cannot be totally eradicated even from conventional instruction, as the college scene has long demonstrated. But safeguards can be placed on non-traditional as well as traditional credits. Major testing programs, such as the College Level Examination Program, have well-established procedures to minimize the possibility of fraud. Verifying prior learning through examinations or interviews conducted by the faculty can limit the effectiveness of falsified records or credentials. Limiting credit to activities approved by a recognized or accredited institution is a further safeguard against fraud and error. And the simple existence of the potential for confirmation of student reports of past experiences limits exaggeration in self-reports.

Beyond these procedural safeguards, the major protection against fraud and error lies in the credit system itself as a counterweight to the importance of the degree system. A system in which the single dominant credential is a diploma certifying completion of a poorly defined, broad set of activities occurring over a period of four years or more, and in which the degree alone carries great weight in admission to desired positions and status, offers both incentive and opportunity for fraud. A system consisting of diversified and clearly defined credentials, each directed to reasonably specific and limited purposes, inherently offers better protection against fraud. Its close relationship between credit and observable performance in the specific activity which the credential certifies makes both fraud and error more readily detectable and fraud less tempting.

Uncertainties of purpose and procedures. The award of credit for learning that is not like that of the traditional college classroom can assume either of two purposes: indicating that the non-traditional experiences have (1) advanced the student to some specifiable point on the path toward whatever a degree represents, or (2) provided the student with the competencies associated with the completion of specified college courses. Either of these determinations is a difficult measurement problem not faced in most college classrooms, although failure to face the problem there does not mean it is not present. In traditional courses, as pointed out before, familiarity has merely led to its being ignored.

More difficulties are encountered in crediting non-traditional learning in terms of progress toward a degree than in terms of specific course requirements, particularly if degree requirements are vague or broadly defined. But if degree requirements can take precedence over course requirements, a quarter spent working in a political campaign, for example, may satisfy a degree requirement for knowledge of American governmental and political institutions even if it is not creditable for the course in American institutions that most students take to satisfy the same requirement. The acceptance of that experience for graduation depends in this case on the purpose of the degree requirement, not on the similarity of the experience to the standard course.

Standardized tests may be used to estimate competence associated with degree rather than course requirements, but they are often supplemented by other kinds of observations—among them, interviews in which the student's previous experiences are discussed, inspection of records of previous activities, examination of samples of the student's previous work, and oral examinations by several faculty members. Judgments reached through several such sources of varied evidence, particularly when criteria are fuzzy, are less likely to involve error or permit fraud than easy decisions based on single measures, not only in assigning non-traditional credit but in regular courses as well. Regardless of how and when learning occurs—on the job, in community service, through foreign travel, or in the classroom—as many different kinds of evidence of capability as possible should be employed. Journals, oral accounts, examinations, physical products or records of an experience, rating scales, checklists, and direct observations of performance are all appropriate for measuring some kinds of competencies and for assessing the results of some kinds of experiences.

If the non-traditional credit is to be associated with a particular college course, comparability can sometimes be based on an examination of the two sets of experiences. For example, the Commission on Accreditation of Service Experiences (1968) examines the content of military training courses to determine their comparability to courses offered in civilian colleges and universities and recommends the number of credits that can reasonably be awarded for each military course and the nature of the most similar civilian course for which the credit should be granted. Validating examinations usually are not required. The award of credit is based entirely on comparability of course content and certification that the military course has been satisfactorily completed.

Increasingly, however, competence in academic areas acquired outside traditional courses is being determined through the use of standardized tests such as those of CLEP or locally prepared written or oral examinations. Standardized tests present a difficult problem in determining the passing score for the award of credit. Even if local norms have been established from scores of students who have passed the regular course, setting the minimum acceptable score is still difficult. A common practice is to give credit if applicants score higher than the twenty-fifth percentile among students who have completed the course, but some colleges set the cutoff point at the fiftieth percentile. Whatever score is adopted as minimally acceptable, the decision is arbitrary and never entirely satisfactory. For example, a cutoff at the twenty-fifth percentile with respect to local norms means that a person who scores above the twentieth but below the twenty-fifth percentile is ineligible for credit yet is more proficient than one in five of the students who have successfully completed the course. And a score at the forty-ninth percentile with a fiftieth percentile cutoff could even more justifiably be considered acceptable performance.

Since no test, even if free of error, is a valid indicator of all the competencies associated with a college course, critics of credit by examination argue that a low test score, even when comparable to that of many successful students, should not justify the award of credit. The fact that students have actually experienced the lectures, discussions, and other activities of a course is a legitimate though imperfect indicator, independent of any test score, that they have acquired some portion of the competencies or understandings associated with the course. But a counter argument can be made that since equivalent courses in different colleges or under different instructors differ substantially in the learning they produce, the score on a standardized test is by itself a better indicator of performance relative to all the equivalent courses offered across the country than is satisfactory performance in any single course. This counter argument is not likely to sway faculty members opposed to offering credit by examination in their own courses, but it illustrates the inevitably arbitrary nature of decisions about the award of credit even with well-constructed standardized tests closely related to the course to be credited.

This difficulty in setting cutoff scores on standardized examinations points to another problem in measuring competence acquired outside college that is expected to parallel that of a college class. Measurement in a class is usually normative in that unsatisfactory and therefore uncredited performance is determined in relation to the performance of other students in that or similar classes. But non-traditional forms of study are at least so varied if not unique that no reasonable normative group is available. As indicated above, using students in regular classes as a norm group is often not satisfactory. More appropriate is some absolute criterion of performance.

During the past decade, interest has been growing in the use of absolute rather than relative standards of performance for the assessment of educational accomplishment at all levels (Glaser & Nitko, 1971). Performance relative to that of other students may be of interest for some purposes, such as comparing the effectiveness of different instructional procedures, but it has little value by itself as an indicator of the competence of individual students. If credit is to reflect student performance or capability, a student's absolute level of mastery of a specifiable learning objective is the attribute that should be assessed (Bloom, 1970).

Criterion-referenced measurement—that is, measurement that assesses a person's competence with respect to a specified performance task—is particularly pertinent for non-traditional study. The usual classroom-based examinations in higher education are norm-referenced—that is, designed to assess the relative standing of students within a course, a college, or some other reference group. But non-traditional study may involve an individualized set of activities for which other students are not available to constitute a reference group, and for reasons discussed earlier, students in traditional classes are not an entirely acceptable reference group for assessing performance in non-traditional study. Thus assessment of a student's capabilities acquired through non-traditional means will often require criterion-referenced measurement. This does not mean, however, that measurement of classroom-based learning should necessarily remain norm-referenced. The requirements for assessing achievement in the two types of learning are not as different as they seem, and neither are the actual practices through which credit is awarded. Both traditional and non-traditional learning require criterion-referenced measurement to a substantial degree unless credit in both kinds of learning is to be awarded on the untested assumption that mere participation in the experiences themselves indicates that the desired learning has occurred.

The necessary specificity of the criteria to be measured leads some instructors to fear that specific criteria will be trivial—that broad goals like understanding will be reduced to something like the recognition of minor facts without a grasp of their interrelatedness—and that the real goals of a course cannot be made as explicit as the requirements of criterion-referenced measurement demand. But specificity does not imply triviality. Criterion-referenced measurement need not be limited to trivial outcomes. In fact, it is one way to ensure that the assessment of performance is not limited with respect to desired course outcomes. If course objectives cannot be made explicit enough to be assessed directly, then no justification can be found for the presumption that any method of instruction, traditional or not, is effective.

Directions for the Future

Whatever form learning experiences take—traditional or non-traditional—assessment of the effectiveness of the experiences and the award of credit must both be related to the purposes the learning experiences are to serve. The importance of educational goals in determining assessment practices is already well recognized at the level of individual courses. In the future it should affect the total degree system as well.

For example, in the previous illustration of crediting a student's participation in a political campaign, the purposes of the expected learning are critical in selecting appropriate examination or measurement procedures. If the purpose is to help the student gain a practical familiarity with the operation of political parties, suitable evidence of achieving this goal may be a record of the student's participation in party activities, testimonials from party officials, or the fact of selection as legislative assistant to a newly-elected state legislator. It may also involve a written or oral examination, a paper discussing the mechanisms through which candidates are selected, an audiotape of selected portions of a state party convention with commentary by the student, or a proposal for revision of party procedures. But if the purpose is to help the student understand conceptually the role of political parties in federal, state, and local government, assessment will more likely rely on an examination, a paper on such topics as the functions of political parties or trends in registrations of voters as independents, a proposal for party reorganization or redirection based on an analysis of voter trends, or a critique of a book on third parties in American politics.

Basing the assessment of achievement on desired educational outcomes demands that the assessment measures be more complex than most current procedures since they will assess a wider range of course-related capabilities than either traditional end-of-course tests or standardized achievement tests. Most faculty members probably agree that performance in their courses cannot be well described in terms of a single, uncomplicated capability. Yet standardized tests are constructed explicitly to be unidimensional measures; and while end-of-course tests may not be unidimensional, they are graded as though they are, and their representation of the various aspects of performance is usually haphazard and unknown. An adequate analysis of the objectives of a course or other segment of an educational program would reveal the different components of learning or performance it is expected to produce. Measures should then be developed to assess each of these components.

As with courses, so with degree programs and credentials. In the absence of a specific educational goal the use of formal recognition of accomplishment is questionable. Because the primary value of a formal certificate of accomplishment is its use as a ticket of admission to some desired activity, usually an occupation or further education, this activity to which the certificate admits its holder should determine the processes that lead to its award. Since higher education is no longer a homogeneous set of prescribed experiences with a limited number of goals, it should provide not only a diversity of programs and a wide range of options within them but also a variety of assessment measures, validational processes, and certificates of performance in these programs.

An example of the need for multifaceted assessment procedures and credentials can be provided by examining the bachelor's degree requirements in political science at a representative public university. One course is required in each of seven areas—American government, state and local government, public administration, political parties and pressure groups, comparative government, international relations, and political theory—plus additional breadth, depth, and skill requirements in order to provide students with "a basis for understanding the political world in which they move" and to help them "gain a foundation for intelligent political action and for advanced study and specialization in political science and the related social sciences." This program is intended to prepare students for careers in public service, business, industry, private research firms, international agencies, teaching, and law.

The nature of assessment in such a program should vary with the purpose of the learning. Students planning to study law might well be assessed for criteria and through procedures different from those for students planning a business career or entering graduate study in political science. The distinctions among these educational goals should be recognized in the certificates that symbolize completion of the program. An attempt to serve all these diverse goals by an undifferentiated program in political science leading only to an undifferentiated bachelor's degree will serve none of the goals adequately.

The credit and degree systems should serve the two purposes of certifying completed educational accomplishment and marking progress toward further educational goals. Despite the recommendation of the Carnegie Commission on Higher Education (1971) to reduce the number of academic degrees (Spurr, 1970), a variety of certificates of competence awarded after varying types and periods of instruction, each specific to some later activity, would accomplish these purposes far more effectively than would a degree system based exclusively on the period of time satisfactorily spent under instruction, which is the present arrangement and the one recommended by the Carnegie Commission. The time-based four-year bachelor's degree indicating broad exposure to a liberalizing educational experience could be retained to represent no more than that. The present demands for a bachelor's degree could be expected to decline, replaced by demands for more meaningful certificates of achievement.

Short programs with specific goals have as legitimate a claim for formal academic recognition as any two-year or four-year degree program. Examples include acquiring enough competence in computer programing to qualify for a job, learning enough spoken and written Italian to start a year of residence in Genoa, or studying enough of the philosophy of Marcuse and his philosophical forebears to understand his appeal for the present generation of college students. Each of these activities constitutes a complete educational experience in itself as well as satisfying current requirements for a bachelor's degree. Recognition of completing such programs need not and should not be predicated on the later completion of additional degree requirements. The existence of a number of alternative certificates within higher education would reduce the present compulsion to earn the baccalaureate that stems from the lack of other forms of academic recognition.

This kind of expansion of options within higher education differs from the recommendation of the Carnegie Commission in *Less Time, More Options* (1971) for "more short-term programs leading toward certificates." The Commission emphasizes easing the movement of students into and out of higher education, but largely by expanding the number of options available to them outside higher education. It proposes modifying college programs themselves only to the extent that formal recognition by means of a degree would occur every two years rather than primarily at the end of four years. Instead of merely revamping an archaic system of time-based degrees, higher education should base recognition of accomplishment on the completion of coherent educational programs, whatever their length, particularly when directed toward specific goals.

A second development that must parallel the diversification of programs and terminal points to meet diverse objectives is the facilitation of transfer among programs. To this end, credits must become units legitimate in their own right and independent of the degree in denoting achievement of a variety of specific educational goals. Easy student movement between programs requires credits that mark achievement in specific, limited regions of a multifaceted but coherent educational domain.

If higher education is to be sensibly organized toward stated goals rather than arbitrarily organized to fill a two-year or four-year time span, credits as well as degrees need more detailed definition. The different meanings or purposes of a degree, such as readiness to continue studies at a more sophisticated level, possession of qualification for employment, or maturity and understanding sufficient for civic participation and leadership, cannot all be served equally well by present definitions and distinctions among credits. "One hour of contact with an instructor plus two hours of individual preparation" in each of ten or twelve or fifteen weeks is the common but inadequate definition of a credit. Distinctions among academic fields and levels—"Political Science 351: Federal Poverty Programs"—gives some but not sufficient specificity to the credits.

Because the primary purpose of a credit system is to convey information about the educational accomplishment of students, the record-keeping and information-handling procedures of more general information systems can be readily adapted for use in a credit system. For example, one suggestive analog to the credit system is an indexing system for classifying and retrieving information contained in books or articles. A comprehensive but limited number of descriptors, organized into various categories similar to those used to identify the content of a document, could be used to indicate the meaning of credits. Academic advisors would be better able to help students select appropriate learning experiences to fill gaps in previous work. Other academic institutions as well as employers would judge students' qualifications more accurately if the credits on students' transcripts carried more information than hours of class contact, field of study, and level of course. To be useful for these several situations, credits should specify in more detail (1) the intellectual content of the credited experience, (2) the general nature of the activities it involved, and (3) the level of competence acquired and displayed by the student. These components of an effective credit system conveyed through the use of descriptors, would increase the utility of credits as devices for the transfer of information.

INTELLECTUAL CONTENT

The academic content to which credits refer could be described by a far more detailed set of descriptors than merely the title of a course. If a student has observed and studied the operation of a federally financed poverty agency, for example, the descriptors could include not just "Federal Poverty Programs" but any of the following: contemporary public problems, poverty, federal-local governmental relations, local government, urban problems, welfare, group processes, special-interest groups, welfare laws, welfare economics, community structure, public administration, the exercise of power, behavior patterns in large organizations, role relationships, community leadership, and influence. Each of these descriptors can be found in course descriptions in existing college catalogs for courses in sociology, psychology, and economics as well as in political science. All of them might pertain to learning activities organized around a poverty agency, yet not all of them would be creditable for every student who participated in such an activity. By making finer distinctions than those possible with course titles, an improved credit system could distinguish among the particular competencies or experiences of individual students in seemingly similar courses.

ACTIVITIES

The nature of students' learning activities can also be an important supplement to information about academic content, even though the process of learning may be, by itself, secondary in interest to the material learned. Knowing that an understanding of community structure was acquired through extended field observation of a model-cities program or through classroom lectures and library reading on urban problems provides additional knowledge about the substance of that understanding. The type of learning activity should also be described, therefore, through the selection of a small number of descriptors, such as observation of poverty agency, participation on local poverty board, bibliographic review, theoretical analysis, written critique, or content analysis of press reports.

LEVEL OF PERFORMANCE

Finally, the level of performance should be reported more fully than in the current practice of distinguishing between upper-division and lower-division courses and adding grades. The most desirable way would be to specify in concrete terms the highest capability the student has shown. This requires development of criteria of performance that can serve as descriptors for reporting type and level of capabilities as well as standards for organizing and assessing students' learning. Hilton, Kendall, and Sprecher (1970), with a group of graduate school faculty members, have developed performance criteria, corresponding rating scales, and a procedure for assessing relevant performance in the graduate study of business. Their work illustrates an effective method for developing criteria and assessing performance that can be applied to individual courses or to broader programs or fields. An example might be, "computes economic projections based on models using partial derivatives." Descriptors for this capability would be computes, economic projections, economic models, and partial derivatives. Variation in the verb, from computes to evaluates, derives, manipulates, recognizes, or some other capability related to mathematical models of economic processes can be used to differentiate among levels of performance.

More than one kind of performance is usually associated with a course or other learning activity. The ability to identify problems and the ability to solve them, for example, may both be performance criteria in a particular course, but they are not necessarily related. The use of such descriptors to identify level of performance with respect to different capabilities would be far more informative than the present system of poorly-differentiated credits and grades assigned to a course as a whole.

Under an improved system incorporating these three elements of intellectual content, activities, and level of performance, the transcript or record of a student's progress would contain more than a specified number of credits in courses with particular titles in designated fields at the upper-division or lower-division level, each with a general grade. The award of certificates or degrees for use in admission to further study or in employment should be based on specified requirements in these three areas—content, activities, and performance—rather than on the number of years enrolled. When a student has performed a set of specified activities with respect to specified academic content at a specified level of performance, any concern for the length of time spent in developing these competencies or the number of units of credit associated with that time period is pointless. For different purposes, requirements in all three of these areas may vary widely. Some graduate departments and employers would expect a wide range of both content and activities at a high level of performance. Others might accept a wide range of content and activities at a relatively low level but be particularly interested in high accomplishment and a moderate range of activities on quite circumscribed content. Still others could be interested only in a narrow range of both content and activities. If the credit system itself were to carry sufficient information, these different purposes could all be served effectively.

Such a credit system could incorporate prior experience and non-traditional forms of study as easily as traditional courses. Their content and type of activity could be determined through interviews or correspondence, and level of performance could be determined by records of experiences, the products of the activity, or by written or oral examinations. This system has advantages over the present credit system in not requiring that these non-traditional competencies or experiences be calibrated to a scale based on the time spent in traditional college courses. Competencies or experiences would be evaluated directly, and the purpose for which the credit is intended would govern the way it is evaluated. This practice would contrast sharply with the present system of automatically accumulating heterogeneous credits, differentiated only very crudely, until some predetermined number is reached.

The present credit system is unlikely to be changed quickly or easily. But a new system could operate simultaneously with the present one, with experience determining the direction in which the new system would evolve and the extent to which it might alone suffice. Uncertainties in the proposed scheme, such as how to judge easily and consistently the appropriate level of a student's performance, could be resolved through use. The present system is inherently less defensible, having acquired its stability and uniformity only through long familiarity. Because the proposed approach would provide better information and let the award of credit be governed by its purposes, with some use and familiarity the advantages of the new system over the old should outweigh the problems to be expected in any new procedure.

Need for New Directions

For three hundred years, American higher education has been organized around the premise that four years of full-time uninterrupted study leads students to a position of intellectual maturity and social grace that merits the award of the bachelor's degree. Except for occasional challenges (Veblen, 1918), this premise has been so widely accepted by American society that a bachelor's degree has itself often led to positions of occupational responsibility and social status. This four-year degree system, and the credit system that developed a century ago to keep the degree system feasible after the adoption of elective courses, have remained essentially unchanged despite enormous changes in other characteristics of higher education, with the following results. A great variety of subjects are offered for study through an extremely limited variety of instructional processes. The system is directed to and used primarily by young people during the four years preceding their first entry into employment and adult responsibilities, but recognition of achievement is not clearly related to either employment or maturity. A universally-accepted system of credits lets students mark their progress toward a degree and, if they desire, shift from field to field and college to college; but these shifts often result in a loss of credit—as much as a full semester for about 13 percent of students changing colleges (Willingham and Findikyan, 1969)—and the degree itself is little more than a poorly defined, arbitrary terminal point. Finally, this system of credits gives institutions a convenient device for allocating financial and personnel resources to instructional activities, for setting instructional fees, and for comparing educational costs and effectiveness; but the credit as a unit of educational output is as poorly defined as the degree.

No rational foundation for the degree and credit structure exists in the higher educational system. Degree programs are made to fit a four-year time span that had its origins at Oxford and Cambridge, that was adopted uncritically by the American colonial colleges, and that continued without substantial change while the nature of the American colleges was changing drastically. The four-year basis for the bachelor's degree is almost the only characteristic of the colonial colleges that still exists, and it may have persisted only because the present programs that were designed to fit it now seem to require it. Thus the time span, the degree, and the credits that mark the path to a degree are self-perpetuating devices for organizing—and inhibiting—higher education.

The mobility and flux of present society is such that an

uninterrupted four-year period of study in preparation for employment and status is unreasonable for a large proportion of the
population. The bachelor's degree as a terminal point for formal
education no longer has validity, if it ever did, other than what
has been uncritically ascribed to it; and even that ascribed value
is now declining. Its award coincides with no stage in human
development in the way that the transitions between elementary,
junior high, and high school are predicated on changes in the social
and psychological development of children. It is associated with no
nonarbitrary point of transition in the social structure, as when a
person leaves his parental home or enters a marital relationship. If
the degree marks a point of entry into full-time employment and
adult responsibility, a situation true at best for a declining proportion of college students, it does so only arbitrarily.

Among the challenges to higher education today, the degree
and credit system are being questioned with an intensity not previously matched in the present century. Yet they are not so much
under attack as being bypassed. The number of nondegree-credit
students increased between 1965 and 1972 at almost four times the
rate of increase of degree-credit students (*A Fact Book on Higher
Education,* 1973); and the numbers of proprietary-school students,
who are primarily interested in goals other than a degree, increased
during the same period at three times the rate of degree-credit students (Moses, 1971).

The combined strains of economic stress, increasingly complex technology requiring highly developed intellectual skills, and
political pressures for social and economic equality are not likely
to permit the four-year degree to remain so dominant a terminal
point in higher education. Instead, a variety of formal terminal
points are likely to develop, based on the pertinence of education
for specific posteducational activities—job entrance, licensing or
certification, further education, or continued personal growth. Although the four-year program combining a liberal general education with moderately intensive study in a single academic area will
probably remain in demand, the diversity of alternatives will reduce
its importance and the intensity of the pressure for its acquisition.

The development of such a multifaceted educational system
will broaden the function and increase the complexity of credits in

some ways and simplify their use in others. This greater diversity of educational programs and purposes will require a more elaborate definition of credits than the present one based on hours per week under instruction. Besides being associated with specified fields of study as they are now, credits could better be differentiated by specific areas of intellectual content, type of activity, and level of performance. But the determination of when the award of credit is justified will be simplified because of the greater specificity of the capabilities to which the credits are attached, however those capabilities are acquired.

Thus far, non-traditional study has had to adapt to an inherently antithetical structure of credits and degrees—one based on time serving rather than demonstrated competence. That problems of crediting non-traditional experiences have been particularly troublesome and have inhibited the expansion of non-traditional programs is hardly surprising. But the non-traditional movement points up so clearly the inadequacies and inequities of the present credit and degree systems that it may reform these systems not only as they apply to new and unconventional educational experiences but also for all of higher education as well.

References

AULD, R. B. "The Cooperative Education Movement—Early Years." *Journal of Cooperative Education*, 1971, 7, 7–9.

BERG, I. *Education and Jobs: The Great Training Robbery.* Boston: Beacon Press, 1971.

BLOOM, B. S. "Learning for Mastery." In J. T. HASTINGS and G. F. MADAUS (Eds.) *Formative and Summative Evaluation of Student Learning.* New York: McGraw-Hill, 1970.

BOK, D. "The Three-Year Degree." *College Board Review,* 1972 (85), 14–16.

Carnegie Commission on Higher Education. *Less Time, More Options: Education Beyond the High School.* New York: McGraw-Hill, 1971.

Carnegie Commission on Higher Education. *The More Effective Use of Resources: An Imperative for Higher Education.* New York: McGraw-Hill, 1972.

Commission on Accreditation of Service Experiences. *Granting*

Credit for Service School Training. 3rd ed. Washington, D.C.: American Council on Education, 1968.

    The Continuing Education Unit. Washington, D.C.: National Task Force on the Continuing Education Unit, 1970.

    ELTON, L. R. B. "The Assessment of Students—A New Approach." *Universities Quarterly,* 1968, *22,* 291–301.

    A Fact Book on Higher Education. Washington, D.C.: American Council on Education, 1973.

    GLASER, R., and NITKO, A. J. "Measurement in Learning and Instruction." In R. L. THORNDIKE (Ed.) *Educational Measurement.* 2nd ed. Washington, D.C.: American Council on Education, 1971.

    HILTON, T. L., KENDALL, L. M., and SPRECHER, T. B. *Performance Criteria in Graduate Business Study: Parts I and II—Development of Rating Scales, Background Data, Form, and the Pilot Study.* Research Bulletin RB-70-3. Princeton, N.J.: Educational Testing Service, 1970.

    HOFSTADTER, R., and SMITH, W. (Eds.) *American Higher Education: A Documentary History.* Vol. 1. Chicago: University of Chicago Press, 1961.

    LORIMER, M. H. "How Much Is a Credit Hour? A Plea for Clarification." *Journal of Higher Education,* 1962, *33,* 302–306.

    MATHIESON, D. E. *Correspondence Study: A Summary Review of the Research and Development Literature.* Syracuse, N.Y.: ERIC Clearinghouse on Adult Education, 1971.

    MC KEACHIE, W. J. "Research on College Teaching: A Review." Report 6. Washington, D.C.: ERIC Clearinghouse on Higher Education, 1970.

    MILLER, S. M. "Education and Jobs: Lessons of the '60's." *Social Policy,* 1972, *2*(5), 43–45.

    MILNER, M., JR. *The Illusion of Equality: The Effect of Education on Opportunity, Inequality, and Social Conflict.* San Francisco: Jossey-Bass, 1972.

    MILTON, O. *Alternatives to the Traditional.* San Francisco: Jossey-Bass, 1972.

    MOSES, S. *The Learning Force: A More Comprehensive Framework for Educational Policy.* Occasional Papers No. 25. Syracuse, N.Y.: Syracuse University, 1971.

    RUDOLPH, F. *The American College and University: A History.* New York: Random House, 1962.

    SPURR, S. H. *Academic Degree Structures: Innovative Approaches: Principles of Reform in Degree Structures in the United States.* New York: McGraw-Hill, 1970.

Union for Experimenting Colleges and Universities. *The University Without Walls: A First Report.* Yellow Springs, Ohio, 1972.

VEBLEN, T. *The Higher Learning in America: A Memorandum on the Conduct of Universities by Businessmen.* New York: Viking Press, 1918.

WILLINGHAM, W. W., and FINDIKYAN, N. "Transfer Students: Who's Moving from Where to Where, and What Determines Who's Admitted?" *College Board Review,* 1969 (72), 4–12.

WILSON, J. W. "Survey of Cooperative Education, 1971." *Journal of Cooperative Education,* 1971, *61,* 790–794.

Avoiding Cut-Rate Credits and Discount Degrees

JB Lon Hefferlin

Anyone planning an unconventional academic program cannot ignore two of the major agents for maintaining educational standards in the United States: state regulation and voluntary accreditation. These legitimizing agencies can pose unsurmountable problems for an off-beat program—just as an unconventional program naturally poses problems for agencies concerned for conventional standards.

Three universities in one southern state illustrate these potential problems in state regulation and voluntary accreditation of non-traditional study. The first of them, regionally accredited as well as state approved, has launched an innovative three-year Ed.D. program for school administrators that involves only three weeks of classes on the university campus. Every month, students through-

This report was prepared at the Center for Research and Development in Higher Education as part of its Non-Traditional Study Program, and thanks are due the Center as well as experts in accreditation elsewhere in the country who contributed the uncited quotations as well as information and suggestions for it.

out the country participate in an all-day seminar run by a university professor in locations near their homes, and their home study is supervised by a local coordinator. The regional accrediting association sees this program as rigorous and well-planned. But educational agencies in some states have blocked its seminar centers in their states, and some school systems have rejected its degree for salary increments and promotions because they do not accept state approval or institutional accreditation as adequate evidence of the quality of the new program.

Less than two hundred miles away, a new university has been created for the sole purpose of enabling experienced educators to earn a doctorate within one year. Its students, among them college presidents, deans, professors, and school superintendents, spend five weeks during one summer at the university and spare time during the following academic year in guided independent study and in writing their dissertation at home; they return to the university the next summer for their examinations and their degree. The university has won a temporary operating license from the state and seeks regional accreditation; but questions have arisen: should it meet the same criteria for approval and accreditation as conventional residential universities? And how can its doctorates best be compared with those of other universities?

Nearby, another "university" has distributed the list of academic degrees from the *College Blue Book* and is taking orders for custom-made diplomas for any degree at twenty-five dollars. Its diplomas, engraved on parchment in Old English lettering with gold and black inks, are embossed with the state seal because the university is a state-chartered corporation. Buyers may not only specify the degree they want and their field of specialization; their diploma can be predated to any convenient time in the past. This university claims that it is exempt from educational regulation because it is simply a purveyor of novelty items rather than an educational institution. But should state officials take the libertarian view that clients of this company are fully aware of the worth of their purchase, or should they move to restrict its trade—if not on behalf of potential clients, at least on behalf of other universities?

Non-traditional study—and especially the external degree—raises questions such as these about quality control in higher education. To remain viable, the non-traditional movement must gain and retain legitimacy; yet the agencies that provide legitimacy— state approval agencies and voluntary accrediting agencies—of necessity operate on a basis of traditional and conventional standards. Non-traditional study thus raises a double problem: how to assure the public of educational quality without restricting the growth of imaginative programs, and how to encourage innovation while safeguarding the interests of the public and existing institutions.

Competence or Chair-Sitting

External degrees and non-resident instruction complicate the task of detecting educational fraud. As long as an academic degree signified not only a certain degree of competence but also a certain amount of chair-sitting, fraud was relatively easy to identify: everyone recognized that truly "earned" degrees were awarded only after a period of inculcative servitude. In contrast to honorary degrees and to purchased degrees, they required resident study.

Thus laws in at least three states—Arkansas, Iowa, and Illinois—prohibit institutions from conferring degrees on students other than those in residence; and the United States Office of Education has been able to warn Americans and foreign nationals about degree mills by proclaiming that "in the United States no reputable institution of higher education confers degrees solely on the basis of correspondence study" (United States Office of Education, 1971). But as the idea has emerged from abroad that academic degrees can signify competence regardless of any period of academic institutionalization, the traditional distinction between "legitimate and reputable" degrees on the one hand and "fraudulent and meaningless" degrees on the other is being reduced and the opportunity for chicanery increased. What is to distinguish the Regents External Degree in New York, for example, from the external degrees of the University of Oklahoma or the University of South Florida or from those of the University of Eastern Florida in Tampa, Indiana Northern University in Gas City, Eastern Nebraska Christian College in Valley, or Golden State University in California? If one degree assures as many salary increments as another, why not buy the least expensive?

As Felix Robb, the executive director of the Southern Association of Colleges and Schools says, "People are trapped financially —familywise and otherwise—by the inability to take time off for residence requirements in traditional programs of established universities. They are looking for a shortcut, but they don't know how short the cut can be between something honorable and legitimate and something that lacks integrity." And as Anthony James Gange, the steamfitter who organized "Greenbriar College" in California, pointed out in explaining its mission, "There seemed to be a crying need. People just wanted to get fleeced, and I wanted to take advantage of the market while it was still hot."

If students want to avoid being fleeced, how can they compare a university doctoral program that involves short-term residence on campus with that of another conducted at a resort hotel? Or how can they weigh a program of "two semesters of field study abroad," that consist of two three-week European tours at $775 each, with another program that involves nothing but a small number of book reports plus a large fee? And how can students know that a non-residential institution will even mail them their degree after they submit their thesis and their five hundred dollars—as the recently closed Marlowe University in Mount Holly, New Jersey, failed to do?

Unless better information is available, the entire field of non-traditional study is likely to be as tarred for the American public by the degree-mill business as conventional American degrees have been tarred for the citizens of other countries by overseas sales of mail-order diplomas. No issue in avoiding the stigma of second-rate education holds more long-term significance for the development of non-traditional study than this need for quality control.

Apart from self-imposed control of quality by each institution, two major means exist for influencing the standards of educational programs in the United States: government support and regulation of educational institutions, and the simple pressure of the market as prospective students are influenced in their choices by lists of accredited institutions, comparative ratings, and guides, by admission standards of more advanced institutions such as graduate and professional schools, and by entrance requirements for the professions and employment generally.

Of these quality controls, government regulation sets *minimal* standards for the conduct of institutional education: it specifies an elemental level of quality beneath which educational endeavors are deemed detrimental to the citizenry and thus illegal. In contrast, voluntary accreditation, admission standards, and employment requirements set the going rate for *mediocrity* in education. They indicate the standards that middling institutions must meet in order to remain academically respectable.

Advocates of non-traditional study thus have an interest in seeing that these mechanisms of quality control do, indeed, measure quality.

State Regulation

State support has greatly assisted the development of non-traditional education—as the funding of innovative public colleges and experimental programs illustrates—but state regulation of education has had relatively little influence on controlling the quality of private education. "It cannot be said that most states exercise even the minimum degree of control for the maintenance of educational quality among private degree-granting institutions," Robert Reid concluded in his 1959 analysis of degree mills for the American Council on Education. "State laws chartering institutions of higher education are not uniform and are actually quite lax in controlling educational malpractice" (Reid, 1959, pp. 62, 8). Until the past two years, this situation improved only slightly. Some states like New York have consistently imposed strict regulations; but some have failed to enforce their existing laws, and others have maintained the view that their citizens should not be prohibited from making fools of themselves by purchasing whatever education and degrees they desire.

Currently a majority of the fifty states extend the privilege of degree-granting to institutions simply on incorporation, with filing fees as low as one dollar in Nevada and requirements ranging as high as a half-million dollars of capital in Michigan or eight full-time professors in Pennsylvania. Less than half of the states require incorporated institutions to be approved by a state agency such as the education department in order to grant degrees.

If *accreditation* in higher education means a process involving periodic reevaluation of an institution or program of study on the basis of certain prescribed standards, and publication of a list of approved institutions or programs, then all of the states practice accreditation of some professional programs such as teacher education, legal preparation, and training in the health professions —although the terms they use to refer to this process range from *approve, certify,* and *classify,* to *license, recognize,* and *register*. But beyond this common practice of state accreditation of professional programs, only a minority of states accredit colleges and universities by periodically reevaluating their entire operations. The rest only require annual reports from institutions, approve vocational courses for state and federal support, or occasionally visit an institution and possibly revoke its charter if scandal develops.

More state attention will probably be devoted to these activities in the future than has been in the past. The state of Florida is a prime example. Until two years ago, Florida permitted any three individuals who wanted to open their own university to pay thirty-seven dollars for filing papers of incorporation and then begin granting degrees. As could be expected, business boomed: only Illinois and California are thought to have rivaled Florida as centers for the degree-mill trade. But after a decade of work by Philip Ashler, the chairman of the Committee on Higher Education of the Florida legislature the 1971 legislature created a new State Board of Independent Colleges and Universities to "protect the individual student from deceptive, fraudulent, or substandard education; protect the nonpublic institutions; and protect the citizens of Florida holding diplomas or degrees" by licensing for annual operation private colleges within the state (Florida *Statutes,* 1971). Indiana, Texas, and Wisconsin have also recently passed regulatory legislation for private or proprietary institutions. The Education Commission of the States has now drafted model state legislation for such approval.

The Commission recommends that every state protect against substandard, transient, unethical, deceptive, or fraudulent institutions, prohibit the granting of "false or misleading educational credentials," and restrict the use of the labels *college* and *university* by empowering a state agency to grant approval to institutions for no more than two years, issue cease and desist orders against detrimental practices, and, if necessary, revoke the authority of an institution to operate. The agency should be authorized to hear complaints against institutions for violating its regulations and to award restitution where warranted, and it should seize and preserve students' academic records from any institution that closes or is forced to close (Education Commission of the States, 1973).

Excellent as this model legislation is, the Commission has not recommended specific regulations and standards for state approval agencies. The most serious potential problem for non-traditional study if states adopt such legislation is the likelihood that their approval agencies will adopt outmoded and irrelevant criteria for approving institutions: standards based on educational convention and tradition rather than on educational quality. State regulatory agencies tend to adopt the existing standards of other states and voluntary accrediting agencies, sometimes just when these standards are being questioned and discarded as adequate measures of quality by the academic community. For example, while the minimum standards of the new board in Florida are admirable in some respects—as in requiring institutional publications to be accurate and realistic, since prospective students "should be able to determine what the college can actually provide" (Florida State Board, 1971)—most of them measure only academic respectability and not educational impact or achievement. The salary schedule for faculty shall reflect a level of income indicative of the importance and worth of college teaching in American society." And similarly, out of eighty-nine issues about postsecondary institutions of concern to the new Private School Accrediting Commission in Indiana, only four involve educational quality in terms of educational outcomes; the rest involve organizational convention. "With what bank do you maintain your major accounts? . . . . List the kind of books, periodicals, and resource materials that you maintain. . . . Show how the organization and presentation of your instructional materials are in accord with sound psychological principles of learning. . . . List the number of toilets, showers, or lounges available to the students. Please do the same for the faculty. . . . Attach a scale drawing of your physical plant, and one photograph of the exterior view of your school" (Indiana Private School Accrediting Commission, 1971).

Only the criteria of the new Educational Approval Board in Wisconsin emphasize the most valid measure of a non-traditional program—that it be consistent in quality of content and instruction with similar existing programs (State of Wisconsin Educational Approval Board, 1972). If other states adopt irrelevant and restrictive criteria in order to decrease the likelihood of fraudulent institutions, they will also decrease the possibility of excellent non-traditional institutions. Even now, the existing regulations of some state approval agencies regarding residency requirements, length of programs, and restrictions on credit need to be updated; laws in the several states that prohibit external degrees need to be modified; and if experimental institutions are to operate in more than one state without unnecessary duplication of difficulties, the lack of reciprocity among states needs to be overcome.

So far, however, state regulations have not seriously retarded the development of non-traditional study. To the contrary, it can be argued that state regulations have far too often been insufficient if not nonexistent. More consistent regulation, including more visible and vigorous state prosecution of unqualified institutions, should help overcome suspicion about unconventional education. But overall, little consistent progress in enforcing minimal regulations can be expected unless all fifty states adopt effective licensing and approval systems. Even if many states seek to protect their citizens' educational investment and the reputation of their chartered institutions by such systems, at least a few of the fifty are likely to continue their laissez-faire neglect of regulation, and in time, although they lack the salubrious climate of Florida or California, entrepreneurs will flock to them from the other states to market discount degrees.

Federal Regulation

Since state regulation will more than likely remain spotty, the federal government will probably continue to play an increased role in the regulation of non-traditional study and consumer protection.

One of its two agencies most directly involved in educational regulation, the Postal Inspection Service of the Postal Service, investigates allegations of mail fraud and brings suit in federal courts against proprietors of fraudulent institutions doing business through the mails whenever aggrieved students lodge complaints. Its difficulties in covering the field adequately with a limited staff are illustrated by the fact that it took four of its inspectors three months full-time to nab Bernard Fuchs and Gershon Tannenbaum at "Marlowe University"—the post office box in Mount Holly, New Jersey, which was closed in 1972 after raking in an estimated two hundred thousand dollars.

The other federal agency directly involved—the Federal Trade Commission—investigates deceptive trade practices in correspondence education and proprietary schools and issues cease and desist orders against institutions that divert substantial trade unfairly from competing schools through misrepresentation of status, program, facilities, fees, or the employment opportunities and earnings of graduates.

Both these agencies deserve commendation for their work as well as further support for it, since the need for their effort is likely to grow with the further development of unconventional education.

The United States Office of Education now plays only an indirect—but significant—role in regulating educational institutions through its recognition of state approval agencies and voluntary accrediting agencies and its financial support for such activities as the task force on model state legislation of the Education Commission of the States. It is unlikely to play a direct regulatory role unless the federal government moves to abandon the use of state approval and voluntary accreditation as a criterion for institutional eligibility for federal funds.

The Veterans Administration conducts annual field reviews of postsecondary proprietary vocational schools in collaboration with state approval agencies, but does not itself undertake institutional evaluation. The only federal agency that does accredit college and university programs is the Federal Aviation Agency

(FAA), which "certificates" aviation maintenance technician schools —such as those at Purdue, the University of Illinois, Western Michigan University, Utah State, San Jose State, and Honolulu Community College—as part of its function of maintaining minimum safety and operational standards in the civilian aviation industry. (Both the FAA and the Office of Education claim that this certification is less than accreditation, but the process involves both evaluation on prescribed standards and publicity about approved programs: technical supervisors from FAA district offices inspect schools on the basis of elaborate evaluative criteria, and the FAA lists certified schools in its advisory circulars.) Other federal agencies could launch similar approval activities in the future for highly sensitive training programs affecting national health and safety— for example, in atomic energy—but none are planned.

As a result, so far no federal regulation has created problems for colleges or universities offering non-traditional programs. Thus unless an advocate of non-traditional study wants to operate an aviation maintenance technician school, undertake mail fraud, violate the regulations of the Federal Trade Commission, or misappropriate federal funds, he is unlikely to run afoul of federal restrictions.

Voluntary Accreditation

While the states seem to be entering a period of increased regulation in their cyclic concern for educational standards, and federal surveillance is increasing as the non-traditional movement expands, voluntary accreditation has been approaching the crest of major upheaval. Not since the 1930s have such significant issues been under debate and such significant changes underway. The Department of Health, Education, and Welfare has called on accrediting agencies to formulate programs "that accept alternatives to formal education for entry into career fields" (Department of HEW, 1971, p. 75). Federal officials have questioned the validity of accreditation as a requirement for institutional eligibility for federal funds on the basis that accrediting agencies are inherently cartels, incapable of meeting the needs of students for objective comparative facts about institutions, incapable of being accountable to the public. Polemists such as James Koerner are continuing to accuse accrediting agencies of being "nothing but old-fashioned trade associations piously pretending to represent the public interest" and claiming that "not merely are they unresponsive to demands for reform in higher education, but they are aggressively protective of the status quo" (1971, p. 51). Two major studies—one by the Federation of Regional Accrediting Commissions of Higher Education itself—have recommended a multitude of changes in agency structure, composition, procedures, standards, and orientation (Puffer and others, 1970, and Study Commission on Accreditation of Selected Health Educational Programs, 1972).

Non-traditional programs and institutions are adding to this ferment a variety of new questions for accrediting agencies. Should these agencies also evaluate certifying agencies like the Regents External Degree Program of New York and test-construction agencies, like Educational Testing Service, that supply standardized tests on the basis of which credit is awarded? And if their accrediting standards and procedures are inappropriate for assessing these new ventures, might they be equally inappropriate for assessing traditional programs and institutions?

Encouragingly, accrediting agencies are responding to these new demands not with dogged intransigency, as critics such as Koerner suggest, but with considered adaptation, aided in the process by the two agencies that accredit accrediting agencies themselves: the National Commission on Accrediting and the United States Office of Education. None of the nationally recognized accrediting agencies approved by either organization tries to discourage experimentation with alternate forms of education; instead, many of them provide means for communicating new educational ideas among institutions and programs. Thus the Federation of Regional Accrediting Commissions of Higher Education (FRACHE) —the coordinating body for the seven regional commissions that evaluate colleges and universities—has adopted this official policy statement on innovation:

> *The Federation of Regional Accrediting Commissions of Higher Education welcomes perceptive and imaginative experimentation which aims at intensifying the effectiveness of higher*

education. The Federation supports no particular theories or style of education or organization. Neither does it prescribe specific rules or formulas. It is cognizant that special requirements may pertain to some institutions, but these should not be permitted to inhibit new approaches and emphases in their educational programs. The Federation insists only that new departures or adaptations be consistent with an institution's purposes and objectives as originally established or as modified to accommodate new conditions (1970).

Among the administrators of twenty-five non-traditional programs interviewed for this study, at least six reported encouragement or assistance from accrediting agencies, and the majority reported no difficulties with any. Only two indicated actual problems, while several stated that they would be prepared to fight the agencies if problems were to develop. And, as Janet Ruyle and Lucy Ann Geiselman reported in Chapter Three, college and university administrators less often view accreditation as a major problem in the development of non-traditional programs than such other factors as the lack of funds, the difficulty of assessing non-classroom learning, and the resistance of faculty.

Few overt constraints on non-traditional study have thus far been imposed by accreditation. Nonetheless, accrediting agencies can impose a variety of restraints on unconventional programs. One unintentional restraint stems from the misrepresentation of accrediting standards by educators for their own purposes—as when administrators claim that the accreditation of their institution will be jeopardized if it adopts non-traditional teaching or grading practices or if its graduate school admits the graduates of unaccredited colleges. Accrediting agencies cannot avoid some misrepresentation of their standards, but they can help reduce this unintended constraint by taking action against any accredited institution where officials falsely claim that accrediting standards preclude innovation.

A more direct restraint stems from the influence of traditionalists as members of visiting teams and commissions. While the permanent staff members of the regional associations are known to be open to experimentation, not as many team and commission

members have been so inclined. This problem probably accounts
for the fact that the most common complaint about the regional
associations, according to a survey of institutional members by the
Puffer committee, is their inhibition of innovation, as illustrated by
the response of one president: "Despite the regional accrediting
association's avowed willingness to view objectively new programs
which are innovative in nature as well as experimental programs,
it is not unknown for team members who are deeply rooted in
tradition to take a negative point of view on such attempts" (Puffer
and others, 1970, p. 317). Here, again, the accrediting agencies
can help reduce constraints, as FRACHE advocates in its recent
recommendation to the regional associations: evaluation committees for non-traditional institutions should include visitors "who
are sufficiently conversant and understanding to review innovations
competently" (1973, p. 1).

Nonetheless, any standardizing agency is likely over time
to be a conservative rather than an innovative force. Claude Puffer
and his associates on the FRACHE study concluded, "Standards
follow the changes in higher education; they do not lead them"
(1970, p. 182). And even the language of accrediting standards
becomes a conserving influence—as when institutional eligibility
is defined in terms of time-serving (for example, in the requirement
that institutions must offer "at least two years" of higher education
at the undergraduate level or "at least one year" at the graduate
level), when non-traditional study is defined as "supplemental"
activity, and when media collections are phrased as "libraries."
Moreover, accrediting agencies that are created and run by the
very institutions they evaluate—as are the regional associations and
some of the specialized professional agencies—must of necessity
espouse conventional standards. If their staffs proceed too far ahead
of the thinking of the majority of institutions or of their most in-
fluential members about what is acceptable or desirable, they will
be challenged and convention standardized. Until 1971, for example, member institutions of the Southern Association of Colleges
and Schools were prohibited by common agreement under the old
"Standard Nine" of its College Delegate Assembly from granting
credit for off-campus study to more than half of a student's total
degree program and were restricted from subsidizing extension

programs that were not self-supporting; and under its new Standard Nine they are prohibited from granting credit "for travel per se" (Southern Association of Colleges and Schools, 1971, p. 25).

But as the 1971 updating of Standard Nine illustrates, changes are occurring; and if they continue, major problems in accrediting non-traditional institutions by the six regional associations will probably be avoided. The six associations are increasingly cooperating in evaluating multicampus institutions that cross regional boundaries, such as Antioch; the regional boundaries are becoming less significant as FRACHE develops national standards for regional implementation; and FRACHE has now adopted useful interim guidelines for the evaluation of non-traditional study. Under these guidelines, the regional associations are to assess the award of non-traditional degrees on the basis of criteria and competence "commensurate with the level and nature of the degrees." They are to assure that the appraisal of student performance rests on explicit standards and objective judgments rather than on merely the learner's self-appraisal; that instructors avoid conflict of interest when working with more than one institution; and that the resources of other institutions and agencies are not used unfairly by the non-traditional institution (FRACHE, 1973).

While problems in accrediting non-traditional institutions by the regional associations are likely to be minimal if FRACHE continues its recent efforts, the prospects are less bright for professional or specialized accreditation. Within five years, non-traditional programs will probably expand from the general liberal arts into professional schools, just as the first New York Regents External Degree —the general associate in arts—is being followed by the bachelor of business and the associate in applied science in nursing. But accrediting agencies of professional programs may not be as ready for non-traditional study in this decade as the professions are.

In comparison to regional associations, the specialized accrediting agencies are devoting far less effort to updating criteria and procedures, and yet they have more work to do. Despite their unique and particular function of helping assure that the graduates of accredited programs possess a minimal level of professional competence, they are not much more competence-oriented; their standards for assessing educational quality are equally questionable;

and they are far more restrictive toward non-traditional approaches to education.

Among their standards that prescribe conventionality rather than quality—all of which are challenged by the development of non-traditional study—are these:

Full-time study required by a majority of students—as when the National Association of Schools of Art ordinarily limits accreditation to schools in which a majority of students "are enrolled regularly full-time in curricula normally requiring at least four academic years."

Specified numbers of clock hours of instruction—as when the Joint Review Committee for Inhalation Therapy Education requires an eighteen-month program with eighteen hundred clock hours specified in thirty-one subjects, including twenty-five hours in microbiology, fifteen in psychology, ninety in physics, and twenty in the practice of ethics and administration.

Limits on the amount of independent study—as when the American Chemical Society limits independent study and research to no more than forty-five of its required three hundred ninety hours or laboratory work.

Specified sequences of courses within clock-hour requirements—as when the Joint Review Committee on Education in Radiologic Technology advocates ten hours of "department administration" to precede six hours of "equipment maintenance" within a four-semester program divided into 114, 91, 106, and 99 hours each.

Required clock hours for general education—as when the Academy of Orthopaedic Surgeons requires orthopedic physicians' assistants to take forty-five hours of American institutions and United States history and ninety of communication or English out of their fifteen hundred-hour curriculum.

Type of required foreign language—as when the American Chemical Society requires scientific German or Russian—a reading knowledge of one and at least an introductory acquaintance with the other (although French is tolerated).

Specified length of program—as when the American Speech and Hearing Association requires a minimum of two academic years for speech pathologists and audiologists, and the American Occupational Therapy Association requires six months of clinical experience for occupational therapists.

Specified residency periods—as when the National Council for the Accreditation of Teacher Education requires one academic year of "full-time continuous residence study" for education doctorates.

Specified student-faculty ratios—as when the American Dental Association specifies five-to-one of six-to-one student-faculty ratios for dental hygiene.

Limits on size of laboratory and quiz sections—as when the American Chemical Society limits sections to no more than thirty students per staff member.

Caution on qualifications of lecturers and proctors—as when the American Chemical Society warns, "All lectures should be given by competent members of the faculty. . . . Quiz sessions should not be placed in the charge of undergraduate students."

Specified seating capacity of the library—as when the Association of American Law Schools expects that "seating accommodations, with generous table or desk space, should be available at any one time for 65 percent of the student body."

Moreover, as if restricting their own professional programs were not enough, a few accrediting agencies have gone so far as to expect professional schools to admit only those students who have completed conventional undergraduate programs in conventional ways at conventional locations. Thus the American Bar Association, despite major improvements this past year in its standards for law schools, continues to specify that "no more than 10 percent of the credits necessary for admission [to an ABA approved law school] may be in courses without substantial intellectual content" (American Bar Association, 1973); and until last year it proscribed military science, hygiene, domestic arts, physical education, and vocal or instrumental music as unacceptable undergraduate courses for admission to law school. It even held that all college work submitted for admission be done in "residence" as an undergraduate—defining residence as work done in class in an approved college or, if done off the campus of the college, as work done in a class meeting in regular sessions each week under the personal supervision and instruction of a member of the instructional staff of an approved college.

Of all such restrictions on non-traditional study among the specialized accrediting agencies, the most common is the requirement of a certain proportion of full-time faculty members rather than practitioners from the field. The American Association of Collegiate Schools of Business, the American Dental Association, the American Psychological Association, the Association of American Law Schools, the National Council for Accreditation of Teacher Education, and the Society of American Foresters, among others, all expect the bulk of teaching to be offered by full-time faculty. Only the American Physical Therapy Association appears to think otherwise: "The question of full-time and part-time appointments," it well indicates in its standards, "is not so important as the qualifications of the instructors" (American Physical Therapy Association, 1955).

This widespread emphasis on full-time faculty naturally poses problems for schools oriented to part-time students. For example, the American Association of Collegiate Schools of Business, which until recently operated as a gentlemen's club of the deans of exclusive schools, has not accredited some largely part-time schools, among other reasons, because they do not meet its standard that 75 percent of their full-time equivalent academic staff serve on a full-time basis. "I plan to go back to them every year until they change," says the disgruntled dean of one such unaccredited school that employs many part-time instructors—three-fourths of them with doctorates—to teach at regional centers. And the president of another major urban university comments:

I have for a long time thought that the part-time faculty, many of them with terminal degrees, who are practitioners in the field, are perhaps better qualified to deal with the adult students who are attending school part-time and holding full-time jobs than some of the full-time faculty. . . . Our part-time program is an important service to the community, and it's an important part of the university. Frankly, if we had to have all full-time faculty carrying on these programs, it would probably force us out of business. I doubt the traffic could cover the tuition rates that you'd have to charge to cover their salaries.

Standards such as this will need to be modified by almost every specialized accrediting agency if the non-traditional movement expands into professional education and if new types of professional training are to be accredited.

Needed Changes in Standards

Some critics of government regulation and voluntary accreditation claim that their criteria for approval are more concerned with "process" than with "product"—that is, with educational procedures more than educational accomplishments. But in fact, to this day regulatory and accreditation standards are not even concerned as much with process—let alone product—as with structure. The imperative task confronting approval and accrediting agencies is to move from structural criteria to those of the efficacy and efficiency of instruction. If they fail this task, their utility will have passed.

From their beginnings, in their concern for standards, regulatory and accrediting agencies have been concerned about standardizing organizational structure. To be a member college of the North Central Association in its early years, for example—and thus to be considered a true college—a midwestern institution had to have eight distinct departments in the liberal arts; each department had to have at least one full-time professor; and no more than thirty students could be enrolled in each class. Ever since then, accrediting standards have defined the basic structural units of higher education, from "semesters"—"fifteen to sixteen weeks (exclusive of time required for registration and examinations)" according to the National Association of Schools of Art)—to maximum permissible "teaching loads"—eighteen hours as of 1912 in the North Central region, lowered to sixteen by 1923, and reduced as much lower as possible since then.

And because of their concern over the stability of institutions in order to assure that an adequate program today would not be disreputable tomorrow, approval and accrediting agencies have naturally emphasized fiscal resources, physical facilities, library holdings, classroom equipment, teaching supplies—and the proper maintenance of all of these belongings. To this day, the Association of American Law Schools requires law libraries to possess "one general unabridged dictionary." The Southern Association expects two-year college libraries to be open sixty hours a week and senior college libraries eighty hours; it prefers open stacks to closed stacks; and it holds that the "architectural design and appearance" of campus buildings should "be in harmony." And the Northwest Association requires that campus bookstores not only maintain complete stocks of required and recommended texts for all courses but that, in doing so, they not undermine "the price structure of local merchants."

This historic emphasis on institutional structure has recently been documented by the Puffer committee for FRACHE. By analyzing reports from the regional accrediting commissions to institutions between 1967 and 1970, Puffer and his colleagues showed that the associations express concern over "libraries, financial problems, administrative organization, physical facilities, quality of faculty, faculty salaries and fringe benefits, and curricular improvements—in about that order" (Puffer and others, 1970, p. 533). Thus in denying correspondent status to institutions during 1968–1969, one of the commissions mentioned inadequate libraries and inadequate preparation of faculties four times each, inadequate financial support three times; overreliance on tuition and fees for income, overextension of courses, and the presence of paid administrators on the governing board two times each—but no other weakness more than once (Puffer and others, 1970, pp. 587–588).

Accrediting agencies have used these structural standards for library holdings, teaching loads, the percent of faculty members holding advanced degrees, and other measures of the educational environment as *inferential* measures of institutional quality. And while these measures obviously correlate with institutional status and renown, and while educators assume that they correlate with educational quality, no one—not even the accrediting agencies— has demonstrated that they correlate with quality in terms of educational impact or achievement—let alone contribute to it or cause it.

Aware of this lack of evidence, accrediting agencies have been turning their attention from institutional resources and environment to institutional "atmosphere" and "processes" as indicators of quality. Now, besides precarious financing and overextended curricula, bad education is implied by the lack of orderly procedures for academic decisions, the lack of official channels of planning, the lack of clear-cut rules and regulations, and the wrong people involved in these procedures. (Thus the Southern Association requires that no financial officials outside of an institution have budgetary control over its educational function; and the Association of American Law Schools will lift its approval of any law school where the university appoints a dean over the objections of the law faculty.)

Thus despite the fact that everyone by now seems to agree that accreditation should somehow assess educational effectiveness or institutional impact, these procedural standards combined with earlier structural ones continue to dominate accreditation. Now, with the growth of non-traditional forms of education that rely on few of the structures and processes formerly deemed necessary in education, the reorientation of accrediting standards—long needed whether or not non-traditional study had developed—has become imperative.

The most significant changes ever made in the standards of accrediting agencies to date—the 1934 revision of the standards of the North Central Association, based on the work of George Zook and Melvin E. Haggerty—stemmed from the collapse of existing standards. In 1922, the North Central Association had decided that member institutions should possess five hundred thousand dollars of debt-free endowment for their first two hundred students and fifty thousand dollars more for each additional hundred students. This standard led to the dismissal of eight member institutions in 1927; the resulting uproar led to the complete reorganization of regional standards—emphasizing the contribution of institutional structures and processes to the self-determined goals of an institution. Little change has occurred in the past forty years, but pressure is building for another major transformation.

The advocates of reform today, led by Alexander Astin (1971), Norman Burns (1972), William K. Selden (1971), and the Puffer committee (1970), together with the non-traditional study movement, have demonstrated the weaknesses of present standards. Just as the accrediting criteria of the 1930s stemmed from the outmoded rigidities of the 1920s, so those of the 1980s will stem from the inadequacies of today. These new standards will focus on two measures of institutional impact: the level of competence students demonstrate at graduation (measures of achievement reached) and increases in the competence of students during their enrollment ("value added" measures). Of these two, the first—that of demonstrated competence—is essential for accrediting credentialing agencies such as the Regents External Degree program, while both of them are necessary for accrediting instructional programs and institutions. With support from the Danforth Foundation, Norman Burns has begun a study for FRACHE of ways to refine these two measures of institutional quality and employ them in accreditation; and unless the regional associations and specialized agencies follow this lead, the assessment of higher education in the future will justifiably become the prerogative of other agencies—most likely, cost-accounting offices in state and federal government.

Since 1952, the United States Congress has authorized the Commissioner of Education to recognize accrediting agencies that he deems to be "reliable authority as to the quality of training" offered by educational institutions and programs; the Commissioner has recognized the seven regional commissions and over forty specialized agencies as such authorities. But it can be argued that the will of Congress has been evaded for twenty years, since only a minority of these accrediting agencies base their decisions on the "quality of training" offered by institutions. The majority still evaluate the quality of institutional structures and procedures: resources, facilities, environment, atmosphere, and decision-making.

Of all the functions of accreditation, the most important for the American public is to insure, as the North Central Association puts it, that students "will receive a fair education for their investment of time and money" and that benefactors, taxpayers, and the state receive a fair return on their invested resources—or, in the vernacular, that students won't be had, and that patrons won't be rooked (North Central Association of Colleges and Secondary Schools, 1961, p. 2). Accrediting agencies must help identify institutions and programs that deserve the time and money of students and benefactors—and, at least by implication, indicate that others may lack this quality. When they fail this function, government regulation on behalf of educational consumers and investors expands to meet it. Unless accrediting agencies want the public to turn to government accountants for the evaluation of educational quality, they will need to demonstrate that they base their judgments on institutional effectiveness in terms of value added and achievement reached and also on the efficient use of their resources: that is, on cost effectiveness. For decades, accrediting agencies have been worried about institutions having enough resources to survive. With the increase of non-traditional institutions, the public will be less concerned about the amount and endurance value of all the resources a college possesses and more concerned about the most effective use of whatever limited resources it has.

Many other improvements in accreditation will increase its utility for the public, such as the publication not only of lists of approved institutions and programs but also comparative information about them, the investigation of supported allegations of institutional bungling as signals of possible educational weakness, and even clarification of the appropriate limits for which accreditation should be used by the public. (For example, should students be eligible to receive survivors benefits under social security only if they attend accredited institutions, as is now true, or should ministers be allowed to become military chaplains only if they graduate from accredited institutions?) But in terms of preventing restrictions on the development of non-traditional study, the most important change will be the modernization of standards.

The most critical problem in this modernization is the possibility that accrediting agencies will adopt separate new standards for non-traditional study while retaining outmoded standards for conventional education. For example, the American Association of Collegiate Schools of Business has been progressive in recently developing new criteria and output measures for evaluating new non-traditional programs in business administration such as the Regents External Degree program in business; but it has planned to continue applying its previous standards to existing schools and part-time programs. If this practice is followed by this association and other accrediting agencies, it will endanger the continued credibility of voluntary accreditation.

While different standards obviously must be applied to organizations that merely examine and certify competence—such as the Regents External Degree program—than to institutions that attempt to educate students—such as Empire State College, accrediting agencies should apply identical criteria of effectiveness and efficiency to every educational institution, be it traditional or non-traditional, residential or external.

Steps for Non-Traditionalists

As these pages have illustrated, the non-traditional study movement is exacerbating long-standing problems of educational regulation and accreditation; these problems awaited solutions before the movement towards non-traditional study had ever developed. Historic inadequacies in state chartering and approval of institutions have merely been dramatized by the boom in discount degrees, just as long-term weaknesses in accrediting standards have now been highlighted by new programs that are achievement-oriented but structurally and procedurally deviant. These facts lead to several specific suggestions for advocates of educational experimentation.

First, in terms of state regulation, if proponents of a new educational idea have a choice of where to implement it, they will be well-advised to introduce it through a publicly supported institution rather than through a private college or university, unless the private institution is prestigious. State regulatory agencies more often are charged to regulate private colleges and universities than public ones—as the new boards in Florida and other states illustrate and as the model legislation proposed by the Education Commission of the States proposes. Thus if state agencies continue to apply outdated and irrelevant standards in their evaluation, an unconventional program will be in greater danger of disapproval under private than public auspices. Moreover, publicly supported experimental institutions, such as Empire State College, Evergreen State College, and Minnesota Metropolitan, carry the aura of public legitimacy, while degree mills and less-than-adequate programs are seen by the public as a phenomenon of private and proprietary education. Thus an avant-garde program is less suspect in a public college than in a private one.

Second, in terms of regional accreditation, advocates of a non-traditional program should be advised to organize it within a large and already accredited institution if they wish to avoid any difficulty—or even much contact—with the regional accrediting association. Unless FRACHE and the regional commissions change their fundamental orientation towards institutional accreditation, the amount of attention that they will devote to non-traditional programs such as the Bachelor of Liberal Studies at Oklahoma or the Bachelor of Independent Studies at South Florida will depend on the significance of the program within the total educational offerings of the institution. The smaller the program proportionally in terms of other institutional offerings, the less likelihood of regional intervention. Thus while institutions are required to report all "substantial" changes such as the creation of a new degree program to the regional commission, the only data that the commission may require on a non-traditional program from a large and well-established institution is that which the institution itself wishes to report. Just as attracting students, faculty, and funds for the program will ordinarily be easier by beginning from a reputable base of operation than by starting from scratch, so will winning the acceptance of accrediting agencies.

Third, in terms of all accrediting agencies, the advocates of a new program should be prepared to challenge a negative evaluation if its standards of quality match those of other existing programs. Since many judgments of the agencies are open to question because of their inferential and undocumented relation to quality, the probabilities are good that an appeal will overcome initial rejection. Illustrating this needed attitude, the president of a totally unconventional public college stated: "We agreed from the start that we would play the accreditation game in the traditional way, but that if it got in our way we would not fall over and play dead— nor would we modify anything that we thought was a fundamental principle simply because some accreditor said we had to change. If we had to, we would fight them. . . . I would be prepared to go to court over the issue, except that I don't think it will be necessary."

If an appeal within the accrediting agency proves futile, the National Commission on Accrediting and the Accreditation and

Institutional Eligibility Staff of the Bureau of Higher Education in the United States Office of Education should be notified, since even if their services do not lead to reconsideration of the case, they can apply pressure by withholding recognition of the agency for future improvements in standards.

Fourth, advocates of non-traditional study should recognize that other forces may be more constraining than are state regulation and voluntary accreditation. For example, all the regulatory agencies and accrediting associations combined have not approached the restrictive power that university graduate schools have held and continue to hold over unconventional undergraduate programs. Just as graduate and professional schools have required graduation from an accredited college as an easy and sometimes illegitimate shortcut in determining the competence and potential of applicants, nothing is to stop them from restricting admission to students who have specialized in conventional majors and classroom study rather than in non-traditional programs. If graduates of accredited non-traditional programs and institutions find that they are thus barred from graduate study or employment despite the fact of accreditation, the non-traditional study movement will wither regardless of accreditation. Conversely, if graduates from un-accredited institutions find that their degrees win them salary increments and recognition despite the lack of accreditation, more and more people will follow their example in obtaining uncertified discount degrees and cut-rate credits.

Fifth and finally, while other forces will thus also affect the non-traditional study movement, proponents of new forms of education should be prepared to help lead the improvement of state regulation and voluntary accreditation—both to assure sufficient monitoring of inadequate quality on the one hand and to avoid illegitimate regulations over qualified programs on the other. If they do so, non-traditional study may be the vehicle that will stimulate solutions to the long-standing problems of regulating and accrediting traditional education.

And here remains the most serious problem. Valid standards of educational quality must be applied not only to new forms of education but also to conventional forms. Unless advocates of non-traditional study succeed in assuring that new standards are applied equally to all types of educational institutions rather than only to the new forms, a historic opportunity for improved regulation and accreditation will be lost. New standards only for new education will prove too little and too late to save accreditation. In the terms of the religious fundamentalists, they will merely whitewash its sepulcher.

References

American Bar Association. *Approval of Law Schools: Standards and Rules of Procedure.* Chicago: Council of the Section of Legal Education and Admissions to the Bar, 1973.

American Physical Therapy Association and Council on Medical Education. *Essentials.* New York, 1955.

ASTIN, A. "Some New Directions for Accrediting." Address at the seminar on "Validation of Accrediting Standards." Washington, D.C.: National Commission on Accrediting, October 27, 1971.

BURNS, N. "The Need for New Techniques for Evaluation." Memorandum for the Federation of Regional Accrediting Commissions of Higher Education. Washington, D.C.: The Federation, 1972.

Department of Health, Education, and Welfare. *Report on Licensure and Related Health Personnel Credentialing.* Washington, D.C.: Government Printing Office, 1971; quoted in *Part I: Staff Working Papers, Accreditation of Health Educational Programs.* Washington, D.C.: Study of Accreditation of Selected Health Educational Programs, 1971, page F-3.

Education Commission of the States. *Model State Legislation: Report of the Task Force on Model State Legislation for Approval of Postsecondary Educational Institutions and Authorization to Grant Degrees.* Report Number 39. Denver, 1973.

Federation of Regional Accrediting Commissions of Higher Education. "Innovation." Statement adopted April 28, 1970. Duplicated. Washington, D.C.

———— "Interim Statement on Accreditation and Non-Traditional Study." Approved March 14, 1973. Duplicated. Washington, D.C.

Florida *Statutes.* Chapter 246, Section 246.011, 1971.

Florida State Board of Independent Colleges and Universities. *Rules and Regulations of Florida State Board of Independent Colleges and Universities.* Chapter 6A-13, 1971–72. Tallahassee, 1971.

Indiana Private School Accrediting Commission. *Rules and*

Regulations of the Indiana Private School Accrediting Commission as adopted November 22, 1971. Indianapolis, 1971.

KOERNER, J. "Preserving the Status Quo: Academia's Hidden Cartel." *Change,* March-April 1971, *3*(2).

North Central Association of Colleges and Secondary Schools. *Guide for the Evaluation of Institutions of Higher Education, 1961.* Duplicated. Chicago: Commission on Colleges and Universities, 1961.

PUFFER, C. E., STEFFENS, H. W., LOMBARDIE, J., and PFNISTER, A. O. *Regional Accreditation of Institutions of Higher Education: A Study Prepared for the Federation of Regional Accrediting Commissions of Higher Education.* Duplicated. Chicago: The Federation, June 1970.

REID, R. H. *American Degree Mills: A Study of Their Operations and of Existing and Potential Ways to Control Them.* Washington, D.C.: American Council on Education, 1959.

SELDEN, W. K. "Research in Accreditation." In *Part I: Staff Working Papers, Accreditation of Health Educational Programs.* Washington, D.C.: Study of Accreditation of Selected Health Educational Programs, 1971.

Southern Association of Colleges and Schools. *Standards of the College Delegate Assembly of the Southern Association of Colleges and Schools, December 1, 1971.* Atlanta, 1971.

State of Wisconsin Educational Approval Board. *Regulations.* Chapter EAB 1–7. Madison, 1972.

Study Commission on Accreditation of Selected Health Educational Programs. *Commission Report.* Washington, D.C., May 1972.

United States Office of Education. "Special Notice." *Accredited Postsecondary Institutions and Programs Including Institutions Holding Preaccredited Status as of January 15, 1970.* Washington, D.C.: Government Printing Office, 1971.

An Annotated Bibliography
with Overviews

WILLIAM A. MAHLER

🙟🙟🙟🙟🙟🙟🙟🙟🙟🙟🙟🙟🙟🙟🙟🙟🙟🙟🙟🙟🙟🙟🙟🙟🙟

*N*on-traditional study is a difficult term to define explicitly and a complex concept to understand, but one way to comprehend its meaning is to review the definitions of others. For example, the members of the Commission on Non-Traditional Study concluded that non-traditional study "is more an attitude than a system"—an attitude that "puts the student first and the institution second, concentrates more on the former's need than the latter's convenience, encourages diversity of individual opportunity rather than uniform prescription, and deemphasizes time, space, and even course requirements in favor of competence and, where applicable, performance" (Commission on Non-Traditional Study, 1973, p. xv). A person unfamiliar with non-traditional study, however, needs some general framework within which to search—even for definitions. The criteria for selecting the documents for this review may serve as a useful starting point: First, only documents about educational programs were chosen and those about purely recreational or entertaining programs were excluded. This criterion does not imply that education cannot be recreational

175

or entertaining, but only that the purposes of any program included in this review include improving, increasing, or altering the knowledge or skills of participants.

Second, the program should be offered at the general post-secondary education level, rather than for elementary or secondary students or adult basic education on the one hand or specialized graduate and professional programs on the other.

Third and finally, the program had to be unconventional. Since there has been no single tradition in American education and unique opportunities for learning have always existed, it is difficult to distinguish between convention and the exception; but for present purposes these programs were considered non-traditional:

(1) Programs for any group, such as mothers with young or grown children, military personnel, fully employed adults, or senior citizens, which faces problems in attending an institution full-time for a specific number of years.

(2) Studies of the learning characteristics and educational needs of these groups.

(3) Programs to provide guidance and counseling for these groups.

(4) Programs which offer learning opportunities in vocational, occupational, or career education; in self-improvement, self-understanding, or self-fulfillment; in problem areas such as ecology or world peace; or in academic subjects taught in non-traditional ways.

(5) Programs which use educational technology to diminish the constraints of time or place, such as broadcast television, video-cassettes, cable television, computer-assisted instruction, radio, and special telephone connections.

(6) Programs which are offered by institutions which have not traditionally been responsible for higher education, such as churches, YMCAS, libraries, proprietary schools, and business and industry.

(7) Programs which grant credit or degrees in non-traditional ways, such as external degrees, credit by evaluation, assessment of work samples, and mastery or criterion-referenced testing.

Not only are these criteria simply a starting point, but this entire review must be considered in the same way. It does not include all of the relevant references: more diversity, innovation and interesting programs exist than can be included in one review. Hopefully, someday there will be a central clearinghouse to accumulate this wealth of information and to assist individuals in answering their specific questions.

The three sources for these references were the personal files of staff members of the research program, materials and recommendations from experts who were interviewed for the project, and the files of the Educational Resources Information Center (ERIC) of the U. S. Office of Education, which contain some one hundred thousand references, more than half of which are unpublished reports unavailable elsewhere. More than ten thousand of these references were found to be potentially related to non-traditional study, but by means of the largest and most complex search strategies ever undertaken of the ERIC files by ERIC/DIALOG—a computerized search process developed by Lockheed Information Sciences—a total of 1755 abstracts were reviewed by the author.

The final phase of the literature survey was to reduce the number of references to the 173 which follow and to categorize them into eight sections in order to make the variety of references more comprehensible.

The list of literature that follows makes it quite obvious that a tremendous amount of innovation is occurring in the area of non-traditional study. All the diversity that non-traditional studies offer, however, cannot be carried on without continual coordination of information. As the Commission on Non-Traditional Study pointed out in its final report, a centralized source of information is needed both by the developers and administrators of non-traditional programs and by students who are seeking the most appropriate source of instruction. The efforts of this research program and the Commission on Non-Traditional Study need to be expanded and continued on a permanent basis. A center on non-traditional study should not try to usurp or even direct all efforts in this area, but it could serve as a clearinghouse of information; it could encourage or undertake needed research and development; and it would provide a setting in which to evaluate existing programs or materials.

The non-traditional movement appears to have changed in recent years from a peripheral to a central concern in education.

But realization of the dream of non-traditional studies—to provide every individual with not only the opportunity, but also the encouragement to develop his or her abilities and to increase her or his knowledge to the greatest extent possible—is not yet accomplished. Many persons and organizations in a great many fields of expertise are needed to carry on these efforts, so that the diverse needs of students, both traditional and non-traditional, can be met.

General

These references deal with the context or totality of non-traditional study; they include commission reports, histories of adult education, predictions and proposals for the future of post-secondary education, discussions of the educational philosophy underlying non-traditional study, and annotated bibliographies.

Five commission reports are of special interest: those of the Commission on Non-Traditional Study (1973; Gould and Cross, 1972; Houle, 1973); the Commission on Postsecondary Education in Ontario (1972); two synopses of the Carnegie Commission on Higher Education (1971, 1972); the Task Force on Higher Education of the Department of Health, Education, and Welfare (Newman, 1971); and the Commission on Academic Affairs of the American Council on Education (1972).

Four documents cover the history and current status of adult education: Carey, 1961; Houle, 1972; Knowles, 1969; and Smith, Aker, and Kidd, 1972. Five references describe various non-traditional programs: College Entrance Examination Board, 1972; Coyne and Hebert, 1972; DeLisle, 1972; Sharon, 1971; and Valley, 1972. Predictions and proposals for the future include the report of the White House Youth Conference's Task Force on Education (1971) and of the entire White House Conference on Youth (1971), the proceedings of the annual seminar on leadership in continuing education (Kellogg, 1968), and the papers by Feinsot (1972), Marien (1972), Hudson (1968), and White (1967). Ashby (1971), Smith (1971), and Vermilye (1972) contain writings about the philosophy of education which underlies the trend toward non-traditional study. Bibliographies include those by the ERIC Clearinghouse on Higher Education (1972), Flaugher and others (1967), Fletcher (1972), and Walkup (1972).

American Council on Education. *Higher Education and the Adult Student, An ACE Special Report*. Washington, D.C., 1972. Accepted as an official ACE statement, this short pamphlet presents forty-two recommendations to educators and others regarding adult students; recommendations on commitment, structure, curriculum, educational resources, technology, credit and degrees, accreditation and licensure, quality, faculty and administrators, research, costs, and adult education organizations are included.

American Vocational Association. *Research Visibility, 1968–69: Reports on Selected Research Studies in Vocational, Technical, and Practical Arts Education*. Washington, D.C., 1969. (ED031598). Research reviews on this volume are a consolidation of "Research Visibility" articles which were regularly published from September 1968 to May 1969.

ASHBY, E. *Any Person, Any Study*. New York: McGraw-Hill, 1971. A noted British educator and member of the Carnegie Commission on Higher Education raises some tough questions in evaluating higher education in the United States from a fresh viewpoint; the title implies his vision for the future.

CAREY, J. T. *Forms and Forces in University Adult Education*. Brookline, Mass.: Center for the Study of Liberal Education for Adults, 1961. (ED047286). Though particularly focused on liberal adult education, this is a detailed study of the range of forces which favor or impede the growth of adult education in American higher education; it explores the history of university adult education, the status of liberal education programing, and such factors as tradition, personnel, financial arrangements, goals and objectives, and community context.

Carnegie Commission on Higher Education. *The Future of Higher Education: How to Get There from Here*. New York: McGraw-Hill, 1971. This catalog gives references and abstracts for the first nine Commission reports, the first twenty-two sponsored research studies, and the first three technical reports.

Carnegie Commission on Higher Education. *A Digest and Index of Reports and Recommendations: December, 1968 to June, 1972.* Berkeley, Calif.: Carnegie Commission on Higher Education, 1972. This book contains digests of the thirteen Commission reports published before June 1972.

College Entrance Examination Board. *Five Articles on Non-Traditional Educational Concepts.* Reprinted from the *College Board Review,* Fall 1972. New York, 1972. These five articles cover the role of the College Board, the vision of non-traditional study, the work of the Commission on Non-Traditional Study, the New York Regents external degree, the Open University in the United States, and the three-year degree.

Commission on Non-Traditional Study. *Diversity by Design.* San Francisco: Jossey-Bass, 1973. This final report of the Commission contains fifty-eight recommendations and extended discussion covering a wide variety of topics related to non-traditional study.

Commission on Post-Secondary Education in Ontario. *Draft Report.* Toronto: Ontario Government Bookstore, 1972. This draft report was published in order to solicit reactions on seventy-one recommendations covering many aspects of postsecondary education; a general discussion, reports on twenty-five public hearings, and 335 briefs from organizations and individuals are included.

COYNE, J., and HEBERT, T. *This Way Out: A Guide to Alternatives to Traditional College Education in the United States, Europe and the Third World.* New York: E. P. Dutton, 1972. This useful guide provides practical suggestions and information for students interested in independent study and brief descriptions of many experimental colleges and foreign study opportunities; information on external degree programs and CLEP exams is included.

DE LISLE, F. H. *Supplement to the March 1972 Compilation of Preliminary Material on Non-Traditional Approaches to Under-*

graduate Education. East Lansing: Michigan State University, Office of Institutional Research, 1972. This second compilation of material on non-traditional study covers new designs and additional information about previously described programs; the classification system is based on non-traditional objectives, content, methods, and evaluation and certification; some evaluation of programs is given.

ERIC Clearinghouse on Adult Education. *Continuing Education for Adults.* Syracuse, N.Y., 1971–1973. This newsletter for university adult educators has brief discussions and references on developments in the field.

ERIC Clearinghouse on Adult Education. *Publications, 1969–1970.* Syracuse, N.Y., 1970. (ED042962). Beginning with general information on the scope and subject coverage of the clearinghouse and on principal periodicals covering the literature, this annotated bibliography lists seventy-four literature reviews and other documents.

ERIC Clearinghouse on Higher Education. *Bibliography on Aspects of Non-Traditional Study in Higher Education.* Washington, D.C.: George Washington University, 1972. This annotated bibliography contains eighty-five references on adult higher education, adult students, continuing education, correspondence and extension study, educational broadcasting, equivalency, evening college, independent learning, institutional studies, the Open University, technology, organizations, and other miscellaneous topics.

FEINSOT, A. *Breaking the Institutional Mold: Implications of Alternative Systems for Post-Secondary/Higher Education.* White Plains, N.Y.: Knowledge Industry Publications, 1972. Experimental colleges, innovative two-year colleges, television colleges, external degrees, proprietary schools, and credit by examination are discussed, and their implications for postsecondary and higher education are predicted.

FLAUGHER, R. L., MAHONEY, M. H., and MESSING, R. B.

Credits by Examination for College-Level Studies: An Annotated Bibliography. New York: College Entrance Examination Board, 1967. (ED016943). This annotated bibliography contains 308 items on transfer students and transfer policy, student accreditation by examination, and sources of instruction for unaffiliated students.

FLETCHER, M. A. *The Open University, the External Degrees, and Non-Traditional Study: A Selected Annotated Bibliography.* Bryn Mawr, Penn.: American College of Life Underwriters, 1972. The seventy-seven references in the bibliography include books, reports, journal articles, news releases, and unpublished papers on the topics listed in the title.

FRIEDMAN, C. H., and others. *Inventory of Federally Supported Extension and Continuing Education Programs: Report to the President's National Advisory Council on Extension and Continuing Education, Part One and Part Two.* New York: Greenleigh Associations, 1967. (ED012415). This extensive listing of all federally supported extension and continuing education programs includes thorough descriptions of community service, adult basic education, manpower development, and vocational education programs.

GOULD, S. B., and CROSS, K. P. (Eds.) *Explorations in Non-Traditional Study.* San Francisco: Jossey-Bass, 1972. The first book-length publication of the Commission on Non-Traditional Study includes essays by Samuel B. Gould, Rodney T. Hartnett, Ernest W. Kimmel, John R. Valley, and K. Patricia Cross and J. Quentin Jones.

HOULE, C. O. *The Design of Education.* San Francisco: Jossey-Bass, 1972. The "system" outlined in this book is designed for adult educators; it provides a history and broad outline of adult education of all types and a method for analyzing individual components or programs.

HOULE, C. O. *The External Degree.* San Francisco: Jossey-Bass, 1973. This publication of the Commission on Non-Traditional

Study attempts to assess the external degree, its historical routes, some of its best-established examples, its rise in prominence, its major ideas and themes, its place in American higher education, and its future.

HUDSON, R. B. "Toward a National Center for Higher Continuing Education." Center for the Study of Liberal Education for Adults, Occasional Papers, No. 17. Syracuse, N.Y.: Library of Continuing Education, 1968. (ED024857). With the closing of the center, a proposal is made to reinstate it and enlarge its concern to include all continuing education, research, demonstration, evaluation, professional training, consultation and program development, publication, development of national policy, and a concern for evolving institutional policies for continuing education.

Kellogg Center for Continuing Education. *Proceedings of the Annual Seminar on Leadership in Continuing Education.* East Lansing: Michigan State University, 1968. (ED021192). Discussions cover demands on educators in continuing education during the final decades of the twentieth century, the relationship of continuing education to society, and the ultimate goals of education in the twenty-first century.

KNOWLES, M. S. *Higher Adult Education in the United States: The Current Picture, Trends and Issues.* Washington, D.C.: American Council on Education, 1969. (ED034145). This paper represents an analysis of the literature of higher adult education from 1960 through 1968 and an attempt to place the field of adult education in perspective.

MARIEN, M. "Beyond the Carnegie Commission: Space-Free, Time-Free, and Credit-Free Higher Education." Syracuse, N.Y.: Syracuse University Research Corporation, Educational Policy Research Center, 1972. This article proposes a greater emphasis on non-credit learning and then discusses non-traditional approaches to alternative types of institutions of higher education, the possible implications of new media, the problems of accreditation, equity for the disadvantaged, and personnel needs; an extensive bibliography and reviews of ten external degree programs are included.

NEWMAN, F., and others. *Report on Higher Education.* Washington, D.C.: U. S. Government Printing Office, 1971. This report attacks many of the basic assumptions of American higher education and proposes several alternatives. The homogenized, professionalized, bureaucratic, mass-scale, monopolistic system is attacked, and suggestions for greater opportunity off-campus, different attendance patterns, and greater diversification are made.

NEWMAN, F. "A Preview of the Second Newman Report." *Change,* 1972, *4,* 28–34. The article reviews the work of the original task force and briefly describes some of the concrete proposals being formulated.

SHARON, A. T. "College Credit for Off-Campus Study." Washington, D.C.: ERIC Clearinghouse on Higher Education, 1971. This paper reviews non-traditional education for which college credit is received, including correspondence study, educational television, military experience, independent study, and credit by examination.

SMITH, A. Z. (Ed.) *Education Recaps.* (For the Commission on Non-Traditional Study). Princeton, N.J.: Educational Testing Service, Spring 1971, Winter 1971–1972, and Spring 1972. Abstracts of articles, books, and reports on non-traditional higher education from a variety of sources are included.

SMITH, G. K. (Ed.) *New Teaching, New Learning,* AAHE *Current Issues in Higher Education, 1971.* San Francisco: Jossey-Bass, 1971. Twenty-seven essays by various educators are grouped into the categories of new teaching contexts, new settings for learning, exits and entrances, paradoxes in decision-making, the professor as employee, and reinterpreting higher education; a broad spectrum of topics about new developments and historical perspectives are included.

SMITH, R. M., AKER, G. F., and KIDD, J. R. (Eds.) *Handbook of Adult Education.* Washington, D.C.: Adult Education Association of USA, 1972. The 1972 edition of this handbook is an attempt to reflect the totality of adult education—its background, function, objectives, and roles: Part One discusses forms, functions, and the future of adult education; Part Two contains papers on institutional forms and arrangements; and Part Three outlines program areas.

United State Office of Education. *Four Years of Research, Development, and Training: A Bibliography.* Washington, D.C., 1968. (ED032432). Citations of final reports of projects funded by the Division of Comprehensive and Vocational Education Research (DCVER) are included in this bibliographic listing.

VALLEY, J. R. *Increasing the Options: Recent Developments in College and University Degree Programs.* Princeton, N.J.: Office of New Degree Programs, 1972. This report focuses on developments since 1969 in degree programs in the United States; descriptions and references are listed under new programs, proposals, major studies and investigations, or related and supporting services.

VERMILYE, D. W. (Ed.) *The Expanded Campus,* AAHE *Current Issues in Higher Education, 1972.* San Francisco: Jossey-Bass, 1972. The twenty-five essays by various educators are grouped into the categories of the Carnegie Commission: point and counterpoint, women and blacks in higher education, the anachronism of the gentleman scholar, breaking time-space patterns, curriculum and instruction, autonomy and control, and an epilogue.

WALKUP, B. S. *External Study for Post-Secondary Students: Original and Supplement.* New York: College Entrance Examination Board, Office of New Degree Programs, 1972. The 244 references, mostly abstracted, in this bibliography are divided into bibliographies and reviews, directories and inventories, innovation, adult and continuing education, correspondence and home study, credit by examination and guidance, College-Level Examination Program, external degree programs, technology, and innovation.

WHITE, T. J. *The Future of American Adult Education.*

Knoxville: University of Tennessee, 1967. (ED014625). The author predicts ten future events that will make the transformation from opportunity to reality of education for all Americans.

White House Conference on Youth. *Report.* Washington, D.C.: U. S. Government Printing Office, 1971. (ED056961). This report covers all aspects of the conference held at Estes Park in April 1971 and contains all proposals and recommendations made by the 914 youth and 500 "establishment" delegates.

White House Youth Conference's Task Force on Education. *Higher Education and National Affairs.* April 16, 1971, 3–5. This fifteen-page report includes ten basic propositions and ten specific recommendations on greater flexibility in educational programs, greater student participation in policy-making decisions and their individual educational futures, less emphasis on credentials, recognition of learning outside of the classroom, better guidance services, better teacher preparation, greater use of modern technology for routine knowledge dissemination, and greater humanization of educational experiences.

Educational Needs

Most studies of educational needs concentrate on vocational education specific groups such as women (Merideth and Merideth, 1971), the aging (Kreps and Laws, 1965), or students interested in vocational and technical education (Office of Programs for the Disadvantaged, 1969). The most important general document is by Johnstone and Rivera (1965), because, like the study by Carp, Peterson, and Roelfs reported in this volume, it reports responses of potential learners from all segments of society.

Adult Education Association of USA. *Continuing Education of Women.* Washington, D.C., 1970. (ED042122). This annotated bibliography of about 150 items on women's continuing education contains descriptions of women's educational needs and some programs to aid them in this country and abroad.

California State Department of Education. *Vocational Education for Persons with Special Needs.* Sacramento: California State Department of Education, 1966. (ED011929). This literature survey covers the vocational needs of a variety of groups with special problems, including aged, culturally deprived, mentally retarded, physically handicapped, and rural persons.

DECARLO, C. R., and ROBINSON, O. W. *Education in Business and Industry.* New York: Center for Applied Research in Education, 1966. (ED015352). Continuing education is discussed as vital to the prosperity of business and industry when technological changes require continual readjustment of job requirements; roles of industry, universities, and government cooperating to provide the resources, materials, and incentives for continuing education are proposed.

GOLDSTAUB, J. (Ed.) *Manpower and Educational Planning: An Annotated Bibliography of Currently Available Materials.* Pittsburgh: University of Pittsburgh, School of Education, 1968. (ED030195). This annotated bibliography of 110 documents deals with various aspects of manpower and educational planning.

JOHNSTONE, J. W. C., and RIVERA, R. J. *Volunteers for Learning.* Chicago: Aldine, 1965. Based on questionnaires sent to eighteen thousand households and interviews with more than three thousand adults, this study presents data on educational experiences of adults, attitudes toward learning, and educational facilities available in selected cities.

KREPS, J. M., and LAWS, R. *Training and Retraining Older Workers: An Annotated Bibliography.* New York: National Council on the Aging, 1965. (ED026472). The 123 annotated listings cover the years from 1943 through 1965 and are organized under headings of general references and government.

MERIDETH, E., and MERIDETH, R. "Adult Women's Education: A Radical Critique." *Journal of the National Association of*

Women Deans and Counselors, 1971, *34,* 111–120. (EJ036302). The authors propose measures to meet the needs of women in universities, including alternative living arrangements and open universities.

MICHAEL, D. N. "The Next Twenty Years: Background Notes for Adult Counseling Planning." Brookline, Mass.: Center for the Study of Liberal Education for Adults, 1965. (ED012054). This address calls for advanced planning and action based on long-range assessments of technological and societal developments, including increased leisure time and ecological considerations.

Office of Programs for the Disadvantaged. *Vocational Training, Employment and Unemployment: Part One—National Trends, Part Two—Profiles on the States.* Washington, D.C.: U. S. Office of Education, 1969. (ED029112). Data on manpower needs, existing programs, and economic factors are given to assist in planning training programs for unemployed youth.

Student Characteristics

All of these references on the characteristics of students who are enrolled in vocational or adult education present data on the backgrounds, preferences, and psychological characteristics of learners, with the exception of the final one (U. S. Office of Education, 1971), which contains statistical information on enrollments in various educational programs which can be considered non-traditional.

BLACKBURN, D. J., and DOUGLAS, M. A. "Method Orientation of Adults for Participation in Educative Activities." Paper presented at the National Seminar on Adult Education Research, Chicago, 1968. (ED017859). This study investigates preferences for various group and individual methods for presentation of a wide variety of adult courses; it reports relationships between preferences and some background factors.

BRINKMAN, F. J. *Analysis of the Characteristics of Selected*

Vocational Students with Implications for Guidance and Counseling. Ann Arbor, Mich.: University Microfilms, (Order No. 70-24, 350), 1970. (ED046388). A literature review and original survey form the basis of this study of mainly students with vocational needs and interests.

COHEN, A., and others. *Adult Education in Metropolitan Toronto, a Situation Report.* Toronto: Board of Education, 1967. (ED011999). A metropolitan Toronto survey seeks to determine the number, preferences, and backgrounds of persons currently pursuing adult education or not participating but willing to attend a proposed twenty-four-hour center.

CROSS, K. P. *Beyond the Open Door: New Students to Higher Education.* San Francisco: Jossey-Bass, 1971. The problems and characteristics of the "new students" who are entering college through open-door policies are discussed on the basis of four large-scale surveys of their interests and goals; special problems of ethnic minorities and women are included.

CROSS, K. P. *Occupationally Oriented Students.* Washington, D.C.: American Association of Junior Colleges, 1970. (ED043328). This research review combines findings of recent studies about junior college students in vocational programs and develops a tentative description of their backgrounds and characteristics.

DUBOIS, P. H., and WIENTGE, K. M. *Factors Associated with the Achievement of Adult Students.* St. Louis, Mo.: Washington University, 1964. (ED003256). This study related biographical data and measures of aptitudes, abilities, interests, and motivational characteristics to the academic success of adult students; results indicated that the use of biographical information, plus the standard battery of tests, formed a good base for achievement prediction.

GARBIN, A. P., and VAUGHN, D. *Community-Junior College Students Enrolled in Occupational Programs: Selected Character-*

istics, Experiences and Perceptions. Columbus: Ohio State University, 1971. (ED057196). The first of four planned publications to be based on a survey of five thousand students at sixty colleges describes the students' personal and background characteristics, experiences, and perceptions. Recommendations on curriculum, guidance, and further research are made.

KAY, E. R. *Vocational Education: Characteristics of Teachers and Students, 1969.* Washington, D.C.: U. S. Office of Education, National Center for Educational Statistics, 1971. (ED050297). This report presents information on the professional qualifications and teaching experiences of teachers; information on students includes individual and family characteristics and plans for the future.

SPIEGEL, J. *Continuing Education for Women: A Selected Annotated Bibliography.* Washington, D.C.: Business and Professional Women's Foundation, 1967. (ED014635). A bibliography on the economic, social, and psychological challenges confronting women in developing their capabilities through continuing education.

United States Office of Education. *Vocational and Technical Education: Annual Report, Fiscal Year 1969.* Washington, D.C.: U. S. Government Printing Office, 1971. (ED060214). Current statistical data on programs and enrollments, discussion of progress toward implementation of the National Education Act of 1963, and discussion of the issues underlying the Vocational Education Amendments of 1968 are included in this annual report.

Guidance

As the report of the General Accounting Office (1972) illustrates, general agreement exists that counseling and guidance must be an integral part of non-traditional study—both the counseling of students with personal or study problems and the guidance of students to appropriate courses, degree programs, sources of information, institutions, and careers. Professional counselors are needed to help with the emotional and psychological problems and the special needs of adults (Adult Student Personnel Association, 1970; Fisher, 1969; Matthews, 1969; National Association for Public Continuing and Adult Education, 1970; Porter, 1969) and vocational students (Brandon, 1969; "Counseling the Technically Oriented Student," 1970; Thoroman, 1968). Various computer-based systems have been proposed for the guidance needs (Brandon, 1969; Hawkins, 1969), and some prototypes are under development (Katz and others, 1972). Super (1970) has descriptions of various systems and discussions of issues in computer-based guidance from a variety of viewpoints.

The remaining articles in this section describe special guidance tests (Crawford, 1966; Holland, 1971) or present data about the guidance services now being offered (Farmer, 1971; Glick, 1969; Kuder, 1971).

Adult Student Personnel Association. *Counseling the Adult Student: Convention Proceedings.* Monticello, N.Y., 1968. (ED025791). A number of papers are addressed to the problems of adult counseling and its implications, future, and relationship with program development.

BRANDON, G. L. (Ed.) *Research Visibility: Guidance and New Careers.* Washington, D.C.: American Vocational Association, 1969. (ED034882). Thirteen research reviews in this issue pertain to occupational information, a pilot computer-assisted guidance program, student selection, guidance and counseling services, and student interests and experiences.

"Counseling the Technically Oriented Student." *Man/Society/Technology: A Journal of Industrial Arts Education.* 1970, *30,* 61–62. (EJ027929). A special survey results in capsule overviews of various counseling procedures.

CRAWFORD, M. L. *Available Tests and Their Use in Research in Vocational Education.* Los Angeles: Los Angeles Trade-Technical College, 1966. (ED012623). Test batteries which include aptitude, intelligence, and personality tests, as well as interviews, have been developed and validated for admissions purposes.

FARMER, M. L. (Ed.) *Counseling Services for Adults in Higher Education.* Metuchen, N.J.: Scarecrow Press, 1971. (ED053365). This book assesses what is needed and what is being done in the field of counseling and in evening college and other higher education programs for adults.

FISHER, J. A. *Educational Counseling for Adults.* Des Moines, Iowa: Drake University, 1969. (ED033419). Personal, noncognitive barriers to education for adults are discussed, and appropriate counseling methods are recommended.

General Accounting Office. *Most Veterans Not Completing Correspondence Courses—More Guidance Needed from the Veterans Administration: Report to the Congress.* Washington, D.C., 1972. Only 25 percent of the veterans who enrolled in correspondence courses completed them, while the rest incurred losses of twenty-four million dollars for uncompleted lessons; more guidance about course requirements and the percentage of veterans completing each course, as well as encouragement to use present guidance services, is recommended.

GLICK, B. (Ed.) *Counseling and Personnel Services in Adult Education: Current Information Sources, No. 23.* Syracuse, N.Y.: ERIC Clearinghouse on Adult Education, 1969. (ED029234). This annotated bibliography contains ninety-four entries arranged under four headings: student personnel services, counseling services; admissions and selection; retention and dropout; and financial assistance.

HAWKINS, S. *Guidelines for Inservice Training: The Bartlesville System.* Stillwater: Oklahoma State University, 1969. (ED029328). The theory underlying this work is that the best guidance programs are those which allow the professional counselor the largest amount of time for counseling; the use of computers in the field of guidance is recommended, to assist the counselors in information storage and retrieval and provide for individualized instruction.

HOLLAND, J. L. "A Theory-Ridden, Computerless, Impersonal Vocational Guidance System." *Journal of Vocational Behavior*, 1971, *1*, 167–176. (EJ034630). A theory of personality types is presented as a basis for the self-directed search for educational and vocational planning—a self-administered, self-scored, and self-interpreted vocational counseling tool.

KATZ, M., CHAPMAN, W., and GODWIN, W. "SIGI—A Computer-Based Aid to Career Decision-Making." EDUCOM: *Bulletin of the Interuniversity Communications Council*, 1972, 7, 12–17. This article describes a computer-based guidance system being developed for use primarily by community college students.

KUDER, J. M. *Past Trends in Student Personnel Services for Adults in Higher Education.* Ft. Collins: Colorado State University, 1971. (ED050403). The author contends that the development of student personnel services for adults in higher education has been extremely painful, erratic, and slow and that there now seems to be a major trend that these services be handled by specially trained personnel.

MATTHEWS, E. E. "The Counselor and the Adult Woman." *Journal of National Association Woman Deans and Counselors*, 1969, *32*, 115–122. (EJ003488).

National Association for Public Continuing and Adult Education. *Counseling and Interviewing Adult Students.* Washington, D.C., 1970. (ED042118). This booklet discusses counseling for adults in the adult school—either by guidance officials or by the teacher.

PORTER, L. "Adults Have Special Counseling Needs." *Adult Leadership*, 1970, *18*, 275–276. (EJ018359). The particular characteristics of adult students, especially those with implications for guidance and counseling, are discussed in this article.

SUPER, D. E. *Computer-Assisted Counseling.* New York: Teachers College, Columbia University, 1970. This collection of essays includes descriptions of working systems and discussions of relevant issues.

THOROMAN, E. C. "The Vocational Counseling of Adults and Young Adults." In *Counseling and the Junior College*. Boston: Houghton Mifflin, 1968. (ED028495). Counseling at community colleges must attempt to fit the individual in a heterogeneous structure which includes academic, vocational, continuing education, and community service courses.

Areas of Learning

The large and growing emphasis on vocational or career-oriented education in curricular revision is illustrated by Mills, 1972; Olean, 1967; Pucinski and Hirsch, 1971; Schultz and others, 1971; Turnbull, 1972; and the United States Office of Education, 1971. Many new vocational/technical programs of less than four years' duration are being offered by community colleges and technical schools (California Coordinating Unit, 1967; and Price and Hopkins, 1970), and many students in baccalaureate and graduate programs are demanding more emphasis on usable skills and knowledge (American Society for Engineering Education, 1972). Knowles and Associates (1972) describe one particular form of vocational education: cooperative education; and Berg (1970) considers the trends toward overtraining and overcredentialing for employment.

Increased leisure time and higher standards of living are creating a demand as well for learning opportunities which have no relevance for career or position (U. S. Office of Education, 1972). Many people are interested in improving their reading skills (Bliesmer, 1971; Ennis, 1965), their interpersonal relations, and their solutions to problems of everyday life (Spitze, 1970).

In addition, many non-traditional students are interested in regular academic subjects, problem-oriented workshops, and interdisciplinary courses. However, these may need to be taught differently or have emphases different from those for regular students.

American Society for Engineering Education. *Engineering*

Technology Education Study: Final Report. Washington, D.C., 1972. Assessment and evaluation of current two-year and four-year programs in engineering guided this study, which includes program descriptions and discussions of the history, goals, and future of engineering technology education.

BERG, I. *Education and Jobs: The Great Training Robbery.* New York: Praeger, 1970. This provocative book examines the relationship between education and degrees on the one hand and job satisfaction, productivity, and financial reward on the other.

BLIESMER, E. P. *1970 Review of Research on College-Adult Reading.* Milwaukee: Marquette University, National Reading Conference, 1971. (ED049007). Over 160 studies are cited, covering reading and study; related skills, traits, and habits—their effects and influences; and evaluation.

California Coordinating Unit for Occupational Research and Development. *Trade, Industrial, and Technical Education: RCU Research Summaries.* Sacramento, 1967. (ED014566). This research review of eighty-one studies covers postsecondary courses and training and retraining courses.

ENNIS, P. H. *Adult Book Reading in the United States.* Chicago: University of Chicago, National Opinion Research Center, 1965. (ED010754). Data from questionnaires, personal interviews of adult reading patterns and preferences, implications, and contributing factors are discussed.

KNOWLES, A. S., and ASSOCIATES. *Handbook of Cooperative Education.* San Francisco: Jossey-Bass, 1971. The history, objectives, and future of cooperative education; programs in the U.S., Canada, and England; how to plan, conduct, and administer such programs; and the special relevance of these programs for ethnic minorities and women are discussed.

MILLS, G. H. *Bibliography on Barriers to Effective Vocational-*

Occupational Education. Denver: Education Commission of the States, 1972. This is one of a series of bibliographies prepared for a Commission-sponsored conference on "Education's Financial Dilemma," Los Angeles, 1972.

OLEAN, S. J. *Changing Patterns in Continuing Education for Business.* Brookline, Mass.: Center for the Study of Liberal Education for Adults, 1967. (ED012428). Educational programs in a variety of businesses, mainly for management and scientific personnel, are described, and possible relationships with universities are discussed.

PRICE, R. G., and HOPKINS, C. R. *Review and Synthesis of Research in Business and Office Education.* Columbus: Ohio State University, Center for Vocational and Technical Education, 1970. (ED038520). This review covers studies on curriculum, instructional materials and devices, learning processes, teaching methods, student personnel services, facilities and scheduling, and other topics in senior high schools and two-year postsecondary schools.

PUCINSKI, R. C., and HIRSCH, S. P. (Eds.) *The Courage to Change: New Directives for Career Education.* Englewood Cliffs, N.J.: Prentice-Hall, 1971. The fourteen contributors to this volume voice different concerns and viewpoints, but they basically advocate that career education must become an integral part of all education, even for college-bound and college students. Using all community resources is also recommended.

SCHULTZ, R. E., and others. *Occupations and Education in the Seventies: Promise and Challenges.* Washington, D.C.: American Association of Junior Colleges, 1971. (ED045852). Five leaders in occupational education express ideas about the place of occupational education in the 1970s and suggest improved programs with relaxed admission requirements in order to meet the needs of the disadvantaged.

SPITZE, H. T. "Adult Education to Strengthen Family Life." *Illinois Teachers' Contemporary Roles,* 1970, *13,* 202–208.

(EJ019896). The responsibility of adult education programs to strengthen family life and prepare persons for their family roles is discussed.

TURNBULL, W. W. (Chm.) *Proceedings of the Conference on Career Education.* Princeton, N.J.: Educational Testing Service, 1972. Twelve speeches cover the role of career education in education, government, and industry including exemplary programs and general implications.

United States Office of Education, National Center for Education Research and Development. *New Thrust in Vocational Education.* Washington, D.C.: U. S. Government Printing Office, 1971. This document contains a description of a project to adapt Air Force training courses for use in schools and colleges in Utah.

United States Office of Education. *Sixth Annual Report on Community Service and Continuing Education Programs.* Washington, D.C., 1972. This report presents enrollment data and expenditures. Anecdotal information on exemplary programs and the impact of the projects is given.

WARREN, J. R. "Changing Students and Constant Curricula." *Educational Record,* 1970, *51,* 182–187. (ED022548). The author recommends a different academic program for the "new" students from the lower classes, which may also benefit the "old" upper-class and middle-class students.

Educational Technology

Summaries of the status of educational technology and its application in postsecondary education have appeared recently in Association for Educational Communications and Technology, 1972; Carnegie Commission, 1972; Commission on Instructional Technology, 1970; and Gosling, 1972. Statistical information on enrollments in mass media courses and program descriptions appear in Everly, 1968; the problems experienced by England's Open University with mass media courses are discussed by McIntosh and Bates (1972); and two general bibliographies on educational technology appear in ERIC Clearinghouse, 1967, and Ohlinger, 1968.

In terms of specific media, broadcast television is covered by Australian Association on Adult Education, 1965; DeKorte, 1967; and Trotter, 1970; videocassettes and related devices are surveyed by Billboard Publications (1971–72), Videocassette Industry Information Service (1972), and Molenda (1972b); cable television is considered by the Sloan Commission (1971) and the bibliography by Molenda (1972a), with brief accounts and specific applications illustrated by Instructional Technology Committee (1969), National Council of Churches (1972), Office of Communication, United Church of Christ (1972), and Stasheff and Lavi (1971).

The potential for computers in higher education is considered by Levien (1972), and the factors which inhibit the use of computers in education are discussed by Anastasio and Morgan (1972). Computer systems already in operation are reported in Alpert and Bitzer, 1969; Dick, 1969; Hammond, 1972; Instructional Technology Committee, 1969; and Volk, 1971. A thorough analysis of important issues in computerization is contained in Holtzman, 1970.

Among other media, radio is covered in ERIC Clearinghouse, 1967; correspondence study by MacKenzie, Christensen, and Rigby (1968) and Mathieson (1971); dial-access resources, such as language laboratories, by Potter (1968); special telephone connections in College Degrees, 1971; and "Teaching by Telephone," 1971; and textbooks by Rojas (1971).

Each medium has unique capabilities and optimal applications. A major factor in keeping accomplishments from equaling potential has been the scarcity of quality instructional materials and resistance by educators. Economic incentives may help with both areas, particularly in encouraging the unique combination of subject matter expertise, knowledge of media capabilities, knowledge of instructional design, and creativity, which are all necessary to produce quality materials.

ALPERT, D., and BITZER, D. *Advances in Computer-Based*

Education: A Progress Report on the PLATO *Program.* Urbana: University of Illinois Computer-Based Education Research Laboratory, 1969. This report describes a large-scale, interactive computer system, and its possible uses in education. The system is being revised and expanded to present courses in grade schools, army installations, community colleges, and universities.

ANASTASIO, E. J., and MORGAN, J. S. *Factors Inhibiting the Use of Computers in Instruction.* Princeton, N.J.: EDUCOM, Interuniversity Communications Council, 1972. Using a Delphi study to elicit opinions from a number of experts, the authors discuss factors which have thus far hindered the development and implementation of computer-assisted instruction and recommend action for the future.

Association for Educational Communications and Technology. "The Field of Educational Technology: A Statement of Definition." *Audiovisual Instruction,* 1972, *17,* 36–43. Based upon inputs from a wide variety of people, this statement attempts to define what is and what is not included in the field of educational technology and attempts to describe the important issues facing the field and its participants.

Australian Association on Adult Education. *Television and Adult Education: Report on Proceedings of the Annual Conference, Sydney, 1965.* Melbourne, 1965. (ED018702). Discussion groups consider such issues as target populations, nature of programs, and use of follow-up materials and methods.

Billboard Publications. *Vid News.* New York: Billboard Publications, 1971–72. This newsletter covers marketing and programing news on the hardware and software of video media: cassettes, cartridges, open-reels, discs, films, and cable television.

Carnegie Commission on Higher Education. *The Fourth Revolution: Instructional Technology in Higher Education.* New York: McGraw-Hill, 1972. This commission report discusses the present status of educational technology and makes a number of recommendations concerning its future.

"College Degrees Off Campus." *Automated Education Letter*, 1971, *6* (5). This article describes the centers in industries in eight cities in Oklahoma, in which students can view televised classes from four universities and converse with the professor.

Commission on Instructional Technology. *To Improve Learning: A Report to the President and Congress of the United States*. New York: R. R. Bowker, 1970. The report of the Commission to the Secretary of HEW and twenty-two papers on the "state of the art" are included; major recommendations include estab- lishment of the National Institutes of Education, the National In- stitute of Instructional Technology, and a National Council of Education and Industry.

DE KORTE, D. A. *Television in Education and Training: A Review of Developments and Applications of Television and Other Modern Audiovisual Aids*. Eindhoven, The Netherlands: N. B. Philips' Gioeilampenfabrieken, 1967. (ED021449). A review of developments in the United States, France, Italy, The Netherlands, and Great Britain shows many successful courses using television and other audiovisual devices; however, unless teachers take truly revolutionary action in adapting themselves, their methods, and their subject matter, they will be unable to take advantage of the new educational tools.

DICK, W. *An Overview of Computer-Assisted Instruction for Adult Educators*. Tallahassee: Florida State University, Computer- Assisted Instruction Center, 1969. (ED033611). A detailed history and definition of computer-assisted instruction, an overview of hardware and software problems, cost data, development and evaluation plans, and an example of an existing adult education course are given.

ERIC Clearinghouse on Adult Education. *Television and Radio in Adult Education: Current Information Sources, No. 1*. Syracuse, N.Y., 1967. (ED014032). This annotated bibliography contains thirty-two items on aspects of educational and instruc- tional radio and television.

EVERLY, J. C. "Continuing Education Instruction via the Mass Media." Paper presented at the National Seminar on Adult Education Research, Chicago, 1968. (ED016924). Statistical data on enrollments are presented, as well as descriptions of teaching methods and course content for courses offered via mass media.

GOSLING, G. W. H. *Telecommunications in Education.* Hawthorn, Victoria: Australian Council for Educational Research, 1972. This study investigates the possible uses of telephone, radio, television, and computer hookups by Australian colleges and universities; present and future hardware systems, as well as present programs and future needs of education, are described.

HAMMOND, A. L. "Computer-Assisted Instruction: Many Efforts, Mixed Results." *Science,* 1972, *176,* 1005–1006. This article briefly reviews many of the existing projects, potentials, and problems of computer-assisted instruction.

HANSEN, M. "Council on Educational Technology." *Congressional Record,* September 11, 1972, *118* (140). Congressman Hansen introduced a bill to establish a council on educational technology, with the purpose of encouraging and assessing the development of educational technology.

HOLTZMAN, W. H. (Ed.) *Computer-Assisted Instruction, Testing, and Guidance.* New York: Harper and Row, 1970. This collection of conference papers by several leaders in the field of computer-assisted instruction, as well as several severe critics, presents a thorough discussion of many of the issues, possibilities, programs, and problems of this field.

Instructional Technology Committee. *Educational Technology in Higher Education: The Promise and Limitations of* ITV *and* CAI. Washington, D.C.: National Academy of Engineering, 1969. This report discusses the future potentials, problems, funding, and the role of engineering schools in relation to computer-assisted instruction and instructional television.

LEVIEN, R. E. *The Emerging Technology: Instructional Uses of the Computer in Higher Education.* New York: McGraw-Hill, 1972. This study, sponsored by the Carnegie Commission on Higher Education, discusses the present and potential roles of computers in instruction, research, libraries, and administration, covering everything from hardware to finances.

MAC KENZIE, O., CHRISTENSEN, E. L., and RIGBY, P. H. *Correspondence Instruction in the United States.* New York: McGraw-Hill, 1968. Based on the comprehensive study starting in 1964, this book covers the history of correspondence instruction, a survey of current problems and practices, analysis and evaluation of correspondence instruction as a method, and a look at the future.

MATHIESON, D. E. *Correspondence Study: A Summary Review of the Research and Development Literature.* Syracuse, N.Y.: ERIC Clearinghouse on Adult Education, 1971. (ED047163). Beginning with a historical review, this literature review covers accreditation and licensing problems, general characteristics of students, educational methods and course design, patterns of student achievement and completion, and innovations in correspondence methodology and suggests limitations of correspondence study and expected trends in the use of programed instruction, broadcast media, films and other audiovisual resources, small groups, special degree programs, and arrangements for course credits and degrees through examinations.

MC INTOSH, N. E., and BATES, A. W. "Mass-Media Courses for Adults." *Programmed Learning and Educational Technology,* 1972, *9*, 188–197. This report by staff members of England's Open University discusses some of the problems of mass media for the producer or designer, educational institution, tutor, and student.

MOLENDA, M. *Annotated Bibliography on the Educational Implications of Cable Television* (CATV). Greensboro: University of North Carolina, 1972a (ED059607). The 156 annotated citations, published between 1967 and 1971, are divided into four sections: status and future, regulation, relation to education, and relation to sociocultural concerns.

MOLENDA, M. *Annotated Bibliography on Videocassettes in Education.* Greensboro: University of North Carolina, 1972b. (ED059608). The twenty-five items in this bibliography include articles in popular magazines during 1970 to 1972.

National Council of Churches. *Cable Information.* New York: National Council of Churches, 1972. This monthly newsletter, begun in March 1972, contains brief reviews of CATV developments in both hardware and programing, reviews of commission reports and studies, and listings of relevant organizations and publications.

Office of Communication. *A Short Course in Cable.* New York: United Church of Christ, 1972. This brief booklet gives the history of cable television, some figures on current use, speculations about the future, and the impact of the 1972 FCC rulings.

OHLINGER, J. *The Mass Media in Adult Education: A Review of Recent Literature.* Syracuse, N.Y.: ERIC Clearinghouse on Adult Education, 1968. This review of 120 references outlines general trends and examines individual media as well as their use in the various areas of adult education.

POTTER, G. "Dial-Remote Resources." In WEISGERBER, R. A., *Instructional Process and Media Innovation.* Chicago: Rand-McNally, 1968. This article describes the advantages and development of dial-remote systems from early language laboratories to complex learning resources centers including a description of such a system at Grand Valley State College.

ROJAS, B. "The Textbook of the Future." *School and Society,* 1971, *99,* 315–317. This article describes the near possibility for individuals to be able to go into bookstores and create their own books from available chapters by using a computerized retrieval system and a cheap reproduction unit; eventually, the computer will generate reading material based upon learning styles and knowledge deficiences of students in computer-assisted instructional courses at the end of each lesson.

Sloan Commission on Cable Communications. *On the Cable: The Television of Abundance.* New York: McGraw-Hill, 1971. This extensive report covers all aspects of cable television, its history, potentials, technology, and politics.

STASHEFF, E., and LAVI, A. *Instructional Television in Industry: A Survey.* Ann Arbor: University of Michigan, Office of Research Administration, 1971. (ED047490). This study surveys several industries hooked up for television communication via microwave from Stanford University and concludes that industry is an environment in which major adult educational activities are taking place and that the formal educational system is not responding to the needs of industry and may be unable to do so.

"Teaching by Telephone." *Higher Education Briefs,* 1971, *4* (6), 6. This article describes the Kansas State University telephone communications system with centers at fifteen locations; any telephone can be used to tie an individual into the system.

TROTTER, B. *Television and Technology in University Teaching.* Toronto: Committee on University Affairs, and the Committee of Presidents of Universities of Ontario, 1970. This extensive treatment of educational television reviews the current literature and applies the findings to the university setting.

Videocassette Industry Information Service. *Videocassette Industry Guide.* North Hollywood, Calif., 1972. This first annual guide lists addresses and brief descriptions of companies involved in all aspects of the videocassette industry.

VOLK, J. *The Reston, Virginia, Test of the MITRE Corporation's Interactive Television System.* McLean, Va.: MITRE Corporation, 1971. This report describes a system using standard television receivers as remote (home) computer-driven displays; the signals are transmitted by microwave link and thence by CATV; home terminal users communicate with the computer through their twelve-button push-button phones.

Institutions and Programs

New institutional arrangements are reported by Gillie (1970), Pond (1965), and Schrupp (1971). Innovative ways of teaching academic subjects are described in Blakely and Lappin, 1969; Burnett and Badger, 1970; NASULGC Council, 1968; and Tolley, 1967. The most complete guide to opportunities in continuing education on a state-by-state and community-by-community basis appears in Thomson, 1972.

Special facilities for the urban disadvantaged are discussed by Cohen (1970) and for the general adult population in ERIC Clearinghouse, 1969; and Hunt, 1968. Community colleges are considered by Davis (1970), Gillie (1970), Harlacher (1969), Johnson (1969), and Schrupp (1971). Proprietary schools are covered by Belitsky (1970). Senior college and university programs are illustrated in Baskin, 1972; California State University, 1972; Empire State College, 1971; Harcleroad and Armstrong, 1972; Minnesota Metropolitan State College, 1972; Policy Institute, 1971; and University of California, 1971. Proposals for a national university are reviewed by Madsen, 1966.

Among other types of institution offering educational programs are correctional institutions (Center for Studies in Vocational and Technical Education, 1968, and Collins and Weisberg, 1966); businesses (Craig and Bittel, 1967); the military (Ducey, 1972, and Turner, 1968); government agencies (Bureau of Training, 1971; National Advisory Council, 1972; and Zetterberg, 1969); and libraries (American Library Association, 1972; Gould, 1966; and Reich, 1971). Rossman, 1972, maintains that these and other alternative sources of education involve as many students as does the traditional system.

American Library Association. *A Strategy for Public Library Change: Proposed Public Library Goals-Feasibility Study*. Chicago: American Library Association, 1972. This report analyzes the present status and immediate history of public libraries, discusses their critical problems and goals, and recommends a plan of action so that public libraries become a more integral part of community life and more responsive to user needs.

BASKIN, S. *University Without Walls: First Report.* Yellow Springs, Ohio: Union of Experimenting Colleges and Universities, 1972.

BELITSKY, A. H. *Private Vocational Schools: Their Emerging Role in Post-Secondary Education.* Washington, D.C.: W. E. Upjohn Institute, 1970. (ED042907). A bright forecast of the future of private vocational schools is based on study findings of a total of seven thousand private, profit-making schools serving an estimated 1.5 million students.

BLAKELY, R. J., and LAPPIN, I. M. *New Institutional Arrangements and Organizational Patterns for Continuing Education.* Syracuse, N.Y.: Syracuse University Press, 1969. (ED040313). Two related parts of this study give findings of questionnaire surveys and interviews in ten middle-sized New York State urban areas and findings of a national study based on interviews, visits, and current literature; the national study indicates a general trend in American society toward applying knowledge to solve social problems and in social action. Specific movements in the use of continuing education by non-educational institutions are reported, along with its progress to a more central role in educational institutions; ten steps to improve the field of continuing education are recommended.

Bureau of Training. *Off-Campus Study Centers for Government Employees.* Washington, D.C.: U. S. Civil Service Commission, 1971. This report describes various cooperative arrangements between government agencies and educational institutions to provide educational, career-related opportunities to employees at agency work sites at relatively low cost.

BURNETT, C. W., and BADGER, F. W. *The Learning Climate in the Liberal Arts College: An Annotated Bibliography.* Curriculum Series No. 2. Charleston, West Va.: Morris Harvey College, 1970. Eighty-seven pages of annotated references about innovative ideas are divided into four sections: the liberal arts approach, curriculum, teaching methods and new media, and the teaching-learning process.

California State University and Colleges. *The 1,000-Mile Campus*. Rohnert Park, Calif.: Commission on External Degree Programs, 1972. This document describes various external and special degree programs being implemented throughout the nineteen member institutions.

Center for Studies in Vocational and Technical Education. *Education and Training in Correctional Institutions: Proceedings of a Conference*. Madison: University of Wisconsin, 1968. (ED037534). Reports from the conference appraise the effects of educational and training programs in correctional institutions and emphasize analytical reports, research findings, and project evaluations.

COHEN, A. O. *Human Service Institutes: An Alternative for Professional Higher Education*. New York: College for Human Services, 1970. (ED049460). Based upon the college for human services in New York City, this alternative model includes work study curriculum with a bachelor's degree awarded after two years, with the emphasis placed on involvement in social change as the moral equivalent of research, and a certification process based on job performance.

COLLINS, J. W., JR., and WEISBERG, R. *Training Needs in Correctional Institutions*. Washington, D.C.: Office of Manpower Policy, Evaluation, and Research, 1966. (ED025601). The bulletin presents a profile of characteristics of prison inmates, some of the handicaps they face in the job market, the kinds of jobs held before imprisonment, the training and education available in correctional institutions, and the employment experience of releases.

CRAIG, R. L., and BITTEL, L. R. (Eds.) *Training and Development Handbook*. New York: McGraw-Hill, 1967. (ED016153). This handbook includes materials for the sophisticated manager of a large training staff as well as the fundamentals of training for the beginning or part-time trainer; the levels of training covered range from apprentices to top executives.

DAVIS, H. E. "Bibliography of Innovation and New Curriculum in American Two-Year Colleges, 1966–1969." Unpublished. 1970. (ED044107). The 165 references in this bibliography deal with general, academic, vocational, and miscellaneous curricula.

DENNIS, J. E. *The Other End of Sesame Street.* Washington, D.C.: American Association for Higher Education, 1971. (ED050672). According to this document, by 1976 the University of North America, a confederation of several radically different regional higher education institutions, will be proclaimed; these institutions, starting with the Open University, pioneered in Great Britain and Japan, will bring a multimedia approach to continuing higher education.

DUCEY, A. L. "Higher Education for the Military." *Change,* 1972, *4,* 27–30. This article presents some of the many programs in the armed forces by which servicemen can get high school and college education or credit or both; the problems of degree attainment are also discussed.

Empire State College. *Bulletin.* Saratoga Springs, N.Y., 1972. This new college with headquarters at Saratoga Springs and learning centers throughout the state offers degrees without residential requirements. New students enroll each month and work with a mentor in developing a learning contract which defines the degree program and the basis for evaluation. Community resources are used for instruction.

ERIC Clearinghouse on Adult Education. *Residential Adult Education: Current Information Sources, No. 25.* Syracuse, N.Y., 1969. (ED032449). This annotated bibliography contains 113 entries, covering the residential method; historical reviews; instructional methods; directories of facilities; program descriptions from such areas as professional education, management training, inservice training, sensitivity training, labor education, family life education, and the contemporary folk schools; and clientele surveys.

EURICH, N., and SCHWENKMEYER, B. *Great Britain's Open University: First Chance, Second Chance, or Last Chance?* New York: Academy for Educational Development, 1971. This pamphlet describes the history and operation of Britain's Open University and places it in the context of the British system.

GILLIE, A. C. *Essays on Occupational Education in the Two-Year College.* University Park: Pennsylvania State University, Department of Vocational Education, 1970. (ED037210). These essays discuss the place of occupational education in two-year colleges and in society and include ideas on curriculum patterns and the future of occupationai education.

GOULD, S. B. "New Era for the Public Library." ALA *Bulletin,* 1966, *60,* 585–590. This article argues that the public library can and must become a vital force in shaping the intellectual, cultural, and humanist developments of society—increased leisure time and advances in science and technology make the need more acute.

HARCLEROAD, F. F., and ARMSTRONG, R. J. *New Dimensions of Continuing Studies Programs in the Massachusetts State College System.* Iowa City, Iowa: American College Testing Program, 1972. This report recommends a new institution, called Open College, which awards degrees and offers instruction via broadcast television, correspondence, and regional learning centers. Credit by examination would also be available.

HARLACHER, E. L. *The Community Dimension of the Community College.* Englewood Cliffs, N.J.: Prentice-Hall, 1969. (ED047226). This volume analyzes the relationship between the community service programs and organizational patterns.

HOOPER, R. *The Open University: A Report.* Albany: State University of New York, Office of Educational Communications, 1970. The author, a member of the BBC Open University staff, discusses a number of problems caused by mass-oriented, television courses of the type planned; conceptual and fundamental questions, as well as practical and logistical questions are raised, and solutions are offered when they are thought available.

HUNT, B. *An Introduction to the Community School Concept.* Portland, Ore.: Northwest Regional Educational Laboratory, 1968. (ED030165). This document attempts to show that community schools have something for everyone, provide opportunities for citizens to apply solutions to problems, and help maintain open channels of communication with the community.

JOHNSON, L. B. *Islands of Innovation Expanding: Changes in the Community College.* Beverly Hills, Calif.: Glencoe Press, 1969. A number of new programs found in community colleges are described and analyzed. The spread of these innovations is also discussed.

MACLURE, S. "England's Open University." *Change,* 1971, *3,* 62–66. Written in a journalistic style, this article deals with the political history behind the Open University, as well as its operation and implications.

MADSEN, D. *The National University: Enduring Dream of the USA.* Detroit: Wayne State University Press, 1966. This historical account traces, from the time of George Washington to the present day, proposals for a national university, an idea that has arisen in various forms many times but never been accepted.

Minnesota Metropolitan State College. MMSC *News.* St. Paul: Metropolitan State College, 1972. This upper division and first graduate degree institution has no campus but uses community facilities. Degree requirements are developed by contract with each student.

NASULGC Council on Extension, Committee on Program Innovation and Action Oriented Research. *1968 Report: Part One, Program Innovations.* Washington, D.C.: National Association of State Universities and Land Grant Colleges, 1968. (ED032463). Ninety-one program innovations by NASULGC member institutions are described.

National Advisory Council on Extension and Continuing

Education. *A Question of Stewardship: A Study of the Federal Role in Higher Continuing Education.* Washington, D.C., 1972. This sixth annual report to the President contains recommendations for federal action regarding continuing education and the first comprehensive survey of all non-military, federally supported programs in this field; titles of all programs, cost data, and brief descriptions of selected programs are given.

Policy Institute of Syracuse University Research Corporation. *Newsletter: External Degree Programs.* Syracuse, N.Y.: Syracuse University, 1971. A consortium of fifteen academic institutions in central New York has established counseling centers with "learning consultants" who provide guidance, referral, assessment of previous learning experiences, and validation of learning opportunities in nonacademic institutions.

POND, M. T. *Occupational Education and Training for Tomorrow's World of Work: No. 5, University Programs.* Columbus: Ohio State University, 1965. (ED014546). This document presents a classification system and descriptions of university-level occupational programs, ranging in length from one-day conferences to two-year certificate programs.

REICH, D. L. "A Public Library Becomes a CLEP Learning Center." *College Board Review,* 1971, *81,* 29–31. This article describes a program in which the Dallas Public Library and Southern Methodist University cooperate to furnish tutorial and counseling help for people interested in taking CLEP exams.

ROSSMAN, M. "How We Learn Today in America." *Saturday Review,* August 19, 1972, *55* (34), 27–33. This article describes the growth, origins, characteristics, and future of an alternative system of higher education.

SCHRUPP, H. A. "A 'Career Ladder' Approach to Junior College Curriculum." Seminar Paper, 1971. (ED051815). The "career ladder" approach is described as career guidance and curriculum programs with exit points to seek employment at any time or to continue education or to do both.

THOMSON, F. C. *The New York Times Guide to Continuing Education in America.* New York: Quadrangle Books, 1972. This guide lists classroom courses, listed by states and cities, and correspondence courses; it also gives information on CLEP exams and the importance of learning.

TOLLEY, W. P. *American Universities in Transition and the New Role of Adult Education.* England: Leeds University, 1967. (ED019556). This document maintains that the greatest trend, with implications for the whole university, is continuing education, which has grown because of more leisure time, the paperback revolution, preparation for retirement, and the demand for new skills in business and industry.

TURNER, C. P. (Ed.) *A Guide to the Evaluation of Educational Experiences in the Armed Services: Formal Service School Courses, Credit and Advanced Standing by Examination.* Washington, D.C.: American Council on Education, 1968. (ED029240). Devoted largely to credit recommendations at the collegiate level, this guide lists formal residential courses and describes two national testing programs, GED and CLEP, through which military personnel may receive appraisal.

University of California. *Degree Programs for the Part-time Student: A Proposal.* A report of the President's task force on the extended university. Berkeley: Office of the President, 1971. This report contains recommendations for part-time, special degree programs at University of California campuses, as well as in-depth analyses of existing programs at ten other universities.

ZETTERBERG, H. L. *Museums and Adult Education.* New York: Augustus M. Kelley, 1969. (ED042085). This report gives a brief history of museums, suggestions on how to provide educational services for adults, and relationships of adult education with other functions, such as youth education and scholarly research.

Credit and Evaluation

There have been several developments in the evaluation of educational progress and awarding of credit (Boyd and Shimberg,

1971; Sharon, 1971). A major direction has been credit by examination, as exemplified by the College-Level Examination Program (College Entrance Examination Board, 1973) and the College Proficiency Examination Program of the New York Board of Regents.

Another major breakthrough is that non-traditional students not only can earn individual credits but can earn degrees more easily. Several references in the general section provide descriptions of such programs, while others can be found in this section (Commission on Higher Education, 1972; Furniss, 1971; Thomas A. Edison College, 1972; Traver, 1969). Blakely (1972) and Troutt (1971) discuss some of the implications and issues.

BLAKELY, E. J. "The External Degree: No Panacea for the Poor." *University of Pittsburgh Times,* May 4, 1972. This article points out potential pitfalls for the poor and disadvantaged with overreliance on external degrees and suggests ways to avoid these obstacles.

BOYD, J. L., and SHIMBERG, B. *Handbook of Performance Testing: A Practical Guide for Test Makers.* Princeton, N.J.: Educational Testing Service, 1971. Brief discussions of the history and philosophy of performance tests are followed by a step-by-step procedure for developing such a test and a listing and description of known performance tests.

College Entrance Examination Board. CLEP *General Examinations and Subject Examinations: Descriptions and Sample Questions.* New York, 1973. This booklet with brief descriptions of and sample questions from the five general and thirty-four subject exams of the CLEP programs, is designed for persons interested in taking these tests in order to gain college credit.

Commission for Higher Education. *Improvement of Opportunity in Higher Education: Alternative Modes for Earning Undergraduate Degrees and College Credit.* Hartford, Conn., 1973. This report describes current practices in the state of Connecticut and in the nation and recommends further action, including a more intensive study of needs and resources and a model, with cost estimates, for granting credit by examination and external degrees.

Educational Testing Service. *Test Collection Bulletin.* Princeton, N.J., 1967–1973. This quarterly digest presents brief abstracts on acquiring complete collections of tests and other measurement devices.

FURNISS, W. T. *Degrees for Non-Traditional Students.* Washington, D.C.: American Council on Education, 1971. Using the example of the problems an army sergeant would have obtaining a B.A., the author describes barriers to higher education for non-traditional students, explains deficiences of traditional and continuing education, and describes some new degree plans.

SHARON, A. T. "The Use and Validity of the GED and CLEP Examinations in Higher Education." Paper presented at the Annual Convention of the American Personnel and Guidance Association, Atlantic City, N.J., 1971. (ED054194). The use and validity of these tests are discussed as measures of non-traditional education for adults.

Thomas A. Edison College. *College Proficiency Examination Program.* Trenton, N.J.: Thomas A. Edison College, 1972. This new college offers no instruction but awards degrees based on previous college credit, successfully completed examinations, and nonresidential learning experiences. It cooperates closely with the New York Regents External Degree Program.

TRAVER, J. L. *A Study of Adult Degree Programs in Selected American Colleges and Universities.* Salt Lake City: University of Utah, 1969. (ED038575). This study investigates the extent of interest and needs of adult citizens of the greater metropolitan Salt Lake City area, insofar as adult degree programs were concerned, and makes a thorough analysis of adult degree programs currently in operation in American colleges and universities.

TROUTT, R. *Special Degree Programs for Adults: Exploring*

Non-Traditional Degree Programs in Higher Education. Iowa City, Iowa: American College Testing Program, 1971. The rationale for special degrees for adults, as well as the history and future of such degrees, are discussed by the Dean of the College of Liberal Studies at the University of Oklahoma, who includes a detailed description of his program.

University of the State of New York. *The Regents External Degree: Handbook of Information for Candidates.* Albany, 1972. This descriptive brochure has information about special degree programs which accept credit by examination, from any accredited college, from the Armed Forces Institute, and through special oral, written, and performance examinations. Applicants need not be residents of New York State.

Governmental Regulation and Voluntary Accreditation

General introductions to state regulation appear in Education Commission of the States, 1972; and Williams, 1970; while introductions to voluntary accreditation can be found in National Commission on Accrediting (no date), Puffer and others (1970); and Selden (1960). The impact of accreditation on adult and continuing education is illustrated by Andrews, 1972.

ANDREWS, G. J. *A Study of Public Service in Higher Education: A Status Study of Accreditation in Adult and Continuing Education Programs.* Unpublished dissertation. North Carolina State University at Raleigh, 1972. This sudy presents a survey of the interest of the 561 member colleges and universities of the Southern Association of Colleges and Schools in adult and continuing education, including the impact of the 1961 Standard Nine accrediting standards on "Special Activities" that led to a major revision in 1971.

Education Commission of the States. *Higher Education in the States.* May–June 1972, *3* (4), 65–120; and September 1972, *3* (7), 177–189. These summary tables of the statutes, amendments, and constitutional provisions—in each of the fifty states—

that form the legal bases for the establishment of educational corporations and private postsecondary institutions provide the most comprehensive data yet compiled on state regulation of higher education.

Education Commission of the States. *Model State Legislation: Report of the Task Force on Model State Legislation for Approval of Postsecondary Educational Institutions and Authorization to Grant Degrees.* Report 39. Denver, June 1973. Recommendations to the states aimed at improved regulation of postsecondary education and the maintenance of adequate standards are offered in the form of a proposed "Postsecondary Educational Authorization Act," drafted by a nine-member task force chaired by State Representative Tom Jensen of Tennessee.

MESSERSMITH, L. E., and MEDSKER, L. L. *Accreditation of Vocational-Technical Curricula in Postsecondary Institutions.* Berkeley: Center for Research and Development in Higher Education, 1969. A survey of 313 administrators of two-year institutions; the survey was requested by the National Commission on Accrediting and the American Association of Junior Colleges; it aimed to solve the conflict between general accreditation by regional associations and specialized accreditation by professional agencies.

MILLER, J. W. *Organizational Structure of Nongovernmental Postsecondary Accreditation: Relationship to Uses of Accreditation.* Washington, D.C.: National Commission on Accrediting, 1973. Recommendations about the future organization of accreditation are based on responses from accreditation experts to a Delphi-technique survey; early chapters contain an excellent summary of the present status of accreditation in higher education.

National Commission on Accrediting. *Procedures of Accrediting Education in the Professions.* Washington, D.C., n.d. A periodically-updated series of looseleaf summaries of procedures is followed by specialized accrediting agencies recognized by the National Commission on Accrediting, with each sheet devoted to a particular field from architecture and art to theology and veterinary medicine.

PUFFER, C. E., STEFFENS, H. W., LOMBARDI, J., and PFNISTER, A. O. *Regional Accreditation of Institutions of Higher Education: A Study Prepared for the Federation of Regional Accrediting Commissions of Higher Education*. Chicago: The Federation, July 1970. This exhaustive study of the standards and practices of the seven commissions of the six regional associations that accredit colleges and universities contains a multitude of facts from the associations, opinions from administrators of regionally accredited institutions, and informed recommendations by the authors.

SELDEN, W. K. *Accreditation: A Struggle over Standards in Higher Education*. New York: Harper and Row, 1960. Although over a decade old, this small volume remains the best introduction to the field of accreditation, putting recent problems in historical and global perspective.

Study of Accreditation of Selected Health Educational Programs. *Commission Report*. Washington, D.C.: National Commission on Accrediting, May 1972. This report, following an eighteen-month study by William K. Selden, Merry W. Miller, and Karen L. Brimm under the direction of a nationally representative commission, contains far-reaching recommendations for reorganization of acceditation in the health fields.

U. S. Office of Education, Bureau of Higher Education, Accreditation and Institutional Eligibility Staff. *Nationally Recognized Accrediting Agencies and Associations; Criteria and Procedures for Listing by the U.S. Commisioner of Education and Current List*. Washington, D.C.: U.S. Department of Health, Education, and Welfare, Office of Education, March 1972. This brochure explains the federal role in recognizing accrediting agencies, lists the standards it employs in recognition, and contains the names of agencies recognized at date of publication.

WARD, C. F. *The State of Accreditation and Evaluation of Post-secondary Occupational Education in the United States*. Center Research and Development Report No. 12. Raleigh: Center for Occupational Education, North Carolina State University, 1970. The most comprehensive study yet undertaken of occupational accreditation focuses on vocational and technical programs beyond high school.

WILLIAMS, R. L. "Legal Bases for Establishment of Private Institutions of Higher Education," *The North Central Association Quarterly,* Autumn 1970, *44* (3), 291–298. This survey of state regulations prior to that conducted by the Education Commission of the States (see U.S. Office of Education, 1972) categorizes the states into three types in terms of their regulations regarding the incorporation of colleges and universities.

⚞⚞⚞⚞⚞⚞⚞ Appendix A ⚟⚟⚟⚟⚟⚟⚟

Survey of
Adult Learning

⚞⚞⚞⚞⚞⚞⚞⚞⚞⚞⚞⚞⚟⚟⚟⚟⚟⚟⚟⚟⚟⚟⚟⚟

*T*he sample was divided into geographic regions of the country according to the Census Bureau categorization of states scheme: *"Northeast:"*—the New England states and New Jersey, New York, and Pennsylvania. *"North-central:"*—Illinois, Indiana, Iowa, Kansas, Michigan, Minnesota, Missouri, Nebraska, North Dakota, Ohio, South Dakota, and Wisconsin. *"South:"*—Alabama, Arkansas, Delaware, District of Columbia, Florida, Georgia, Kentucky, Louisiana, Maryland, Mississippi, North Carolina, Oklahoma, South Carolina, Tennessee, Texas, Virginia, and West Virginia. *"West:"*—Arizona, California, Colorado, Idaho, Montana, Nevada, New Mexico, Oregon, Utah, Washington, and Wyoming.

The sample was also divided into urban and rural sub-samples: "urban" included all urban or central city residents in Standard Metropolitan Statistical Areas (SMSA's) as defined by the Bureau of Census, and also residents of cities in counties with a minimum population of 50,000 in 1970; "rural" respondents included all residents of sparsely populated areas and residents living outside of cities and urban areas in SMSA's.

Percentages may not add to 100 because of rounding or

219

because more than one response was possible for some questions. These figures supersede those reported in *Diversity by Design,* which were based on preliminary data. The tabulations on the left are based on a weighted N of 3910.

Section I

In this section, we want to find out about your interest in learning new things.

1. Is there anything in particular that you'd like to know more about, or would like to learn how to do better? If yes, circle 1; if no, circle 2.

Percent of 3910   *N*

77   3001   1. Yes—*go on to Question 2*
23   909   2. No—*please skip to Section II, Question 14*

2. Listed below is a wide variety of subjects and skills which people might wish to study or learn. If you had your choice, and didn't have to worry about cost or other responsibilities, which ones interest you enough to spend a fair amount of time on them? Circle the numbers next to *all* the subjects or areas on this page and the next which you would be interested in learning.

AREAS OF LEARNING

Percent of 3001*

11   1. Agriculture, farming
6   2. Architecture
13   3. Basic education, such as reading, basic math, writing
8   4. Biological sciences, such as biology, botany
26   5. Business skills, such as typing, accounting, bookkeeping
17   6. Child development, such as parenthood, child care
4   7. Citizenship, Americanization
12   8. Commercial art, such as design, fashion
14   9. Community problems and organizations
14   10. Computer science, such as data processing, programming
15   11. Consumer education, such as buying, credit

* 3001 = number responding "yes" to Question 1.

10	12. Cosmetology, such as beauticians
27	13. Crafts, such as weaving, pottery, woodworking
13	14. Creative writing
10	15. Education, teacher training
9	16. Engineering
8	17. English language training
15	18. Environmental studies, such as ecology, conservation
16	19. Fine and visual arts, such as art, photography, filmmaking
11	20. Flight training
26	21. Gardening, flower arranging
11	22. Great Books
25	23. Home repairs
16	24. Humanities, such as literature, philosophy, art/music appreciation
22	25. Industrial trades, such as welding, carpentry, electronics
29	26. Investment, such as money, finance
4	27. Journalism
16	28. Languages, such as French, German, Chinese
12	29. Law
16	30. Management skills, such as business administration, hotel management
10	31. Medical technology, such as x-ray technician, dental assistant
5	32. Medicine, dentistry
13	33. Nursing
7	34. Occult sciences, such as astrology, tarot
14	35. Performing arts, such as dance, music, drama
15	36. Personal psychology, such as encounter groups, psychology of everyday life
26	37. Physical fitness and self defense, such as exercises, karate
6	38. Physical sciences, such as physics, math, chemistry, astronomy
12	39. Public affairs, such as current events, world problems
11	40. Public speaking
15	41. Religious studies, such as Bible, yoga, meditation
16	42. Safety, such as first aid, water safety
7	43. Salesmanship
27	44. Sewing, cooking

9   45. Social sciences, such as ethnic studies, economics, government
28   46. Sports and games, such as golf, bridge, swimming, boating
19   47. Technical skills, such as auto mechanics, t.v. repair, drafting
22   48. Travel, living in foreign country
3   49. Other, please specify ....

3. Of the areas listed in question 2, which would you *most like* to study or learn? Please write in the names or numbers of your first, second, and third choices in the spaces below.

First Choice ....

Second Choice ....

Third Choice ....

AREAS OF LEARNING—FIRST CHOICE

Percent
of
3001

3   1. Agriculture, farming
1   2. Architecture
4   3. Basic education, such as reading, basic math, writing
1   4. Biological sciences, such as biology, botany
9   5. Business skills, such as typing, accounting, bookkeeping
4   6. Child development, such as parenthood, child care
1   7. Citizenship, Americanization
2   8. Commercial art, such as design, fashion
1   9. Community problems and organizations
2   10. Computer science, such as data processing, programming
1   11. Consumer education, such as buying, credit
2   12. Cosmetology, such as beauticians
3   13. Crafts, such as weaving, pottery, woodworking
1   14. Creative writing
1   15. Education, teacher training
2   16. Engineering
1   17. English language training
1   18. Environmental studies, such as ecology, conservation
2   19. Fine and visual arts, such as art, photography, filmmaking
2   20. Flight training
2   21. Gardening, flower arranging

Percent
of
3001

0	22. Great Books
2	23. Home repairs
2	24. Humanities, such as literature, philosophy, art/music appreciation
4	25. Industrial trades, such as welding, carpentry, electronics
4	26. Investment, such as money, finance
0	27. Journalism
2	28. Languages, such as French, German, Chinese
2	29. Law
3	30. Management skills, such as business administration, hotel management
2	31. Medical technology, such as x-ray technician, dental assistant
1	32. Medicine, dentistry
4	33. Nursing
0	34. Occult sciences, such as astrology, tarot
2	35. Performing arts, such as dance, music, drama
2	36. Personal psychology, such as encounter groups, psychology of everyday life
1	37. Physical fitness and self defense, such as exercise, karate
0	38. Physical sciences, such as physics, math, chemistry, astronomy
0	39. Public affairs, such as current events, world problems
0	40. Public speaking
3	41. Religious studies, such as Bible, yoga, meditation
0	42. Safety, such as first aid, water safety
1	43. Salesmanship
4	44. Sewing, cooking
1	45. Social sciences, such as ethnic studies, economics, government
2	46. Sports and games, such as golf, bridge, swimming, boating
5	47. Technical skills, such as auto mechanics, t.v. repair, drafting
2	48. Travel, living in foreign county
1	49. Other, please specify ....

*Please answer Questions 4 through 10 by thinking about the area
you listed first in Question 3.*

4. Would you like to get credit toward a degree or some other certificate of satisfactory completion for learning this area? Circle *one* of the following numbers.

Percent of 3001

32	1. No, doesn't matter, don't care
21	2. Certificate of satisfactory completion
5	3. Credit toward high school diploma
20	4. Credit toward skill certificate or license
4	5. Credit toward a two-year college degree (AA)
8	6. Credit toward a four-year college degree (BA)
5	7. Credit toward an advanced degree (MA, PhD)
1	8. Other, describe ....

5. There are many ways in which people can take a course of study. How would you want to learn this area if you could do it any way you wanted? Circle the *one* which best describes how you would like to study this field.

Percent of 3001

28	1. Lectures or classes
13	2. Short term conferences, institutes or workshops
8	3. Individual lessons from a private teacher
8	4. Discussion groups, informal book club or study group
2	5. Travel-study program
21	6. On-the-job training, internship
3	7. Correspondence course
1	8. T.V. or video cassettes
1	9. Radio, records, or audio cassettes
3	10. Work on a group action project
7	11. Study on my own, no formal instruction
0	12. Other, please specify ....

6. There are many places people can go to study or learn. Where would you want to go to learn the area you chose first in Question 3? Circle *one* choice.

Percent of 3001

16	1. Public high school, day or evening
10	2. Public two-year college or technical institute
8	3. Private vocational, trade or business school
8	4. Four-year college or university

3	5. Graduate school
10	6. Community run "free school"
5	7. Business or industrial site
5	8. Employer
2	9. Religious institution or group
3	10. Community or social organization, such as YMCA
4	11. Correspondence school
2	12. Government agency (federal, state or local)
1	13. Library or other cultural institution, such as a museum
3	14. Fine or performing arts or crafts studio
1	15. Recreational or sports group
5	16. Individual instructor
10	17. Home
1	18. Other, describe _____

7. How often would you want to attend classes, training sessions, or study on your own? Circle *only one*.

*Percent
of
3001*

23	1. One evening a week
26	2. Two or more evenings a week
6	3. One morning or afternoon a week
11	4. Two or more mornings or afternoons a week
2	5. One full day a week
9	6. Two or more full days a week
2	7. One weekend day a week
0	8. Both weekend days a week
8	9. One or two evenings a week plus occasional weekends
4	10. One or two evenings a week plus one or two weeks during the summer
2	11. Two weeks to a month during the summer
4	12. Other, specify _____

8. How long would you want to continue your training or study in this area? Circle *only one*.

*Percent
of
3001*

2	1. Less than one month
15	2. One to three months
17	3. Four to six months
5	4. Seven to nine months
17	5. Nine months to a year

17   6. One to two years
19   7. More than two years

9.   Still thinking of your first choice in Question 3, how important is *each* of the following reasons to you for wanting to learn the area? Respond in columns A, B, or C for each reason listed below. Please circle *one* number in each row.

	A Not at all Important	B Somewhat Important	C Very Important *Percent of* *3001*
Help get a new job			25
Help to advance in present job			17
Become better informed, personal enjoyment and enrichment			56
Meet new people			19
Meet requirements for getting into an educational program			13
Be a better parent, husband or wife			30
Get away from the routine of daily living			19
Work toward certification or licensing			27
Better understand community problems			17
Be better able to serve my church			12
Meet the requirements of my employer, profession or someone in authority			24
Become a more effective citizen			26
Work toward a degree			21
Learn more about my own background and culture			14
Feel a sense of belonging			20
Curiosity, learn for the sake of learning			35
Become a happier person			37
Work toward solutions of problems such as discrimination and pollution			16
Get away from personal problems			11
Improve my spiritual well-being			19
Other _____			4

10.   If there were a charge for this course or activity, how much would you be willing to pay?

Percent
of
3001

23   1. Nothing
30   2. Less than $50

20 3. Between $50 and $100
9 4. $100 to $200
13 5. More than $200

11. Many things stop people from taking a course of study or learning a skill. Circle *all* those listed below that you feel are important in keeping you from learning what you want to learn.

Percent
of
3001

53 1. Cost, including books, learning materials, child care, transportation, as well as tuition
46 2. Not enough time
21 3. Amount of time required to complete program
5 4. No way to get credit for a degree
15 5. Strict attendance requirements
5 6. Don't know what I'd like to learn or what it would lead to
7 7. No place to study or practice
11 8. No child care
16 9. Courses I want aren't scheduled when I can attend
35 10. Don't want to go to school full-time
16 11. No information about places or people offering what I want
8 12. No transportation
10 13. Too much red tape in getting enrolled
3 14. Hesitate to seem too ambitious
3 15. Friends or family don't like the idea
32 16. Home responsibilities
28 17. Job responsibilities
9 18. Not enough energy and stamina
17 19. Afraid that I'm too old to begin
12 20. Low grades in the past, not confident of my ability
6 21. Don't meet requirements to begin program
12 22. Courses I want don't seem to be available
9 23. Don't enjoy studying
6 24. Tired of going to school, tired of classrooms
2 25. Other, describe _____

12. If you were to complete the area of learning you listed first in Question 3, would you want to have any of the agencies or persons listed below informed about your completion of or achievement in this activity? Circle *as many* as you want to know about your study or training.

*Percent
of
3001*

10	1. One or more universities, colleges, or other schools
20	2. My employer
30	3. Possible employers
12	4. One or more government agencies
7	5. Award granting agencies for scholarships, grants
13	6. A licensing agency
6	7. Certain teachers or professors
10	8. Certain people in my community
38	9. My family
27	10. My friends
53	11. Myself
1	12. Other, please describe ....

13. People often need information and advice before beginning a course of study or during a course. Some people find it most helpful to talk with professional counselors at a school or college or at a community, government or social agency. Others would rather talk with employers, friends or members of their family. With whom, if anybody, would you want to discuss *each* one of the matters listed below? Respond in colunms A, B, C, D, or E for each kind of problem. Please circle *one* number in each row.

	A Counselor at a school or college Percent of 3001	B Counselor at social, government or community agency Percent of 3001	C Employer Percent of 3001	D Friends or family Percent of 3001	E Nobody Percent of 3001
Availability of educational programs	39	16	5	8	17
Paying for studies	15	15	7	22	24
Enrollment procedures	46	14	2	5	16
Planning a degree program	38	6	2	5	31
Choosing a course	35	9	2	12	24
Improving study habits or techniques	39	8	2	8	26
Employment possibilities as a result of training	16	17	19	5	25
Uses of training or study	24	15	12	7	23
Other, please describe	2	1	1	1	12

Section II

Now we are interested in your actual education experiences.

14. Are you enrolled in school or college at the present time?

Percent of 3910

0	1. Yes, full-time
4	2. Yes, part-time (half-time or less)
94	3. No

15. Circle the *one* item below that shows the amount of formal education you have had.*

Percent of 3910

14	1. Eight years of school or less
19	2. One to three years of high school
38	3. High school diploma
4	4. Business or trade school
3	5. One year of college
3	6. Two years of college
1	7. Two-year college degree
2	8. Three years of college
5	9. Four-year college degree
3	10. Some graduate or professional school
2	11. First postgraduate degree (law degree, MA, MSW)
1	12. Doctorate degree (PhD, MD, EdD)

16. If you had the opportunity, what educational degrees or certificates would you like to get in the next ten years? Circle *all* those you want.

Percent of 3910

39	1. None
16	2. High school diploma
22	3. Certificate or license needed for an occupation, such as electrician, beautician, real estate salesman
9	4. Two-year college degree (AA)
12	5. Four-year college degree (BA)

* For statistical analyses reported in this volume, respondents to items 4 through 8 were combined as "some postsecondary education" and to items 9 through 12 as "4-year college graduate."

8   6. Master's degree (MA)
4   7. Doctoral degree (PhD, MD, etc.)
1   8. Other, please specify ....

17.   Within the past 12 months, have you received (or are you receiving) instruction in *any* of the following subjects or skills? Please include
evening classes, extension courses, correspondence courses, on-the-job
training, private lessons, independent study, T.V. courses or anything
else like that. Please do not include subjects you have studied as a full-
time student. Circle *all* that apply.

Percent of 3910	*Percent of 1207**	
1	4	1. Adult basic education, such as reading, basic math
1	3	2. Citizenship, Americanization
1	3	3. Agriculture, farming
2	7	4. High school level courses
3	11	5. College level courses
2	5	6. Graduate level courses
6	18	7. Technical and vocational skills, such as typing, auto mechanics
3	10	8. Managerial skills, such as hotel management, business administration
3	9	9. Professional skills, such as law, teaching, medicine
1	4	10. Civics and public affairs, such as consumer education, ecology
4	14	11. Religion, such as Bible study, ethics, meditation
3	10	12. Safety, such as first aid, water safety
4	13	13. Home and family living, such as home repairs, gardening, child care
4	11	14. Personal development, such as personality, physical fitness
8	25	15. Hobbies and handicrafts, such as photography, weaving, music
4	13	16. Sports and recreation, such as bridge, boating, golf
2	7	17. Other, describe ....

* 1207 = number who circled one or more of the areas in Question
17 (31 percent of all respondents).

If you circled one or more of the areas in Question 17, please answer Questions 18 through 25; if you circled none of the areas, please skip to Section III, Question 26.

18.   Consider the area circled in Question 17 on which you spent the most time in the past 12 months. How was this course or activity conducted? Circle the *one* which best describes how you learned this area.

*Percent
of
1207*

35	1. Lectures or classes
8	2. Short term conferences, institutes or workshops
6	3. Individual lessons from a private teacher
4	4. Discussion groups, book club or study group
0	5. Travel-study program
14	6. On-the-job training, internship
5	7. Correspondence course
0	8. T.V. or video cassettes
0	9. Records or audio cassettes
2	10. Work on a group action project
17	11. Study on my own, no formal instruction
2	12. Other, please specify ....

19.   Where did you go for this course or activity? Circle *only one.*

*Percent
of
1207*

9	1. Public high school, day or evening
6	2. Public two-year college or technical institute
3	3. Private vocational, trade or business school
6	4. Four-year college or university
2	5. Graduate school
3	6. Community run "free school"
5	7. Business or industrial site
13	8. Employer
6	9. Religious institution or group
6	10. Community or social organization, such as YMCA
2	11. Correspondence school
5	12. Government agency (federal, state or local)
2	13. Library or other cultural institution, such as museum
0	14. Fine or performing arts or crafts studio
2	15. Recreational or sports group
4	16. Individual instructor

17   17. Home

2   18. Other, please describe ....

20.   What kind of credit did you get (or do you expect to get) from this course or activity?

Percent
of
1207

61   1. No formal credit

15   2. Certificate of satisfactory completion

4   3. Credit toward high school diploma

7   4. Credit toward a skill certificate or license

2   5. Credit toward a two-year college degree (AA)

3   6. Credit toward a four-year college degree (BA, BS)

2   7. Credit toward an advanced degree (MA, PhD, etc.)

2   8. Other, please specify ....

21.   How many hours a week on the average did you devote to this course or activity?

Percent
of
1207

19   1. Less than two hours a week

33   2. Two to four hours a week

44   3. Five or more hours a week

22.   How long did this course or activity run?

Percent
of
1207

12   1. Less than one month

25   2. One to three months

16   3. Four to six months

9   4. Seven to nine months

30   5. More than nine months

23.   Did you complete this course or activity?

Percent
of
1207

49   1. Yes

33   2. No, still taking course

10   3. No, stopped taking course

24.   Who paid for this course or activity?

Percent
of
1207

31   1. Course was free

39	2. Myself or family
18	3. Employer
4	4. Other, describe ....

25. Why did you take this course or activity? Circle *all* that apply.

*Percent
of
1207*

18	1. Help get a new job
25	2. Help to advance in present job
55	3. Become better informed, personal enjoyment and enrichment
18	4. Meet new people
4	5. Meet requirements for getting into an educational program
19	6. Be a better parent, husband or wife
19	7. Get away from the routine of daily living
14	8. Work toward certification or licensing
9	9. Better understand community problems
10	10. Be better able to serve my church
27	11. Meet the requirements of my employer, profession or someone in authority
11	12. Become a more effective citizen
9	13. Work toward a degree
8	14. Learn more about my own background and culture
9	15. Feel a sense of belonging
32	16. Curiosity, learn for the sake of learning
26	17. Become a happier person
9	18. Work toward solution of problems, such as discrimination or pollution
7	19. Get away from personal problems
13	20. Improve my spiritual well-being
2	21. Other, please describe ....

Section III

BACKGROUND INFORMATION

26. Here are some reasons people have given for not taking more courses or instruction. Circle *all* those reasons that apply to you.

*Percent
of
3910*

19	1. I'd be interested in taking some type of course, but there's nothing like that available around here
3	2. The courses I've heard about sound pretty dull
5	3. I can learn all I need to know without taking courses to do it
37	4. I'm much too busy with other things right now, and just wouldn't have the time
15	5. I'm interested in a lot of things, but I really don't enjoy studying
31	6. Right now, I just couldn't afford it
17	7. I've never thought about taking a special course
7	8. Other, please describe ....

27.   Indicate your sex.

*Percent
of
3910*

52	1. Female
48	2. Male

28.   Your age.

*Percent
of
3910*

18	1. Under 25
14	2. 25–29
12	3. 30–34
22	4. 35–44
23	5. 45–54
12	6. 55 and over

29.   Your race

*Percent
of
3910*

87	1. White
10	2. Black, Negro
1	3. Latin-American, Chicano, Puerto Rican
1	4. Asian, Oriental
0	5. Native American, American Indian
0	6. Other, please specify ....

30.   What is your marital status?

*Percent
of
3910*

12	1. Single
79	2. Married
3	3. Widowed
5	4. Divorced, separated

31.   How many children, 17 years or younger, do you have?

*Percent
of
3910*

20	1. One
21	2. Two
10	3. Three
5	4. Four
5	5. Five or more
36	6. None

32.   Approximately what was the combined income of you and your spouse (if married) last year (before taxes)?

*Percent
of
3910*

12	1. Less than $3,000
7	2. $3,000 to $4,999
8	3. $5,000 to $6,999
6	4. $7,000 to $7,999
11	5. $8,000 to $9,999
23	6. $10,000 to $14,999
13	7. $15,000 to $24,999
4	8. $25,000 and over

33.   Did you have any paid job as of May 15, 1972?

*Percent
of
3910*

55	1. Yes, a full-time job
9	2. Yes, a part-time job
34	3. No

34.   Please write in below a short description of the kind of work you usually do (for example: electrical engineer, stock clerk, typist, student, homemaker).

These descriptions were coded according to the following Bureau of Census classifications:

Percent
of
3910

20	1. Housewife
7	2. Unskilled worker or laborer
13	3. Semiskilled worker
2	4. Service worker
15	5. Skilled worker or craftsman
17	6. Sales or clerical worker
7	7. Owner, manager or partner of small business; lower-level administrator
6	8. Profession requiring a bachelor's degree
1	9. Owner or high-level executive of a large business or governmental agency
2	10. Profession requiring an advanced degree
2	11. No usual occupation
0	12. Student

❧❧❧❧❧❧❧ Appendix B ❧❧❧❧❧❧❧

Inventory of Institutional Resources

❧❧❧❧❧❧❧❧❧❧❧❧❧❧❧❧❧❧❧❧❧❧❧❧❧❧

*I*talics indicate categories compiled from survey responses but not contained in the survey instrument. Percentages may not add to 100 because more than one response was possible for some questions or because the percentage that did not respond to a specific question is not listed. These figures supersede those reported in *Diversity by Design,* which were based on preliminary data.

Part I. Non-Traditional Programs (641 programs)

The Commission needs to know if your institution offers any specially-designed programs *based on new or unconventional forms of education free of the time or place limitations of traditional classroom instruction.* They may be unconventional in any of the following ways:

Type of Student Enrolled—such as working adults, housewives, young and older adults motivated to study independently, or others who cannot easily come to the campus or do not wish to devote full-time to classroom work.

Location of Learning Experience—such as regional center offerings, field work, home study, or other off-campus programs.

Method of Instruction—such as non-lecture or non-classroom teaching and learning methods, distinctive from those common in higher education.

The content of the program may either be different from or the same as conventional courses or programs; but in either case it must be a program offered for non-typical groups of students or at an unusual location or in a novel way.

If your institution currently offers *no* such program, please skip to Question 29 inside.

If your institution is planning such a program, there will be an opportunity for you to report such plans on the last page of this form.

PROGRAMS TO EXCLUDE

You DO NOT need to mention any of the following types of programs:

Non-Credit Programs—such as one-shot weekend workshops and non-credit lecture or concert series.

Conventional Programs for Regular Students—such as interdisciplinary majors, cluster colleges, independent study for full-time students, January intersessions, and remedial or compensatory education.

Professional Programs at the Graduate Level—such as medical school innovations or continuing education for the bar.

1. LIST OF NON-TRADITIONAL PROGRAMS: If your institution currently offers any non-traditional programs apart from the three types mentioned immediately above, please identify up to three of them below by title or brief description and check the characteristics that make each of them particularly unconventional. (If your institution offers more than three, check this box [ ] and list the three most significant programs below.)   (5)
   Non-Traditional or Unconventional Features (Please check as many as apply)   (6–11)
   1. Type of student   70%
   2. Location of instruction   67%
   3. Method of instruction   57%
   4. Content of program   48%

Please provide information on the remaining items in Part I for *each* of the programs you listed above.

2. DEGREE LEVEL: Check all certificates or degrees awarded in the program.   (12–14)
   1. Not a certificate or degree program   12%
   2. Certificate less than degree level   11%

3. Associate degree only 21%
4. Bachelor degree only 25%
5. Graduate or Professional degree only 8%
6. Other (please indicate) 6%
   More than one degree or certificate 17%

3. LENGTH OF PROGRAM: Check the amount of work required for completion of the program. (15–17)
   1. Less than six months 4%
   2. Six months to one year
      (up to 30 semester credits) 17%
   3. Up to two years (60 semester credits) 33%
   4. Up to three years (90 semester credits) 4%
   5. Up to four years (120 semester credits) 16%
   6. Other (please indicate the length) 25%

4. FOCUS OF THE PROGRAM: Check all the areas of content that are emphasized in each program. (18–23)
   1. Same content as traditional curriculum 42%
   2. Occupational and career orientation 62%
   3. General or liberal studies 38%
   4. Social problems (ecology, etc.) 28%
   5. Recreation or leisure activities 9%
   6. Other (please indicate content) 8%

5. PRINCIPAL LOCATION OF LEARNING ACTIVITIES: Check the *one primary* learning site for each program. (24–26)
   1. Main campus 35%
   2. Regional learning or extension center 13%
   3. Business or industrial site 7%
   4. Community center, agency, or library 6%
   5. Home 5%
   6. In the field 13%
   7. Other (please indicate site) 9%
      Multiple sites 12%

6. TYPES OF STUDENT FOR WHOM THE PROGRAM IS DESIGNED: Check *all major* groups for which the program is aimed. (27–32)
   1. Same age students as in
      conventional programs 50%
   2. Military personnel 14%
   3. Special occupational group 41%

4.	Housewives and working adults	45%
5.	Unemployed and economically disadvantaged	26%
6.	People confined or beyond commuting distance	18%
7.	Independent learners of all ages	30%
8.	Others (please identify the group)	5%

7. AGE OF PROGRAM: Check the approximate number of years the program has been in operation. (33–35)

1.	Less than one	26%
2.	One to two	36%
3.	Three to five	24%
4.	Six to ten	7%
5.	More than ten	7%

8. CURRENT ENROLLMENT: Check the approximate number of students enrolled in the current academic year. (36–38)

1.	Under 25	19%
2.	25 to 100	42%
3.	101 to 500	26%
4.	501 to 1000	4%
5.	Over 1000	6%

9. PLANNED ENROLLMENT: Check the direction that enrollment in the program is expected to take *next* year. (39–41)

1.	Much greater	13%
2.	Somewhat greater	48%
3.	About the same	35%
4.	Smaller	1%

(42–56)

Part II. Policies and Practices in One Non-Traditional Program (351 programs)

Even if you listed more than one program above, please answer the question in this Part for the *one undergraduate program* that seems likely to receive the greatest resources and support at your institution in the near future. Identify it by circling the appropriate letter:

Program　　a.　　b.　　c.

10. ADMINISTRATIVE ORGANIZATION: To what office or division of your institution is the program directly responsible

(such as the Office of the Vice President for Academic Affairs, Division of Liberal Studies, Office of Continuing Education, etc.)?

Executive office	20%
Conventional office	46%
Separate, special organization	28%

11. POLICYMAKING: How extensively do regular faculty committees participate in decisions concerning this program?   (57)

    58%   Same involvement as in conventional programs
    22%   Less involvement, but some participation
    13%   Little if any involvement

12. INTERINSTITUTIONAL RELATIONSHIPS: Is the program conducted by your institution alone or as part of a cooperative interinstitutional operation?   (58)

    58%   Conducted by institution alone
    18%   Part of a cooperative operation with other educational institutions
    16%   Part of a cooperative operation with non-educational organizations (business or industrial firms, hospitals, etc.)
    4%   *Combination*   (59–79)
                                                          (80) 1

13. ADMISSIONS RESTRICTIONS: Please check *all* criteria used as admissions requirements for this program.

    23%   Minimum age (please specify)   (5)
    3%   Sex (men only or women only)   (6–14)
    2%   Ethnic background (specific ethnic group)
    7%   Low socioeconomic background
    47%   High school diploma or equivalent
    7%   Must have completed lower division work at least
    7%   Meets state education code requirement
    11%   Satisfactory scores on standardized examinations (ACT, CEEB, etc.)
    4%   Certain rank in high school class
    34%   Other (please specify)

14. SEX OF STUDENTS: What proportion of the students in the program are male?   (15)

    13%   Few or none
    11%   About one-quarter

    40%   About one-half
    14%   About three-quarters
    14%   All or almost all

15. STUDENT AGE: Are *most* of the students in the program from any particular age group? (16)

    12%   Information unavailable
    32%   Primarily 18 to 22 year olds
    13%   Primarily in middle to late 20s
    24%   Primarily in 30s and 40s
    13%   Approximately equal range of all ages
    6%   Other (please specify)

16. CURRICULUM: If a brochure or statement describing the nature of the program is available, please enclose a copy in the return envelope along with this form. If not, please briefly describe the program's distinctive content or focus. (17–18)

17. CURRICULAR OPTIONS OR REQUIREMENTS: Please check *all* of the following features that apply to the curriculum of this program. (19–27)

    28%   Students may begin the program at *any* time
            (as opposed to *start of term* only)
    31%   Students design their own unique programs
    44%   Most or all of the curriculum is structured
            or prescribed
    28%   Learning contracts are devised between
            students and faculty
    29%   Concentration or major is required
    30%   Distribution among courses (e.g., general
            education) is required
    57%   Pacing of program is determined by students
            individually
    33%   Course work at several different campuses
            is possible
    56%   Students may earn degree or complete the
            program entirely on a part-time basis

18. LOCATION OF LEARNING ACTIVITIES: In Question 5 above you reported the *principal* location for learning in this program. Please indicate the extent to which other locations are also used. (28–34)

Much use	Some use	No use	
46%	30%	19%	Campus
17%	21%	57%	Regional learning center or community center
1%	29%	65%	Public library
11%	27%	57%	Business or industrial site
21%	28%	46%	In the field
10%	19%	66%	Home
11%	7%	77%	Other (please specify)

(35–79)

(80) 2

19. LEARNING OPTIONS: Please indicate how much each of the following learning situations is used in the program. (5–18)

Much use	Some use	No use	
38%	41%	17%	a. Traditional classroom lectures
19%	46%	31%	b. Tutorial
11%	33%	52%	c. Programmed instruction
1%	12%	83%	d. Computer-assisted instruction
10%	36%	50%	e. Tape cassette instruction
1%	6%	89%	f. Talk-back telephone instruction
2%	9%	85%	g. Closed-circuit live talk-back television
2%	18%	76%	h. Closed-circuit TV or video-tapes with no immediate feedback
2%	9%	85%	i. Broadcast radio or television
28%	38%	30%	j. Field work or cooperative work study
6%	15%	75%	k. Correspondence
7%	22%	67%	l. Occasional short-term campus residency
14%	6%	76%	m. Other (please specify)

20. PRINCIPAL LEARNING OPTION: Which of the above

methods constitutes the major means of learning in the program? (Circle the appropriate letter)   (19–20)

a.   b.   c.   d.   e.   f.   g.   h.   i.   j.   k.   l.   m.

21.   SCHEDULED INSTRUCTION: When is instruction in the program scheduled? (Check as many as apply)   (21–26)

     56%   Daytime
     62%   Late afternoon and evening
     23%   Weekends
     10%   One weekday
     21%   Blocks of several days periodically
     17%   Other (please specify)

22.   ATTRITION AND COMPLETION: Approximately what proportion of students who start the program complete it?   (27)

     43%   Information unavailable
     28%   All or almost all
     20%   About three-quarters
     6%   About one-half
     2%   About one-quarter
     1%   Few

23.   RECOGNITION AWARDED: What type of recognition is awarded the graduates of the program?   (28)

     10%   Certificate or other non-degree award
     51%   Regular degree, similar to that awarded for
             conventional programs
     4%   Special degree, distinct from those for
             conventional programs
     28%   Other (please specify)

24.   ACADEMIC ADVISING: Who provides academic advice to students in the program?   (29)

     28%   Faculty advisors
     6%   Counseling staff members
     7%   Administrative staff
     6%   Others (please specify)
     47%   *Combination of above*

25. EDUCATIONAL COUNSELING: How frequent is academic and educational advisement and counseling?   (30)

     19%   Primarily at enrollment and registration periods
     25%   Occasional between registration periods

47% Intensive and continual throughout the program
3% Other (please specify)

26. FACULTY: Who comprise the faculty for the program?

(31–34)

Majority	Minority	None	
			Regular faculty, who teach conventional programs
62%	17%	16%	as well
			Separate faculty of the
13%	18%	64%	institution
			Special instructors from the community, professions, business, industry,
16%	39%	40%	or the arts
4%	3%	88%	Other (please specify)

27. FINANCING: What is the primary source of funding for the program? (35)

39% Self-sustaining through student fees and grants
25% Primarily institutional subsidy
14% Primarily foundation or other outside grant
13% Other (please specify)
3% *Combination of above*

28. OPERATING COSTS: Are the costs of conducting the program roughly comparable to those for conventional programs of your institution? (36)

22% Information unavailable
41% Yes, generally similar
20% No, generally *less* than conventional programs
17% No, generally *more* than conventional programs

Part III. Other Opportunities for Non-Traditional

Undergraduates (1185 institutions)

In addition to specially designed non-traditional programs, the Commission on Non-Traditional Study is concerned with opportunities at your institution for young people and adults to enroll in regular undergraduate programs on an intermittent or occasional basis. The following questions to these opportunities.

29. INTERMITTENT STUDY: For your undergraduates, is continuous progress generally expected, or are leaves of absence and "dropping in" and "dropping out" encouraged? (37)

    17% Continuous registration or progress is expected

    48% Dropping in and out is facilitated but *not* encouraged

    28% Neither practice is encouraged nor discouraged

    4% Dropping in and out is encouraged

30. PART-TIME DEGREE STUDY: Can any student earn your principal undergraduate degree *entirely* by part-time study? (38)

    68% Yes, entirely by part-time study

    8% Yes, although some short-term intensive campus residence is required

    15% No, but some work may be taken on a part-time basis (please specify the proportion of part-time work permitted)

    6% No, full-time study is required entirely

31. OLDER STUDENTS: Are people over 25 actively encouraged to enroll? (39)

    73% Yes, into *regular* programs with younger undergraduates

    5% Yes, but ordinarily into *special* undergraduate programs for part-time students

    17% No, no active encouragement or recruitment

    3% *Combination*

32. RECRUITMENT: What are the major means used to recruit older students and other potential students (e.g., dropouts)? (Check those most used) (40–46)

    31% No active recruitment of older students

    57% Literature available

    46% Newspaper of broadcast advertisements

    34% Industrial, professional, military, and other occupational contacts

    20% Employment counselors, unemployment and welfare offices, churches, etc.

    15% Special facilitating services for adults (low fees, counseling, etc.)

    8% Other (please specify)

33. ADULT COUNSELING: Are adult students advised and counseled by different faculty or staff members than younger students?

                                                                   (47)

    8%   Yes, separate counseling and advisement services

    8%   Varies (please indicate differences)

    81%   No, same staff and services for all students

34. FINANCIAL AID FOR PART-TIME STUDENTS: What financial aids are available to your part-time students? (Check all that apply) (48–54)

    28%   Grants (scholarships, fellowships, and other non-repayable awards)

    27%   NDEA loans

    27%   Federally-insured loans

    22%   Other loans

    25%   Work-study jobs

    10%   Other (please specify)

    34%   No financial aids are available to part-time students

35. TUITION AND FEES: Are tuition and fees for part-time students charged on a per-credit basis or a flat-fee basis? (55)

    80%   Per credit or unit basis

    7%   Varies (please specify)

    3%   Reduced-rate flat fee

    3%   Same flat fee as full-time students

36. CHILD CARE: Does your institution provide child care for students' children during classes and study hours? (56)

    3%   Yes, without extra charge

    7%   Yes, with extra fee

    16%   No, but assists in locating child-care facilities

    70%   No, no provisions exist for child care or for assistance in locating such care

37. HOURS OF SERVICE: What services are available to evening and weekend students before or after their classes? (57–71)

    55%   Counseling services

    33%   Business office

    24%   Financial aids office

    24%   Job placement service

    58%   Bookstore

   82% Library
   34% Computer terminals or centers
   54% Laboratories
   75% Study areas
   73% Student lounges
   54% Cafeterias
    8% Institution's museums
   22% Health services
   39% Physical education facilities
   63% Free parking

38. IDENTIFICATION OF CREDITS: Are credits earned in part-
   time programs, such as evening or weekend classes, identified
   distinctively on transcripts?   (72)

       7% Yes, distinctively
       8% Some distinction, but obvious only to
                institutional specialist
      77% No

39. FLEXIBILITY OF CREDITS: Are credits from your part-
   time degree program applicable to the regular full-time degree?
                                                                  (73)

       7% No part-time degree program
      85% Yes
       1% Limited (please indicate limits)
       1% No

                                        (74–79)   (80) 3

Part IV.   Policies Regarding the Award and Acceptance
   of Credit for all Undergraduates (1185 institutions)

       The Commission needs information on activities deemed by
your institution to be academically "creditable" for *all of your undergraduate degrees.*

40. CREDITABLE ASSESSMENTS AND EXPERIENCE: Please
   check the kinds of assessments and experience for which your institution *actually awards* course credit to undergraduates.
       STANDARDIZED EXTERNAL EXAMINATIONS: (5–31)
       64% Advanced Placement Program examinations
       27% CEEB Achievement Tests or ACT tests

64%   CLEP (College Level Examination Program
        of CEEB)
11%   CPEP (College Proficiency Examination
        Program of New York State)
14%   Cooperative Test Services (ETS) or
        Cooperative Foreign Language Tests
38%   USAFI Subject Standardized Tests
14%   Testing programs in the professions
        (nursing, office management, etc.)
 5%   Statewide standardized examinations
54%   Credits awarded by other colleges or
        universities for passing standardized tests
        such as the above

INSTITUTIONAL ASSESSMENTS: (14–17)

51%   Institutional proficiency or equivalency
        examinations
24%   End-of-course tests without course enrollment
46%   Special departmental tests
18%   Oral examinations or interviews

NON-COURSE WORK (possibly credited through independent study):   (18–30)

28%   Volunteer work in community agency
 6%   Classes at local free university or
        local experimental college
10%   Student body officer or active participant in
        institutional governance
14%   Participant in local community theater,
        orchestra, or civic activity
 7%   Sensitivity training or encounter group
        experience
17%   A completed work (book, piece of sculpture,
        patent, etc.)
35%   Military courses recommended for credit
        by the Commission on Accreditation of
        Service Experience (CASE)
14%   Formal courses of instruction conducted by
        business, industry, or government agencies
28%   Course work completed at an *unaccredited*
        college

35%   Cooperative work experience
16%   Study abroad sponsored by groups other than
          educational institutions
 6%   Unsupervised foreign travel
 8%   Other (please specify)

41. LIMITS ON CREDIT BY EXAMINATION: How much credit is allowed toward a degree through examinations only?

(31)

12%   No credit awarded for examinations alone
 6%   Less than one quarter or one semester's
          full-time credit
 9%   Not more than one quarter or one semester's
          full-time credit
25%   Not more than one year's full-time credit
19%   More than one year's full-time credit is possible,
          but some course attendance required
 7%   No limit: possible to earn undergraduate
          degree *entirely* by examination
14%   Other (please specify)

42. ENCOURAGEMENT OF CREDIT BY EXAMINATION: Please check any ways your institution encourages students to earn credit by examination.   (32–37)

41%   No real encouragement to earn credit
          by examination
26%   Wide publicity that the institution awards
          credit by examination
39%   Examinations administered on campus for
          student convenience
 2%   Institution waives or pays examination fees
16%   Students contacted individually and encouraged
          to take examinations
 7%   Other (please specify)

43. FEES FOR EXAMINATIONS: If students can earn credit by taking end-of-course exams without having enrolled in the courses or by taking special departmental tests, what fees are charged for these examinations?   (38)

18%   No credits permitted to be earned this way
16%   No fees

18% Examination fee to cover the cost of
     providing the test
4% "Recording" fee to record credits on transcript
11% Fee *equivalent* to the fee for the credits granted
4% Fee *greater than* the fee for the credits granted
15% Other (please specify)

44. CREDIT FOR PRIOR WORK EXPERIENCE: Please check
whether any of the following four students would ordinarily receive any credit for their work experience *without* having to take
a special examination or test.   (39–42)

8% A 25-year-old student with two years' teaching
     experience in the Peace Corps or Vista
7% An older man with ten years' investment
     counseling experience
5% A middle-aged wife with five years' volunteer
     social-worker experience
7% A sophomore who dropped out of another
     college after his freshman year and worked
     in a newspaper office for a year

45. RESIDENCY REQUIREMENT: What is the usual minimum
amount of work that an undergraduate must complete at your
institution to earn its degree?   (43)

4% No residency required
20% *Less* than one academic year's work or
     less than 30 semester hours' credit
57% One academic year's work or 30 semester
     hours' credit
14% *More* than one academic year's work or more
     than 30 semester hours' credit

46. THREE-YEAR BACHELOR'S DEGREE: Many institutions
now permit students to complete the bachelor's degree in less than
four years. Has your institution moved far enough in this direction to publicize a "three-year degree" program? (785 institutions)
                                                   (44)

20% Yes
31% Not yet, but the issue is under consideration
43% No

47. MEANS OF SHORTENING THE PROGRAM: How can a

student receive a degree in a reduced length of time? (Check all that apply) (45–50)

4% Not possible

74% Year-round attendance with no reduction in credits

69% Heavier student course load with no reduction in credits

63% Credit by examination with no reduction in credits

3% Reduced number of credits in a revised curriculum (please indicate the number of credits required in this curriculum)

6% Other (please specify)

Part V. Problems and Plans in Non-Traditional Study (1185 institutions)

48. PROBLEMS: Please check any of the following issues which have posed difficulties or obstacles for your institution in the development of non-traditional programs, opportunities for non-traditional students, or new policies regarding the award and acceptance of credit: (51–68)

15% No evident demand or need for such developments

12% Recruitment of students

13% Recruitment of appropriate faculty

12% Inadequate preparation of students

21% Lack of interest within the institution

32% Faculty resistance

34% Institution's concern about its academic standards

20% Suspicion of passing fad

12% Lack of interest among institution's constituency

41% Lack of funds

25% Problems of budgets based on FTE units

40% Difficulty in assessing non-classroom learning

19% Lack of approved examinations or other assessment techniques

10% Accreditation

    9%   Licensing and certification

    7%   Employers' concerns about graduates'
           qualifications

   18%   Acceptance of graduates into advanced
           education or graduate schools

    6%   Other (please specify)

49. STUDIES: If any studies are available from your institution about the areas touched upon in this questionnaire, or if any market surveys have been completed to determine needs and interests in these areas, please indicate how or from whom they can be obtained. (69)

50. PLANS: If significant changes are planned at your institution for the coming 1972–73 year in the areas of this questionnaire, please describe them briefly for the information of the Commission: (70)

(71–79)

(80) 4

Name Index

Subject Index

A

Academy of Orthopaedic Surgeons, 162

Accreditation: bibliography on, 215-218; decisions on appealed, 171-172; of non-traditional programs, 7-9, 157-173; professional or specialized, 161-165; regional, 158-161, 171-172; standards for, 160-161, 162-163, 165-170, 172-173; state, 153; voluntary, 157-165

Adults: bibliography on education for, 178; learning interests and experiences of, 11-52; learning needs of, 95-98; opportunities for, 55-59, 66-67, 90, 91; technology in education for, 95-115

Advanced Placement Program, 64, 65

Aging, the, needs of, bibliography on, 186-188

Agriculture, courses in: credit for, 38, 39; interest in, 19, 21, 22, 23, 24, 25, 26, 27

American Association of Collegiate Schools of Business, 164, 169

American Bar Association, 163-164

American Chemical Society, 162, 163

American College Testing, 64

American Dental Association, 163, 164

American Occupational Therapy Association, 162-163

American Physical Therapy Association, 164

American Psychological Association, 164

American Speech and Hearing Association, 162

Antioch College, 122, 161

Assessment: future of, 135-142; measures of, 7, 9; multifaceted, 136-137; of non-traditional study, 126-128; problems in, 125-135; of traditional learning, 126-128

Association of American Law Schools, 163, 164, 165-166, 167

Audio cassettes, 29, 30

C

California, University of: at Davis, 97; at Irvine, 122

California State College at Dominguez Hills, 122

Career-oriented education. *See* Vocational education